LIFE AFTER MARRIAGE
Scenes from Divorce

WORKS BY A. ALVAREZ

General
UNDER PRESSURE
THE SAVAGE GOD: A STUDY OF SUICIDE
LIFE AFTER MARRIAGE: SCENES FROM DIVORCE

Novels
HERS
HUNT

Criticism
STEWARDS OF EXCELLENCE
THE SCHOOL OF DONNE
BEYOND ALL THIS FIDDLE
SAMUEL BECKETT

Poetry
LOST
APPARITION
PENGUIN MODERN POETS No. 18
AUTUMN TO AUTUMN AND SELECTED POEMS 1953–1976

Anthology
THE NEW POETRY
(*Editor, and Introduction by*)

Life After Marriage

⸻◦∞◦⸻

Scenes from Divorce

A. Alvarez (Alfred)

M

ISBN 0333 24161 4

First published in the United States of America 1982

First published in The United Kingdom 1982 by
MACMILLAN LONDON LIMITED
4 Little Essex Street London WC2R 3LF
and Basingstoke
Associated companies in Auckland, Dallas, Delhi, Dublin
Hong Kong, Johannesburg, Lagos, Manzini, Melbourne, Nairobi,
New York, Singapore, Tokyo, Washington and Zaria

Printed in Great Britain by
Redwood Burn Limited
Trowbridge, Wiltshire

*For Terry and Joan Steinhouse,
Colin and Kay Lanceley*

Contents

Now my father . . . was musing within
himself about the hardships of matrimony,
as my mother broke silence.—

'—My brother Toby, quoth she, is
going to be married to Mrs. Wadman.'

'—Then he will never, quoth my father,
be able to lie *diagonally* in his bed again as
long as he lives.'

Laurence Sterne,
Tristram Shandy

Preface

My original intention was to write a book on divorce rather like my study of suicide: a kind of critical meditation, with some history and philosophy, but above all literary and personal. My secret title was *The Savage God Meets Frankenstein's Daughter*.

It seemed a natural progression, since for me suicide and divorce were closely linked. My bungled attempt at the former, twenty or so years ago, was followed within a few months by a remarkably unacrimonious experience of the latter. Unacrimonious not because my then wife and I parted as friends, but because by the time we reached the divorce court all acrimony was spent. The suicide attempt had destroyed the marriage more effectively than I ever could have guessed. After it, divorce was the only way out.

For me, there were other similarities between divorce and suicide: they produced the same private depression and public failure, the same need to come to terms with the split between my romantic ideals and the reality I had managed to create for myself, between what I had thought I wanted and what I had somehow arranged to get. Later I came to think of them as my rites of passage, taking me from my unnaturally protracted adolescence—I was thirty-one and a father when they happened —into something like the real adult world. There didn't even seem much difference in their degrees of unhappiness; I was just as miserable before and after my divorce as I was before and after my attempt to take my own life.

Yet when it came to writing, the problems were utterly dissimilar. Where suicide seemed to reach out continually toward the imagination and a whole world of literature, including Hamlet's most famous soliloquy, divorce seemed above all a matter of theological and legal argument. Perhaps I should have known, since I myself had learned how to cope with it not from Shakespeare or Donne or Lawrence or any of my other literary heroes of that time but from a passing comment in a book called *The Education of a Poker Player* by a retired American cryptographer and intelligence agent, Herbert O. Yardley: "A card player should learn that once the money is in the pot it isn't his any longer. His judgment should not be influenced by this. He should instead say to himself, Do the odds favor my playing regardless of the money I have already contributed?" What applied so cogently to money in a poker pot applied equally to the feelings I had invested in my disastrous personal affairs. The lesson of divorce had nothing to do with the dark side of the creative imagination and everything to do with learning how to cut one's losses gracefully.

As a matter, literally, of life and death, suicide has always provoked intense speculation. Camus called it "the only truly serious philosophical question" and Wittgenstein thought it the pivot on which every ethical system turns. Divorce, on the other hand, is nobody's philosophical question and everybody's problem. It is about making a decent life, not an afterlife. "If you can get a good wife," said Socrates, "you become happy; if you get a bad one, you become a philosopher." Philosophers, however, rarely philosophize about marriages, good or bad. I suppose it would be like philosophizing about the weather or the common cold or any other incurable condition of this life. Marriage—even the Christian sacrament of marriage—is essentially a temporal arrangement; divorce has the power of making it also temporary.

The wrangling about both began with the theologians but

was swiftly handed over to the lawyers, even if the distinction between the two professions was often unclear during the Middle Ages when the courts of law were administered by ecclesiastics. With the separation of Church and State at the Reformation, divorce became increasingly secularized, a question of civil law and social prejudice. Although the Catholic and Anglican clergy continue to argue, Canutelike, against the rising tide of modern divorce—by mail order, by government office license, without lawyers, sometimes even without the consent of one of the parties divorced, and always without any notion of guilt—what remains of the larger issues has been handed over to the social historians and sociologists, the social psychiatrists, social workers and statisticians. Speculation has been replaced by concern, which is at best a dignified, public name for worry. With the notable exception of W. D. Snodgrass's beautiful sequence, *Heart's Needle*—which is, anyway, an extended love poem to the child he left behind after a divorce—the poets haven't really bothered.

I discovered all this in the months I spent researching the history, reading sociological studies and boning up on the law and statistics of divorce. I went to Stockholm where, thanks to the generosity of the Swedish Institute, I talked to government officials and experts in various fields. I did the same, although less formally, in England, the United States and other Scandinavian countries, and even less formally in Italy. In the process I learned a great deal of interest. Yet not much of it had to do with divorce as it is experienced by people going through it. As with suicide, the statistics, tendencies and theories seem to flourish apart from the distress on which they are based and which they are supposed to illuminate. Perhaps because I am not a journalist and so lack those specific gifts—the flair for facts, a nose for the clean, simple story line—I found I was unable to use all my carefully collated data in any very interesting way. In the end, I suppose, it bored me. Instead, I found myself fascinated by the people I talked to privately, without benefit of theories or statistics. Their confusions and contradictions seemed to say more about what really happens in divorce than all the figures and charts. Even in Sweden, for example, I learned more from a long, informal conversation with a casual acquaintance just be-

fore I left Stockholm than from the endlessly helpful and infor-
mative experts. Or perhaps the informal conversation finally
made sense of what the experts had told me.

I spoke to dozens of men and women who had been divorced
or were in the process of divorcing or were considering divorce.
I also heard stories about dozens more. Almost everyone seemed
to have been touched by the subject, involved at one remove or
another and astonishingly willing to talk about it: not just about
their grudges and complaints, their excuses and self-justifica-
tions, but also about their doubts and guilt and grief for what
they had lost. It often seemed as if divorce were the clue they
had been waiting for to make sense of their submerged lives, and
now that they had it everything was falling painfully but miraculously into place.

From all that I heard I have blended voices, incidents, hints,
partly to preserve the anonymity of the people who spoke to me,
partly in the belief that re-creation, in the end, is more convincing than unedited fact. "All cases," Freud said of neuroses, "are
unique and similar." Similar to the observer, unique to the par-
ticipants. By letting these composite voices have their different
say, I hope to give some sense of the uniqueness which lies at
the core of what, in the last decade, has become a depressingly
commonplace experience.

In her postscript to *The Future of Marriage* the sociologist
Jessie Bernard tells how she came, almost reluctantly, to es-
pouse the feminist cause when her research began to show her
that, contrary to the myth of the carefree bachelor, men seemed
to do better in marriage than women. According to her charts
and figures, they were happier, healthier, less prone to nervous
stress than their wives. By chance rather than by scientific
method, I too encountered a number of admirable women who
had come out of miserable marriages stronger than they went in
and seemed to thrive in their new lives. But then, their husbands, when I knew them, also seemed better off than before.
Nobody, in short, benefits from a bad marriage—except maso-
chists who would be miserable in a happy one, and the children
for whom there is no such thing as a good divorce.

Yet despite the research and the rhetoric, I came across
almost no women, even among the liberated, who blamed their

troubles simply on the institution of marriage. They blamed their husbands, of course, just as the husbands blamed their wives, but they also blamed themselves, if only in a halfhearted way, and if only for their ignorance in choosing the wrong man, their innocence in allowing their lives to be twisted into shapes they had never envisaged. Had I been writing a different book— about monogamy instead of divorce, or even about patience—it would have been equally easy to come up with very similar examples in which both the women and the men found in each other whatever convoluted happiness they were after. I am not attempting to prove anything in this study; people interest me more than theories. As Louis MacNeice wrote, "World is crazier and more of it than we think, Incorrigibly plural." I also believe that the hesitant, double-tracked, qualified answers which emerge from a conversation between two consenting adults are fundamentally different from those a researcher gets when he peers over his clipboard and asks, "In your marriage are you: Very happy? Happy? Average? Unhappy? Very unhappy? Tick one."

Over the years I have come down, rather to my surprise, on the side of marriage, although I suspect that for a number of people, including myself, it may be necessary to marry wrong before you can marry right. Unlike love at first sight or Calvin's grace, a decent marriage is neither sudden nor God-given. It has to be worked for like everything else worth having, and paid for in grinding small change, by compromise and growing older. There are no shortcuts to it, as suicide is a shortcut to dying. And unlike dying, not everyone finishes up married. But most do, despite the alarming divorce statistics, even if the obstinate only get there out of sheer weariness, having exhausted all the other possibilities.

Minette est de mauvaise humeur, parce que je ne veux pas veiller le soir. Il est clair que je serai forcé de me marier pour pouvoir me coucher de bonne heure.

Benjamin Constant

(Minette is in a bad temper because I do not want to stay up late in the evening. It is clear that I will be forced to marry in order to go to bed early.)

If goodnesse leade him not, yet wearinesse
May tosse him to my breast.

George Herbert

I

Introduction

Two generations ago divorce was so scandalous and out of the ordinary that it was scarcely even contemplated as an alternative to conventional misery within a respectable marriage. Divorce was for millionaires, aristocrats, film stars—the lucky few who no longer had to care about what other people thought of them and were powerful enough to enjoy the publicity. At the other end of the scale, the socially invisible poor simply lit out for the Territory, leaving deserted wives and children to chase them for maintenance. But for the vast majority in between— the various shadings of middle class, from upper to lower—divorce was not a thinkable option.

Even one generation ago, after the epidemic of rash marriages and morning-after separations provoked by World War II, it was still a grave social misdemeanor, agonizing, suspect and against the moral grain. It damaged Adlai Stevenson's presidential chances in the 1950s and Nelson Rockefeller's in the sixties. As late as 1968, when London was in full swing and the French students were on the barricades, Buckingham Palace caused a stir when it appointed the anodyne but divorced C. Day Lewis to the anodyne but Establishment post of Poet Laureate.

Yet within a dozen years, Princess Margaret was divorced, America had a divorced president, while another presidential hopeful did not even bother to marry the lady he traveled with. Nobody notices because everybody is divorcing. It is now rare to meet anyone who has not been through it, or who is not married to someone who has been through it, or who is not, at the very least, yearning or plotting to go through it at any moment. In the United States a minimum of one marriage in three ends in divorce (one in two in California); in Britain one in four; in the USSR, even more spectacularly, one marriage in three breaks up *within the first year*. The figures are overwhelming and rising.

They are also misleading. In his authoritative book, *The Family, Sex and Marriage: England 1500–1800*, Lawrence Stone has written:

> It is a curious fact that, if one adopts the reasonable criterion of durability, marriages in the mid-twentieth century were more stable than at any other time in history. . . . Indeed, it looks very much as if modern divorce is little more than a functional substitute for death. The decline of the adult mortality rate after the late seventeenth century, by prolonging the expected duration of marriage to unprecedented lengths, eventually forced Western society to adopt the institutional escape hatch of divorce.

In other words, marriage has always been a shifting, transitory arrangement; only the appearances have changed, and the problems. "Till death us do part" used to be a realistic assessment of the odds; now it is wishful thinking. The more efficient medicine becomes, the longer a couple has to change and grow apart, and the more likely it is that the fantasy or affection which once held them together will be eroded, like rocks in the desert, by time.

According to Professor Stone, the premodern couple protected themselves against the shock of haphazard and premature death in the family by investing very little emotion in each other or in their children. He quotes Montaigne, a man of prodigious understanding and sensibility: "I have lost two or three children in infancy, not without regret, but without great sorrow." Indifference was a preemptive strike against grief. The early family was a loose, open structure, more concerned with property, lineage, domestic management and relatives than with the feelings of the husband and wife. In contrast, the modern couple is private and exclusive. They may or may not need each other economically, but in other practical matters they can get along perfectly well alone, with laborsaving machines, supermarkets and the state to do the cleaning, providing, nursing and educating for them. They are held together neither by necessity nor by convenience, but by feelings. And feelings shift and change unpredictably, sometimes deepening, more often withering, since endurance is as rare as any other virtue and habit not always a substitute for it. In the crumbling world of emotion and free choice, divorce is a preemptive strike against age and disillusion.

So the divorce figures continue to climb and couples split up on every side, bewilderingly. Not just young people, infected by restlessness and fashionable sensuality, but also the middle-aged and the elderly who, in a more settled time, would have dealt themselves out of the game. They have survived together the death of their own youth and the unspeakable adolescence of their children and seemed to have settled, creaking, on a bedrock of disillusion. Yet now they, too, are caught up on the rising tide and swept off into divorce. But eagerly and with relief, as though not wanting to be excluded from the possibilities of the age. We have reached the point where a good marriage seems as unusual, almost as scandalous in some devious way, as a divorce did a generation or two ago. We wonder what the lucky couple are hiding or denying or missing out on, and what they are secretly doing about this aberration in their lives. Do they have religion? Lovers? Booze? Dope? Cancer? The possibility that they might enjoy each other's company, make each other laugh occasionally and be friends as well as lovers seems too remote to contemplate. Easier to assume that they are suffering from some obscure, undiagnosed sickness which has made them fatally dependent on each other. "The rocks in his head," said Gore Vidal, "fit the holes in hers."

Envy plays a part in these responses, or what in England is now called "the politics of envy": a desire to change things not out of any idealism but because the sight of other people's contentment is not to be borne. But so does a sense of superiority.

Those who have been through a divorce come in time to think of themselves as forming a shop-soiled but proud freemasonry of a kind which has been described with innocent enthusiasm by Morton and Bernice Hunt in a book called *The Divorce Experience*. According to the Hunts, the divorced—code-named FMs, Formerly Marrieds—have their own world, their own rituals, their own clubs and network of communications. And there are millions of them, although most are in transit from one marriage to the next. Meanwhile, they huddle together for warmth and comfort, like sheep in a fold. In the United States, where money can be made from anything, even unhappiness, FMs join singles clubs like Parents Without Partners, consult computer dating agencies, visit singles bars, subscribe, if they live in or near New York, to the magazine *Singles World*, place and answer advertisements in the *Singles News Register* or *The New York Review of Books*, according to temperament. For those who provide the services all this may be good business, but it is also a serious business for those who use them. The Hunts quote an officer of the Huntsville, Alabama, chapter of PWP: "We are like the genuine aristocracy of old."

He meant, in fact, that his organization tried to keep out the cads and the gold diggers and was more concerned with helping than with making a fast buck. Yet the idea that he and his fellow members constitute an unacknowledged elite is accurate as well as touching. Secretly, the divorced think of themselves as initiates, although into what they are reluctant to say. Unhappiness, presumably, since for those lucky enough to avoid the larger horrors the twentieth century has to offer, divorce is the one certain experience of pain democratically available to everyone. To the initiates, then, it seems in retrospect almost desirable, part of the process of growing up, a necessary insight into the way the world is run: which is, they have learned, not specifically for their convenience. "Divorce," wrote William Carlos Williams, "is the sign of knowledge in our time."

But knowledge of this order is rarely welcome and it jolts the system in odd ways. Often, for example, it provokes bouts of intense promiscuity, although always for the most plausible reasons: they are making up for lost time; they are taking revenge on the partners who rejected them; they are proving to themselves that they are attractive to the opposite sex, despite the evidence of their marriages; they are also proving to themselves that they are free at last to do what they want, without alibis, without accusations and, even more miraculously, without any particular emotional involvement. The newly divorced sleep around just because they want to, as the fancy takes them and because there is no one to stop them.

They are responding to the contemporary image of the good life as it is projected everywhere: in movies, television serials, magazine stories and advertisements for after-shave, perfume and Smirnoff. Behaving selfishly, for the simple hell of it, is a proof that they are now free agents, paid-up members of the glossy, swinging world they have been led to believe exists. It is also a natural response to the eruption of divorce into previously restricted lives. After years in a closed domestic universe—children, schools, illnesses, family budgeting and annual holidays, the pleasures or troubles of the marriage bed, the few friends who become fewer as the horizon tightens with age—the walls suddenly fall away. The newly divorced are both lonely and, at the same time, overwhelmed by the numerousness, the sheer busyness and indifference of what had been swarming out there all along, just outside the front door.

An example: one afternoon on Hampstead Heath I saw a woman who had recently separated from her husband after twenty years of marriage. I knew this only from a passing remark by a mutual friend, since neither she nor her husband was more than a casual acquaintance of mine. But where he was talkative and easygoing, she was a woman who rigorously kept her own counsel: taciturn, disapproving and with a knack of making people feel they had interrupted her in the middle of something important. That afternoon—it was late May and the air was sweet with the scent of hawthorn—she was sitting on the bank of one of the ponds, watching a flock of pigeons bathe themselves in the shallows below her. The birds were shaking the water over their smoky-blue feathers and shifting their raw pink feet about, oblivious of her and unafraid. I nodded to her as I passed, expecting the usual curt nod in return. Instead, she called out, "Aren't they lovely?" I stopped, but before I could answer she went on, "Twenty years I've lived near the Heath and I've never looked at them. Now I can. It's a matter of choice, you see. Either I stay at home and listen to the children squabbling or I come out here and watch the pigeons. I didn't seem to have that choice while he was around." She hesitated, as though expecting an answer, then returned abruptly to her study of the birds. "Pigeons are better," she said.

It was like a door opening for a moment onto a private world, then slamming shut again. Yet she did not seem to be making a bid for sympathy. There was nothing pleading in her voice, nor any sudden intimacy. Instead, she sounded perplexed, curious, as if the pigeons primly splashing themselves, the sunlight, the heady scent of the hawthorn trees under their avalanches of white blossoms, were a theatrical set which had been wheeled into position while her back was turned. The world was not what she had been led to believe. It was larger, richer and devastatingly more impersonal.

It was also more interesting. The need to cope with feelings beyond the usual call of domestic duty—private pain, public humiliation and hatred for the partner who is the cause of both—transforms habit into drama. Lives which had previously been drowned in trivia and routine suddenly acquire a narrative line, with beginnings, middles and ends. The dull family faces, once so familiar that they were scarcely seen, come abruptly alive with character and intent; they become heroes and heroines, villains and betrayers, while demanding children turn into irreplaceable lost loves. Life, in short, becomes interesting again, as it was in one's youth when it still seemed about to happen.

"Indeed, we are but shadows," wrote Hawthorne; "we are not endowed with real life, and all that seems most real about us is but the thinnest substance of a dream—till the heart be touched. That touch creates us—then we begin to be—thereby we are beings of reality and inheritors of eternity." He was talking about love and the infinite promises of marriage. But the death of love and marriage at the end of its tether can each, in its way, be equally transfiguring. Those transfigurations are the subject of this book.

II

Myself
When Young

(i)

"The understanding partakes of death."—Coleridge

"Anyone . . . discussing the future of marriage," wrote the sociologist Jessie Bernard, "has to specify whose marriage he is talking about: the husband's or the wife's. For there is by now a very considerable body of well-authenticated research to show that there really are two marriages in every marital union, and that they do not always coincide. . . . There is usually agreement on the number of children they have and a few other such verifiable items, although not, for example, on the length of premarital acquaintance and of engagement, on age at marriage and interval between marriage and birth of first child. Indeed, with respect to even such basic components of the marriage as frequency of sexual relations, social interaction, household tasks, and decision making, they seem to be reporting on different marriages."

The narrative that follows is no exception and makes no pretense to be anything except partial and subjective. This is how I remember the marriage from my point of view and from a distance of more than twenty years. It is a story about myself when young—very young and very literary and, in every other way, very ignorant. It is also a story about two people who no longer exist—or rather, they continue to exist only in the way carvings in sandstone exist, weathered by the years into unrecognizably different shapes.

(ii)

Something was wrong and I already knew it on the first morning when I went downstairs to make a cup of tea while my young wife slept on. The wedding night had not been a success. Which should not have come as a surprise, since we had met only seven weeks before and married in a dream. It seemed to be the thing to do in the fifties, particularly for a young literary man who had read too much Lawrence and Leavis. I had this terrible lust for premature maturity, this irresponsible desire for responsibility before I had any idea of what maturity involved or had tasted the pleasures of irresponsibility.

I was twenty-seven but young for my age, having hardly been outside the academy: boarding school, Oxford, research in England and America, university teaching. A narrow and opinionated life, led mostly at second hand, through books. As for my wife, she was just young: we married on her twentieth birthday.

I had already met her mother and extraordinary grandmother in America, so finding her seemed like a marvelous piece of luck. She was a tall, headlong girl with brown hair over her shoulders and wide green eyes which seemed to contain endless depths of feeling. More, perhaps, than I was experienced enough to cope with, although I was too naive to understand this.

Her parents were wiser but tactful. When we announced we were getting married, her father shook his head in wonder.

All her mother said was "Isn't this a bit sudden?"

But when we pooh-poohed her caution she shrugged and did

not bother to argue. Perhaps she and her husband suspected how it would turn out before it had even started.

With us, it took a little longer. First we had to go through the ceremony at the registry office, the afternoon party for the family, the drunken brawl for friends in the evening, the wedding night, the first unhappy sleep, then the first and even unhappier experience of waking up with someone who is still an utter stranger. Although we had had no revelations before the marriage, I suppose we expected the sex to be all right on the night, like amateur dramatics. It wasn't and, without anything being said, it seemed unlikely it ever would be.

Now this beautiful, unknown girl whom I had absurdly married slept on, her mouth slightly open, her thick hair spread across the pillow. The early-winter sunlight flooded in. Outside, the last leaves hung in the still air. I watched her as I pulled on my dressing gown, but she did not stir. Then I went downstairs to make breakfast.

I moved about the kitchen thinking, What have I done? I felt guilty, as if I had committed a crime: against her, against myself, but above all against common sense. All the doors had slammed shut around me. "For better and for worse, for richer and for poorer, in sickness and in health, till death us do part."

"Till death us do part." I was overwhelmed by the finality of my mistake, by its endlessness.

I set the kettle on the gas ring, put the dirty glasses in the sink, then went into the sitting room to get the stove going. It was my usual routine, but now it felt different. Someone else was part of it, someone I scarcely knew.

I loved her, or so I told myself. I had imagined myself into one of those grand and sudden passions that change everything. Just like my idols, Lawrence and Frieda. I pictured her as the Dark Goddess, the Muse, the Jungle Jane to my Sensitive Poet. She instinct, me intellect. The Great Passion, Mark II. And I really believed it, however absurd and sad it now seems to have been once so young. What I was too dumb to understand was that although Great Passions may be possible without actually liking each other, marriages aren't.

I collected the empty bottles and carried them out to the dustbin, tidied and swept the sitting room and did the washing up. Just like Lawrence, I tried telling myself. Tidy as a sailor. But somehow it didn't seem much of a consolation.

Then I made toast and carried a breakfast tray upstairs. She was still sleeping. I put the tray down on the bed and gently shook her shoulder. She opened her astounding eyes reluctantly.

I assumed a breezy but affectionate manner that seemed appropriate for a newlywed. "Breakfast," I said. "And I've cleaned up downstairs."

She levered herself slowly into a sitting position and did not reply. The expression in her eyes was puzzled, as if she were having trouble understanding why she was there.

I poured tea. "It's a lovely morning," I said. Her silence was making me nervous.

She bit into her toast, then put it down in dismay. Her first words that morning were "You didn't cut off the crusts."

I looked at her blankly.

"The crusts. You have to cut the crusts off to let the steam out."

Surely that wasn't what Frieda had said to Lawrence on their first morning in Metz? More like what she had said to her first husband after *their* wedding night.

It's the wrong script, I thought in a panic. I racked my brains to think of what my other literary heroes had said:

"And now good morrow to our waking souls . . ."

"It was the lark, the herald of the morn,

No nightingale . . ."

Neither seemed appropriate in the circumstances. So I settled for "Pardon?"

She did not reply.

I went back downstairs to eat my breakfast alone in the beautiful little studio, with the stove glowing away in one corner and the spidery Windsor chairs which seemed to float on the bloodred linoleum. I had rented the place from a painter friend, and over everything was the curiously rousing smell of oil paint and turpentine—the smell of art, the smell of bohemianism, the smell of the kind of bachelor life to which, after so many years in the academy, I now aspired. Or rather, had achieved for a few weeks and had now impetuously blown. In the three months since I got back from the States I had been moving from one bachelor pad to another while their owners were on holiday: no job, no money in the bank, no fixed address. But I had the better part of my first book written and was reviewing and broadcasting enough to scrape a living of a kind, though not necessarily the married kind.

When I told my barber I was going to get married, he looked at me quizzically and said, "Well, sir, from now on your penny bun is going to cost you tuppence."

I wouldn't believe him. Didn't they say, "Two can live as cheaply as one"? As it turned out, we had trouble living as cheaply as three, even before the baby arrived. But that was because we were so uneasy together that staying quietly at home rarely seemed to me possible.

Meanwhile, the life I had finally organized for myself before our marriage seemed like a paradigm of bachelorhood: hand-to-mouth and in transit, from one place to another, one girl to another. Or that is how it would have been a few years later. But this was 1956, and they ordered these things differently then. When two young people got together on a regular basis they may have had just one traditional thing in mind, they may even have gone to bed together, but the other beast they had in view was marriage: the wife, the kids, the little home and the dog. Everyone was doing it.

As a literary man, I worded it differently, although it came to the same thing in the end. There were Lawrence and James, there were Leavis and Trilling, and behind them there was Matthew Arnold. From them we derived our slogans—"maturity," "reverence," "poise," "the quality of felt life," "the free play of the vital intelligence"—a whole cliché-ridden but insidious concept of literature as a moral discipline, as a substitute for religion. To be a literary critic, even more than to be an author, was to be a priest into whose hands the spiritual and moral welfare of society had, we believed, been entrusted. I suppose the psychoanalysts felt the same, although their catch phrases were different. Since the politicians were so patently drab, or corrupt, or both, it was up to us literary folk to show the moral way. We lusted after responsibility as fiercely as the swingers of the sixties or the punks of the next decade lusted after psychopathology. For an ambitious literary-critical young man like myself,

marriage was not just a way of settling down and legitimizing
my sex life, it was something meaningful and heroic, a career, a
vocation, a vindication of my values.

Not that I want to blame literature for the deformations in
my character. But it went a long way toward dignifying my
yearnings and endowing my perfectly ordinary youthful senti-
mentality with a fine moral edge. For those of us who were
brought up in the days when Leavis and Trilling kept the flame,
getting married was a gesture of cultural solidarity, joining us
to the Great Tradition.

My own case was complicated by an overdose of D. H. Lawrence which I had come by in a not altogether literary way. Not
long before I met my future wife I had been helplessly in love
with a German girl—pale, blond, skinny and very subtle—who
was a few years older than myself and unhappily married. Since
we were all literary beyond the call of duty or reason, she inevitably imagined herself to be a latter-day Frieda, and for a time
I became her Lawrence. I had never been so in love or so miserable or so flattered. I hung around her in agonies for a whole
academic year, gratefully feeding off whatever scraps she threw
me. When the long summer vacation came, she went home to
Germany and I followed: to a tiny primitive village with oxcarts
in the streets and deep forest all around. We were just like
Frieda and Lawrence, we told each other continually and without any irony at all. But it didn't work out and in the end she
returned abruptly to her husband, while I sailed, brokenhearted,
to the States.

I had a grant from the Rockefeller Foundation which insisted, in the politest possible way, that I spend the first six
months at Harvard. But I was uneasy there since it reminded
me of Oxford: Oxford without the architecture and without the
German girl. So as soon as my time was up I lit out for New
Mexico, the country of Lawrence's heart. Because the critical
book I was writing included—of course—a chapter on Lawrence, my official excuse was that I wanted to talk to his widow.
But in truth, I was still under the spell of the German girl and
her potent, contagious literary imaginings. Since she had cast
me in the role of Lawrence, then Lawrence I would be—as far
as that was possible for a middle-class London Jew with good

academic qualifications and a visiting fellowship from an un-Lawrentian research foundation. I would see his widow, live in a place he had loved, and try to play the part. It was literary infatuation expanded into the realm of dementia. It was also a demented misjudgment of my own abilities and temperament.

Frieda was away in Mexico when I arrived in Taos, and by the time she returned I was already lost to the place itself. I had managed to rent a cabin that had once belonged to Dorothy Brett, Lawrence's disciple. High up on the flank of the Sangre de Cristo mountains, twenty miles north of Taos and a mile from the then deserted Lawrence ranch, it was a little log cabin on two floors, light and airy, with an old wood-burning range for cooking and heating. The water came from a stream a few yards from the back porch. The Lobo Mountain went up behind it, slowly at first, then suddenly steeper, covered with pinewoods and swarming with wildlife: deer, porcupines, jackrabbits, the occasional bobcat and rattler. Beavers had built an elaborate dam in which I used to dunk myself on hot afternoons and there were also said to be bears, although I never saw one. But the other animals came regularly in the evenings, rustling around the cabin, sometimes faintly outlined in the starlight. They were my only company. A little downhill, Bill and Rachel Hawk, Lawrence's old friends, raised alfalfa and a few head of cattle; they were friendly but elderly, shy and not forthcoming. Four miles away in the valley was another elderly, more beady-eyed couple who ran a tiny general store and post office. Apart from them, the mountain was empty that year.

I had never been in a place so isolated, so peaceful, so beautiful. The woods dropped away below the cabin, and beyond them was a vast blue sagebrush plain, sliced in the distance by the gorge of the Rio Grande and rimmed by violet mountains. On this desert plain, far off, rose two or three little volcanic cones, also blue, as though from the surface of the moon. To the left, the Sangre de Cristo mountains swept on toward the south. Occasionally, I would slog up to the top of the Lobo and look down toward Taos, twenty miles away. The air was so clear that I imagined it would have been possible, with binoculars, to pick out people moving about the streets.

In that limpid Dantesque light and silence I felt happier than

ever before, and hungry for work. I got up when the sun woke
me, rising from behind the Lobo in the pure pale sky, washed
myself in the chilly stream, then wrote for five or six hours.
After lunch, I drove down to collect the mail, then wandered
about the mountain or went off in my ancient car to explore the
canyons and ridges up and down the range. Once a week I drove
into town to shop, and occasionally I spent the afternoon with a
Taos sculptor whose passion was hunting. Every so often I drove
the hundred miles into Sante Fe for an evening with the gifted
poet Winfield Townley Scott and his wife, Elly.

But mostly I kept to myself, and as the summer went on—
blazing days, clear cold nights—I think I went a little dotty from
sheer isolation. Some evenings I would catch myself in long and
intricate conversations with my own shadow. Then I would get
into the car, bump off down the dirt road and drive into Taos to
see the sculptor and his wife. But often my nerve would fail
before I arrived and I would finish up in one of the shabby little
bars on the outskirts of town where impoverished Spanish-
American farmers drank and "Anglos" were not welcome. I
would tuck myself into the darkest corner, sip a beer and listen
to the voices. It was reassuring to know that the world still
contained other people, even if they were speaking a language I
hardly knew in an accent I could not penetrate. Then I would
drive back up the mountain to the moonlight and the silence:
only the creaking of the car as it cooled and the faint breathing
of the little stream. The rickety gate squeaked as I opened it,
the sound of my footsteps was outrageous, the back of my neck
was stiff with the sense of being watched by whatever creatures
had retired into the piñon when my car's headlights climbed the
hill.

I was used to the monastic but peopled loneliness of boarding school and university; despite a few affairs, I had never lived
with a woman, regularly and day to day. But the loneliness I
experienced up in that cabin in New Mexico was different: lit-
eral, physical, and augmented by the vast indifference of the
desert landscape. Underneath, I suppose, it scared me, though
I would never had admitted this.

One morning after breakfast, I started to read a paperback
translation of Bédier's *Romance of Tristan and Iseult.* Instead

of going to my desk, I took it outside and read it straight
through, lying on my back under the blazing sun. Then I turned
over on to my stomach and read it through a second time. It was
the story of the German girl all over again—young, blond, passionate, with her besotted lover and elderly, not quite complaisant husband—but transformed into poetry and nobility and
doom.

> "And what is it that you know, Iseult?"
> She laid her arm upon Tristan's shoulder, the light of her eyes
> was drowned and her lips trembled.
> "The love of you," she said. Whereat he put his lips to
> hers. . . .
> . . . The lovers held each other; life and desire trembled
> through their youth, and Tristan said, "Well then, come Death."
> And as evening fell, upon the bark that heeled and ran to King
> Mark's land, they gave themselves up utterly to love.

As for me, when evening fell I reeled back into my lonely
cabin, starving hungry, red as a freshly boiled lobster, but utterly content. So that was what it was all about; that was what
I had been waiting for. All night I didn't sleep because of the
sunburn. I twisted about, trying to find a position that was not
altogether agonizing, and fantasizing about the German girl and
the future and about Frieda, who was due back in Taos a day or
two later. The dottiness incubated by my isolation had reached
a fine and florid climax. "Well then, come Death." I was ready
for any stupidity. No rashness was beyond me.

As it turned out, Frieda's return was an anticlimax. Not
only because nothing could have survived my expectations, let
alone lived up to them, but because she celebrated her homecom-
ing by gorging herself on rum babas and dark German beer at
Taos's one good restaurant, then promptly collapsed with a severe attack of diabetes. So it was a couple of weeks before I
finally met her. By then her younger daughter had arrived from
England to visit her.

In style and size they were an odd couple, but affectionate
with each other and close—closer even than Frieda seemed to
the handsome, strutting Italian she had lived with since Lawrence's death. She herself was ironic and easygoing but frail, as

though diminished by age and her recent illness. All that was left of the exuberant Wagnerian of the legend were her vivid blue-green eyes and a German accent which all those years in England and America had never managed to thin. She also laughed like a young woman, throatily and easily, and as a tribute to youthful vanity still rinsed her hair in saffron to keep it yellow. Her daughter Barbara was a tall thin woman in her early fifties, nervous as a thoroughbred, with quick gestures, a sensitive Bloomsbury face and a fine line in casual wit, mostly at her own expense. I fell for them both in a good-humored, filial way and did my best not to bore them with the dogged, scholarly questions Frieda had come to dread. Not that I had many questions; I had come to drink at the fountain, not to analyze the water. I was also relieved that the heroine of the most famous literary love affair of the century was now simply a determined, vivacious old lady with a past she was proud of.

She died a couple of months later. I was back in London by then, so I telephoned Barbara, who had also returned to England, to say I was sorry. "Come to lunch on Sunday," she said. "My little daughter will be here."

The little daughter turned out to be nineteen years old, with dramatic good looks, Frieda's green eyes and a gift for keeping quiet which, to someone as talkative as I was, seemed both awe-inspiring and profound. My Lawrence mania grew overnight even more florid: I saw her not as the young woman she was but as the reincarnation of her marvelous, scandalous grandmother. I imagined that she believed as fervently as I did in the myth of the Great Passion, that we had that dream in common, and arrogance enough to think it would get us through. Common sense was a vulgar and pedestrian virtue, and I was nothing if not an emotional snob. We married seven weeks later, on her twentieth birthday.

Sitting up in bed, her hair falling round her face like a nomad's tent, she peered at the offending slice of toast, then at me.

"The crusts. You have to cut the crusts off to let the steam out."

"Pardon?" I said.

But she did not reply, then or ever.

At first her angry silences disconcerted me; later they scared me. They were so remote from the noisy scenes my parents used to stage and from my own similar habit of raging briefly, then forgetting all about it, that I was unable to cope. And that made me seem dismissible in my own eyes as well, I imagined, as in hers. She would look out at me from under her glowing mane of hair, her broad face stiff with distaste, her mouth heavy, her eyes like green stone. She made me wonder what I had done with my life, chucking it away thoughtlessly, as a gesture. She made me wonder why I had ever been born—to make her miserable, apparently.

In my romantic innocence I had thought that silence was womanly and somehow superior: "She hath a prone and speechless dialect such as moves men." Instead of realizing that some people are taciturn and others not, irrespective of sex, I consoled myself with cultural precedents: the *Mona Lisa*, the Sphinx or Ghirlandaio's beautiful women who watch and keep their own counsel and have their own different wisdom. At that time, art still had the power of validating reality for me and making it palatable.

So I told myself we would get over it. Everyone knew there was a "period of adjustment" when each reluctantly gave up his and her unmarried habits to make room for the other person. As the Stalinists blandly remarked while they were liquidating the Kulaks, "You can't make an omelet without breaking eggs." Give it time, I thought. And I'm sure she thought so, too. Secretly, I was astonished to be so unhappy.

After three weeks of bewilderment, the painter returned to reclaim his flat, so we went off for a belated Christmas honeymoon. In memory of Lawrence and Frieda, I insisted we go to Germany. We even stopped in Heidelberg to visit Frieda's sister Elsa, a shrewd and splendid bluestocking, then in her eighties, who had lived for years with the great sociologist Max Weber. When she asked me what I was doing, I proudly chirped up, Lawrence-fashion, "Writing a novel."

She looked at me with amusement, sizing me up. "Novel-writing is a heartbreaking business." Her voice was guttural, authoritative. "And if it doesn't break your heart, it isn't any good."

I felt curiously reassured by this. Maybe all our unhappiness was going to be justified, after all. But it didn't feel like that.

It felt, instead, like the unhappiness of children: endless, with no before or after. The expectations I had brought to the marriage were disproportionate to a degree which was more or less inhuman. The sense of failure which followed almost instantaneously was equally disproportionate and left no room for qualities that might have saved us: patience, tolerance, a sense of humor.

In my ignorance and emotional snobbery, I didn't even know marriage was supposed to be about those things. I thought of it as a heroic act, as symbolic in its literary way as the traditional marriage of the Church with Christ. It was also a kind of professional qualification. For a mathematician to fail as a husband had no bearing on his ability as a mathematician. But a literary critic spent his time pronouncing on moral subtleties, sensitivity, insight, maturity; if he couldn't handle his drab little life, what right had he to lay down the law on those values literature was supposed to embody?

Matthew Arnold had been right: literature had taken over where religion left off. As for me, I felt like a priest who has failed his faith.

At the center of that religion of marriage was a cult every bit as hallowed as that of the Virgin: the cult of the orgasm, mutual and simultaneous. It descended to the young people of my generation from both Lawrence and Freud as the Inner Mystery, something they all aspired to, a sign of grace. Because of it I had impossible expectations of my marriage, my sex life, myself. I was an absolutist of the orgasm before I had had enough experience to ensure even sexual competence.

Maybe everybody is, in varying degrees, copulation being the one thing you are supposed to do perfectly from the start. No one ever tells you that it is like every other activity: whatever your natural ability, it gets better with practice. Somebody once said of sex, "When it's good it's marvelous, and when it's bad it's still pretty good." Not so young sex. More often than not, it is messy, fumbling, confused and, even when legal, more than a little furtive. Indeed, it may be that legality makes it more furtive, since it reminds you of the only other marriage you know well: your parents'. So perhaps you bring to it all the curiosity and sense of forbidden delights which accompany a child's fantasies about how and why and when his father and mother fuck.

Whether or not that is what happened to me, I cannot now tell. All I know is, there were no revelations. Given my sexual idealism and ambitiousness, and my total intolerance of human imperfection which only the true believer possesses, it was not surprising we failed to achieve the Inner Mystery. Nevertheless, I was surprised.

When the sex had been poor with the German girl she had smiled reassuringly and told me not to worry. "It's often like that at first," she had said. "Be patient."

I had believed her, then remembered what she had said and believed it again with my young wife. After all, we had a lifetime ahead of us. But it did not get better, and the worse it was, the more our loneliness increased, until loneliness became the defining condition of our life together: loneliness awake and asleep, in public and in private, in bed and out.

Yet our case, I know now, was in no way peculiar. The figures and reports published by the various social services which cope with marital problems indicate that a vast number of young men and women are physically incompatible. It seems to be a major cause of unhappiness in young marrieds even after the so-called "sexual revolution." But in those days you couldn't say so. The social services were less conspicuous than they are now. There was nowhere to go, no one to ask.

And if there had been, I would not have known what to say. The subject was unmentionable and humiliating. Even my wife and I never talked about it. It seemed too private, too laden with guilt, too insulting. As a result, it not only became the main source of our devastating loneliness, it also became such an obsession that, although I thought continually about sex, I no longer associated it with enjoyment. It was not until I left my wife and—abruptly, ironically—my nervousness vanished, and with it my incompetence, that I began to understand the pleasures of sex: the touch, tastes, smells, sounds which make up the whole experience of lovemaking, as distinct from the single crisis of the orgasm more or less in isolation, certainly in despair. Until then I did not enjoy sex or understand it, I was simply obsessed by it. Obsessed, appalled and struck dumb. But as Bob Dylan used to sing, "We never did too much talking anyway." Nothing was said, and in the silence all our fears and anger turned inward and rancid.

After we got back from Germany we borrowed a flat from the friend of a friend in Victorian North Oxford. It was there that the seething dissatisfactions erupted into the first of our many savage rows which stopped short just at the edge of violence, then rumbled on for weeks. I no longer remember what it was about, but afterward I wrote a poem about it which reads like an elegy on a love affair that has been dead for years. We had been married for less than three months.

I was scraping a living from reviewing and teaching two evenings a week at the American bomber base at Greenham Common. English I, I think it was called, and it meant the basics. My students ranged from a portly major who took great pride in his copperplate handwriting to a semi-illiterate black cook who wrote "flour show" when he meant "floor show." It was a great relief after teaching Oxford undergraduates. But the journey was by local train and very slow. The evening after that fight, I took with me my battered copy of *Tristan and Iseult*, hoping to squeeze a little comfort from all that poetical misery. Instead, I had trouble remembering what the fuss had been about. "The light of her eyes was drowned and her lips trembled." It seemed a long way from hard toast, messy sex and other people's furnished rooms. I read on less and less hopefully, while the train puffed slowly toward Reading. The night outside was raw and foggy. The compartment smelled of soot and stale cigarettes. When I next looked up we had stopped just outside Reading station, opposite a big bleak slaughterhouse. Its doors were open, and men in long rubber aprons and gumboots were moving about in the yellow light, hosing down the floors. I watched them for a while, then went back to my book:

Now a woman's wrath is a fearful thing, and all men fear it, for according to her love, so will her vengeance be; and their love and their hate come quickly, but their hate lives longer than their love; and they will make play with love, but not with hate.

So now I knew: there would be no forgiveness. Instead, there would be these black, fixed rages and a life stopped short. Two lives, come to think of it.

I watched the slaughterhouse workers hosing muck from the stone floors. They worked vigorously and seemed to be enjoying themselves. Then the train moved slowly into Reading station, where I had to change to an even more local line. So that's that, I thought. I was never going to star in a poetic tragedy. It was time to change the script. While I waited on the foggy platform, I pondered the alternatives. All I could come up with was Kafka's *Metamorphosis*.

I felt cheated. Sheer owlishness had made me miss my wild oats during my student days. While other youths of my age were researching the intricate fastenings of girls' bras, I was beavering away in the great libraries: the British Museum, the Bodleian, the Widener, the Firestone. While they were dancing, necking, copulating, I was dutifully scribbling away at constipated poems, romantic stories and unfinished novels, but mostly at criticism—high-minded, hard-hitting and grim as nightfall. Even after I finally managed to lose my wearisome virginity— one month and four days after my twenty-first birthday—I still seemed to miss out on the fun and games. With two or three lucky exceptions, there had been no lighthearted, casual fucking in my life.

I see now that for my wife, it must have been even worse. She had not missed her twenties; she had married on the day they were supposed to begin. Instead of the droves of admirers, the parties, the usual stupid mistakes that can be recouped, she had got me: a mistake on a larger scale and not so easily erased. Not that I felt sorry for her; I had too much to do feeling sorry for myself.

We continued to shift about for months. When the owner of the flat in Oxford returned, she lent us a cottage a few miles away, just outside a fading little country town full of lovely, decaying seventeenth- and eighteenth-century houses. The cottage was pure picture-postcard: whitewashed walls, half-timbered and thatched, with genuine roses round the door and a big open fireplace in the living room. My wife made herself a German peasant dress to go with the place: lace-trimmed blouse, black velvet waistcoat, dirndl skirt. She tied her beautiful hair in long plaits and looked ravishing. We used to walk the muddy lanes into town, singing folk songs—just like Lawrence and Frieda. Perhaps I hoped the romantic atmosphere would help us. It didn't.

When the days began to lengthen and the weather turned warmer, the owner decided she needed her cottage again. So she put us in touch with a colleague who lived in a bungalow not far from Newbury, where the empty downland begins to roll southward to Salisbury Plain. It was the north edge of the Hardy country, the uplands from which Jude sighed toward Christminster. The friend had a glorified two-room shanty in her garden, shaped like a brick and made of asbestos. But we scrubbed it out and painted it in bright colors, hung fishnets across the ugly pitched ceiling, bought a couple of rugs, arranged our books and went on fighting like wolves. Good taste and bad blood: a deceptive combination, like my wife's dramatic good looks and my own minor but respectable reputation as a clever young writer, which made us appear to outsiders a rather glamorous couple.

Our landlady was not taken in. She was a tough, stringy woman who lectured and researched something medical at Oxford and still bobbed her hair, 1930s style. She also had the upper-class egalitarianism—a sense of fair play translated into political terms—of the thirties left-wing intellectuals. She chain-smoked and coughed ferociously, which impressed me in a doctor. Although she never mentioned it, she must have heard us quarreling—it was impossible not to—since her casual generosity increased as the tension between us grew. She pretended not to notice and disguised her kindliness by being witty about neutral subjects. If she felt sorry for us, she was too well-mannered to say so. I was grateful to her on both counts. Talking to her made me feel wistful for the sane world where people laughed and joked, were fond of each other and got on with their work.

Then one morning we had one of those fights that seem like the end of the world, and my wife marched off to stay with a family friend, an old-style bohemian who was into rural living and organic food years before they again became fashionable. I drove her to the station, then spent the rest of the day tramping across the downs, wondering what I had done with my life. The sun shone, the wind blew, the skylarks sang their hearts out, dipping up and down as though balanced on jets of water. It says a lot for the degree to which I had been brainwashed that even then it never occurred to me we would do better to get a divorce.

The next day I damaged my car—an ancient ex-racing MG which made a vast amount of noise but was not quite fast enough to do much harm. The incident, however, sobered me up abruptly. A day later my wife was home again, and a couple of months after that, in the calm that followed the storm, our child was conceived.

That made divorce even more impossible, although the marriage was no better. We dragged our unhappiness after us like some large and obtrusive pet until it became, I felt, a source of considerable social embarrassment. And we led a disproportionately social life. The emptier our private world became, the more crowded we made it. While we were living in the country we trekked up to London for every trivial invitation, and when we eventually moved back to town we seemed to do nothing except give parties or go to them: dinner parties, bottle parties, publishers' parties, fancy-dress parties, even poets' parties. I judged the success of each inversely to the bitterness of the fight we had staged during it. In one way or another we kept on the move, knowing that if we paused for a moment and looked at each other, there would be nothing to see except misery.

"All happy families are more or less like one another; every unhappy family is unhappy in its own particular way." When I first read *Anna Karenina* I was just taking the measure of my own unhappy marriage and was much impressed. Later I became less convinced. Perhaps Freud was nearer the truth when he said that all neuroses were "unique but similar." Everywhere I looked I saw fellow members of the club: attractive young couples trying to disguise the fact that they were tearing each other apart. Each seemed to be signaling to whomever they were with, "Admire me," "Laugh with me," "Love me," as if the response of other people might convince their partner of their worth. But at heart they had no hope, so they shifted about anxiously, piling charm on charm, while the tension between them vibrated in the air almost audibly. It is called "putting on a good face." It might also be called "the continuation of marital warfare by other means."

The arrival of our son steadied us for a time by giving us someone else to think about. But in the end it changed the nature and seriousness of the conflict without making it any less a battle to the death. Divorce was now even more unthinkable than before, for the small creature seemed to tap in me all the reserves of tenderness which might otherwise and in better circumstances have been shared with my wife. Or perhaps it was our frozen, embattled state that deepened my feelings for the child. Either way, a baby is so defenseless and so absolute in its affection that it demands in return an equally absolute love and devotion. I found myself responding willingly and without afterthought—to my surprise, since I had never been smitten by other people's children.

We shared the nappy-changing and, after he had gone on to the bottle, the feeding. I took him for walks in his pram and later sang to him every night when he went to bed—softly, to disguise my tuneless voice—a constantly growing repertoire of gloomy folk songs, all of them about frustrated love. We grew very close, and in the end, leaving him was the hardest part of the divorce. I suppose I am not cut out for a loveless life, although that is a burden no child should have had to bear.

I had the impression that my devotion to the kid seemed to my wife faintly suspect. Literary to the death, I saw myself, as the marriage disintegrated, in the role of Weekley to some faceless Lawrence, as Karenin waiting nervously for another Vronsky to arrive on the scene. But with this difference: unlike Frieda or Anna, she would have taken the child with her.

So I hung on, telling myself that this was a Great Passion and everyone knew how rough the course of that brand of true love always runs. "Well then," said Tristan, "come Death."

That is how I justified myself at the time; it seemed a specious, even dignified excuse for doing nothing. But the truth is, love had very little to do with our situation. Her power over me was more elementary and harder to get away from: she got under my guard. She was the first person I had ever been in-

volved with who seemed, I thought, to take no account of what
I could do, either professionally or in terms of the kind of person
I was or might have been. How accurate that impression was I
have no means of telling. All I know for sure is that I projected
onto her my own overpowering sense of inadequacy and was
convinced that nothing I could ever do would redeem me in her
eyes. I had judged myself by the gospel according to Saint Lawrence and condemned myself without appeal.

I see now that that must have been what I wanted. Secretly,
I believed that the charmed early life I had led was undeserved
and sooner or later would have to be paid for. I was an indulged
only son, with doting parents, doting nanny and two older sisters
who, though sometimes less doting, were careful to hide their
resentments. I was also precocious, so that at school, where a
clever child is hard to find, I could get away with murder. (As
for the other boys: their standards were largely athletic, so I
concentrated on games and made up in energy and ambition
what I lacked in natural talent.) At Oxford, where cleverness is
always at a premium, I acquired all the outward signs of a brilliant career: a First, a research scholarship, a couple of visiting
fellowships to the States, my articles and poems immediately in
print, an undergraduate talk broadcast on the BBC Third Pro-
gramme. And so on. The trouble was, I myself had never quite
believed in it. In my heart I had known it was an illusion, a con
trick, an intellectual sleight of hand. Perhaps that is how everyone feels about whatever it is they do most naturally: it can't be
worth much if it comes easily. They also feel guilty toward those
who can't do it so well. So I was impressed, maybe even relieved,
when my twenty-year-old wife, who had never sat an examination in her life, seemed to call my bluff without even trying. I
was an intellectual snob who had been brought up by other intellectual snobs to believe in the absolute value of intellectual snobbery. Then I found myself married to a young woman who, I
thought, behaved as if the whole thing were a worthless sham. I
had been outsnobbed.

The baby had been born in the United States, so when summer came we drove out to my beloved New Mexico to spend
time on the Kiowa Ranch in the cabin where Lawrence and

Frieda had originally lived thirty years before. It was a small, run-down little shack, infested with pack rats. Bats nested over the rickety porch and hissed maliciously together when disturbed. But the seediness added to the romance of the place, like the buffalo painted on the outer wall by an Indian the Lawrences had befriended. It was a pilgrimage, not a holiday, and it should have been some kind of consummation; instead, it made things worse by showing how far we had fallen short of my original ideal. All that lonely beauty and silence—the only sound was the wind moving in the huge ponderosa pine that overshadowed the house—made our emptiness more complete.

After a few weeks of this we drove to San Francisco to visit friends. When the time came to return to Taos, we decided to drive south down the then beautiful coast road which twisted past Big Sur toward Los Angeles, then cut straight across the desert to Gallup. We got as far as Ventura on the first evening, then woke late and dawdled over breakfast. So it was ten o'clock before we left and midday when we hit the Mojave Desert. The heat was like a visitation, supernatural. We trundled along in our weary old Studebaker through a shimmering, baking, fading emptiness. My wife, who didn't drive, slumped in the passenger seat, dozing or trying to read. I sweated and itched and kept an eye anxiously on the temperature gauge. Only the baby, stretched out on the back seat in his carry-cot, seemed unperturbed; he slept most of the time and woke cheerful. The hot dust sifted into the car, clogging our eyes and drying our mouths. When the furnace blast from outside became insupportable we drove with the windows up, inhaling our own sweat and stale tobacco.

It was dark when we reached Flagstaff, where we planned to spend the night. But when I looked at the map, I realized that if we stopped, it would be high noon again when we crossed the Painted Desert. Better to go on in the relative cool of the night than endure another day of inferno. So I drank four cups of coffee, filled the car's tank, then lumbered on into the huge, shadowy vacancy of the desert. My wife slept, the baby slept, I blinked and yawned and thought about nothing.

It was ten o'clock when we drove into Gallup the following morning. I had been driving for twenty-four hours straight and had covered a thousand miles. We checked into a motel for a few hours' rest, ate, bathed the child, showered ourselves and flopped into bed. I was beyond fatigue, but vaguely pleased with myself for having spared us the horrors of another day in the desert. It was only six hours' drive to the pinewoods and cool mountain air of the ranch.

The baby fell asleep again instantly. I rolled over toward my wife and said, "Let's make love." My efforts, I felt, deserved some gesture of thanks.

She tilted her head reluctantly in my direction and stared at me for a moment with an expression somewhere between astonishment and distaste, then turned her back on me and went to sleep.

Eventually, I too slept a little, but we scarcely spoke again until we reached Taos that night. The next day I started to write a long-overdue essay on Henry James and "The Art of Travel." Try as I would, I was unable to connect his leisurely, regal progress round the cultures and monuments of late-nineteenth-century Europe with my own sweating, sleepless grind across a thousand miles of blank desert. Although I slipped back automatically into the familiar, comforting, not quite real world of judiciousness, exquisite discrimination and the poised, elegant put-down, my heart wasn't in it. For the first time in my life the fatigue would not go away. My hands shook, my head buzzed, my bones ached; even the marrow inside them seemed to hurt. Up until that point I had always thought, I'm young, I'm fit, I'm tough, I can take whatever life dishes out. Now I knew I was beaten. The rest was only a matter of time.

We went back to London that fall to a new but slightly seedy flat on the shabby edge of Hampstead, and a social life like rising hysteria. "Love of one singularly, with desire to be singularly beloved, [we call] THE PASSION OF LOVE," wrote Thomas Hobbes in *Leviathan*. "The same, with fear that the love is not mutuall, JEALOUSIE." As the strain between us increased under the pitched roof of our attic bedroom, my jealousy grew into an obsession. I imagined that every man she spoke to was her lover and every moment she was out of my sight was seething with intrigue. I was like Othello without the dignity, drowning and pulling her down with me.

I can remember the precise moment the madness began in me. It was an early evening in October and I was on my own, driving into town to a theater, having become, for reasons still obscure to me, a drama critic. On the leafy road beside Primrose Hill I saw my wife's most insistent admirer driving toward me. I caught his eye as we passed each other and nodded politely. But he looked away quickly, pretending not to see me. He's going to her, I thought, without any reason at all. I sat through the play taking nothing in, spoke to none of my fellow drudges during the interval and broke most of the rules of the Highway Code in my race to get home.

By the time I arrived my wife was already upstairs asleep, but there were two unwashed glasses in the kitchen sink.

"Trifles light as air / Are to the jealous confirmations strong / As proofs of holy writ," said Iago.

So now I knew.

Or thought I knew.

Or refused to know.

Or hoped I knew.

The intricacies, permutations and perversions were endless: rage, despair, fascination, lust. It was as if every sick fantasy that had been stored away since earliest childhood were finally being dragged out into the light.

After that I was locked to her by a strange bond of distrust, paranoia, prurience and need. I began to read her letters on the sly, search her drawers and cupboards, grill her ruthlessly each time she went out alone. I felt we were like two starving prisoners feeding off one another's flesh. But in a perverse way, I was probably closer to her during the two demented years of mutual torture before we separated than I was during the first couple of years when I was trying to make a go of the marriage.

Belatedly, I began to grow up—that is, grow less confident that I knew all the answers. The moral and literary certainties on which I had battened for years no longer convinced me. I began to see that the world was run in ways that had nothing to do with the insular British virtues of decency, gentility and politeness, nor with the rhetorical elegance and intellectual superiority of the French. I immersed myself in the history and literature of the concentration camps and became obsessed with all the little self-enclosed hierarchies of power—hospitals, schools, ships, prisons, armies—that shut off their inmates from the sane and indifferent world. Out in the street I used to look with amazement at people going about their business and wonder how many of them were really free, how many of them secret prisoners, secret warders like myself.

Prisoner, warder: the parts were interchangeable. I watched her relentlessly, timed her arrivals and departures and invented fictions for the pleasure of not being believed. Whenever she went into town, for example, I was convinced she was going to meet a man and would force her to play out the same charade. Over lunch she would mention casually that she felt restless; maybe looking at pictures for a couple of hours in the National Gallery or the Tate would clear her head. I would glower at her, fail to think of some killing witticism, then shrug and go back to my typewriter. She knew what I was thinking and each time dutifully brought home a sixpenny postcard reproduction of a famous painting, like a stamp on her passport. Those postcards were a constant puzzle to me in my frenzy: had she laid in a store of them, or did each purchase involve a hurried, expensive detour by taxi? Did her admirer also take one home to his wife? If there was an admirer and if he had a wife. Were the same steps being trodden in an ever-expanding dance all over London? Or was it all my paranoia? A year or two before, the BBC had first broadcast Beckett's *All That Fall;* one line stuck in my mind: "Christ what a planet!"

We were locked in a perfect circle: my suspiciousness made her life a misery, which made her cast around for sympathy, which increased my suspiciousness, which made me in turn cast around, which increased her suspiciousness. It was all perfectly logical. But it also killed off whatever tiny spark remained between us. During our last two years together we shared the same bed without touching one another.

I no longer slept more than a couple of hours at a stretch. I would wake abruptly about 2 A.M., then lie for hours listening to my wife's deep, slow, underwater breathing, sniffing the heavy smell unhappy adults exude while they sleep, watching the moving inks of the night sky against the windows, waiting for the dawn chorus and trying to think what could be done, or how I could get out without losing the child, or trying to remember what it was like to be free. What I tried not to think about was why, of my own free will, I had done this ridiculous thing to my life.

Finally, I would hear the first sleepy chirping of the birds slowly turning into a full, wild chorus of greeting. Made it again, I'd think, then would doze for an hour or two before going off to swim in the pond on Hampstead Heath. The rustling song of the birds as they woke and the sharp, muddy-tasting water of the pond kept me going that summer and the next.

In the end—it had to come—I went to a psychotherapist, although I was shamefaced about it, since in England in those days to ask for that kind of help was neither a usual nor an easy thing to do. He was a plump, kindly man with a punctured face, a heavy Middle European accent and, I was told, a special interest in writers. He even turned out to have read my stuff, which seemed a minor miracle. We arranged to meet once a week: better than nothing, although nothing like enough.

I had the impression that my wife resented those weekly meetings and the idea of all that talk grated on her unreasonably, particularly since she must have assumed we were talking about her. Which was partly true. The problem was that most of the time I did not talk at all. It took me half or more of each session to get back to the point where we had left off the week before.

The meetings continued sporadically for eighteen months, between two trips to America. Although it was a relief and a reassurance, neither the analyst nor I thought of the treatment as anything more than a holding operation. I saw him as I saw my friends, through the wrong end of a telescope, and I remember what went on less distinctly than the setting: the gloomy, overstuffed room lined with books mostly in German, poetry and novels and existentialist philosophers, as well as the texts of his trade; his desk littered with notes in a microscopic hand and letters from a firm of stockbrokers. Isolated images to go with that of my wife dancing to the music of Dave Brubeck, languidly, as though almost asleep, her hair blotting out her partner's shoulder; or of the way her mouth and jawline seemed to thicken when she was angry; or of the hot, anxious voice of my small son describing a nightmare; or of the cleansing chill of the pond where I swam.

Then one day, after about twelve of the eighteen months with the analyst had passed, I was jolted briefly out of my apathy.

"Tell me," said the formal Germanic voice from just behind my right ear, "why don't you leave your wife?"

I lay still for a moment to attend to this, then rolled over on the couch and stared at the doctor's plump thighs, at his round, sad belly, at his sad owl's face. He watched me attentively.

I said, "It's never occurred to me."

"Please," he replied, "we do not have time for games. We meet only once a week. It is not enough. It is not nearly enough. But in that short time we must do what we can. Frankness is essential."

"I was being frank. It has frankly never occurred to me."

"Please," he repeated wearily. "For one year you have been coming to me. For all that time you have complained, when you have spoken at all. True, you do not always complain about your wife. Much of the time you complain about yourself. But always I am thinking that you tell me about yourself only what your wife makes you believe. In all that time you have tried to present me only with your wife's image of you, or what you believe it to be. At last it seems you are growing tired of that image. Or should I say, you are growing out of it?"

"But I couldn't leave my child. I'm too much of a Jewish father for that."

"And please do not blame your Jewishness. For an intelligent man, you are strangely conventional. You will not cease to be a father by living apart. You may be more of one."

"Perhaps," I said doubtfully.

There was a silence. A subdued bell rang for the next patient. I could hear discreet murmurs as he was shown into the waiting room. I felt old and tired and tremulous; I wanted to cry for no good reason. So this was where all that Great Passion and moral ambition had led me: to a weary, unanswerable voice with a funny accent asking why I hadn't got the hell out.

The subject was never mentioned again, and it was another

year before I eventually upped and left her. We moved house,
then went to America again, where we fought even more bitterly
until my wife left prematurely for England, taking the child with
her. I wandered around in a state of shock, like an amputee,
another casualty of the war I'd been too young to fight in. I came
back to England for Christmas, made even more of a mess of
things, then went back to finish the term at the American university where I was teaching. By the time I returned to London
in February, it was all over bar the formalities. She had her life,
I acquired mine, although we continued to share the same bed,
sleeping back to back, night after lousy night.

The crisis came at my beloved pond. It was a hot summer's
day, and I had arranged to meet a girl there. We swam out to
the raft and lay stretched in opposite directions, head to head,
discreetly untouching. Then I looked up and saw my wife marching across the causeway to the pond.

I sat up and said, "That's torn it."

The girl promptly dived in and swam back to the landing
stage.

My wife swam sedately out to the raft, stared at me with
loathing, then swam sedately back again. Nothing was said;
there was nothing to say. I sat on for a moment, not knowing
whether to call to her or to stay where I was.

Finally, I dived in and swam after her. But by the time I
reached the landing stage she was already in the ladies' changing
room, and by the time I had changed she had gone.

I caught up with her on the hill back to our house. We
shouted at one another incoherently; we pushed each other
about. She ran; I ran after her. More shouting and pushing and
stumbling around. The passersby stared.

Then it was all over. I left her standing on the pavement,
hurried home, packed a suitcase, hugged my child and was gone.

A few days later she and our son left for a holiday in Greece
which we had already planned. I went to Poland with a Uher
tape recorder and a ticket paid for by the BBC. When I returned
she was still away. I took my books, clothes and most of the
paintings I had had before we married. Everything else I left:
four years of accumulated furniture and knickknacks, each chosen and put in its place with care; four years of records, hi-fi,

cutlery, crockery, glass, linen, towels; the new washing machine I had bought six weeks earlier; all the tedious impedimenta of setting up home. When I closed the door on that silent, elegant house, bought for us by her mother, I had never felt so free in my life.

I phoned the painter who had rented me the studio where we were married, and he lent me another flat. Later, I even got the beautiful studio back.

When I told my parents what had happened, my father, who had a weakness for the ladies and also a way with them, nodded judiciously: "A beautiful girl . . ." He paused. "But . . ." He had the thoughtful, inturned air of a connoisseur testing a dubious vintage. ". . . but too big for you."

"We're the same height, for God's sake."

"Are you?" said my father, the expert. "Are you really? Ah, well."

For the first time in months I began to laugh without afterthought, without restraint.

It was at that moment that I realized that perhaps divorce might be the luckiest thing that could happen to either of us. God alone knew what kind of warped and diminished creatures we would have become if we had remained locked together in combat. But the moment passed quickly, and the heartache returned in a different form. I felt ashamed. Not taken aback, not angry, not socially embarrassed—I left that to my parents, although they never complained—simply ashamed at such undeniable, comprehensive failure. Until then I had thought I could do anything if I tried: write books and poems, climb rocks, mend things, even play club rugby. And because I had a small gift in one area and competence in several, I assumed everything would be forgiven and forgotten. Now I discovered that my account had been scrupulously kept and I had to pay the whole score: the evasions, the sleights of mind and tricks of style, the white lies, missed appointments and unanswered letters. All of them had been called in by this marriage. Failure in that canceled out the successes elsewhere and revived failures I thought I had forgotten or hadn't even recognized. Every last one of them.

While we were living together, putting each other down was our own special form of intimacy. But for me, the collusion did not end when we separated. Instead, as often happens after a divorce, I adopted the role and characteristics I had projected onto her in my jealous fever: I gave up reading and devoted myself to a deliberate and dreary bout of promiscuity. As if by some perverse magic, my sexual insecurity had disappeared as soon as I left her, but I didn't believe it and was afraid that this double gift of competence and pleasure might vanish as abruptly as it had arrived. So I set about trying to test it on every girl I met, dourly, as though my existence depended on it. Which in a way, perhaps, it did.

I couldn't get over the sense of freedom. After four years eyeball to eyeball, I was astonished not to be accountable to someone else for every moment of my day. I was also certain it could not last. For a whole year I filled my diary with cryptic scrawls against times and places, and telephone numbers identified by initials that now mean nothing to me. The only appointments not made in code were those to collect my son from school or take him to a Saturday-afternoon movie or a Sunday trip to High Rocks or Harrison's. Guided tours of Heartbreak House, beginning excitedly, ending in exhaustion. I took care never to have a girlfriend around when he was there, and he took equal care not to mention his mother. But the effort to maintain tact of that order left him drained for years. Then and later, school bored him and seemed trivial, rather in the way Vietnam made life back home unreal for so many young American soldiers.

Meanwhile, there were the technicalities of divorce 1961-style to get through. And in that, the previous rules of our game did not apply. Nothing became him in his wife like the leaving of her. It was as though the real divorce had taken place when we stopped even pretending to make love, and we then had two years to endure the bitterness of divorce while still nominally married. When it finally happened we both behaved well out of sheer relief, although she, being more relieved, behaved better. Whatever else she had cared about, she had never cared about money. There was hardly enough to quarrel about, and I was willing to give her what I could for the child's sake. Since she wanted to wash her hands of the whole unsavory business as swiftly as possible and there was nothing to be gained by provoking us, even her lawyer scarcely bothered to argue.*

In those days before the Divorce Reform Act, mutual consent was not a legal ground for dissolving a marriage; someone had to be guilty, someone innocent. I gladly volunteered to play the villain. Had there been money involved, my wife's lawyer would have had to hire some poor ferret to discover me in a hotel room with a girl—also hired for the occasion. Statements would have been taken from me, from the girl, from the chambermaid, the porter, the receptionist, each of whom would have been paid a fee. Then the statements would have been transcribed, turned into affidavits and read out in court. All of which takes time, which in turn takes money.

Since that style of bedroom farce was beyond our means, we had to settle for do-it-yourself adultery. I got together with my steadiest girlfriend—a funny, disorganized redhead from Australia who wrote novels and talked even more than I did—we took out our diaries and picked some dates at random. "Enough?" she asked when we had half a dozen. "Seven's a lucky number," I answered. "The last of the big spenders," she said. But after I had sent the dates to the lawyer for him to turn them into a solemn deposition, she telephoned to say that her own lawyer had warned her that being cited as my corespondent might prejudice the judge in the divorce case she was bringing against her husband, whom she had not seen for two years. "Don't worry," she said, "I have a friend."

The friend was a pale, stubby girl with large hands and the gentle, puzzled air of someone who has been permanently ill-used by life. She lived in an almost unfurnished house in Notting Hill with a very small boyfriend and a very large baby. She was devoted to both of them, despite the fact that her parents had begun her troubles in life by naming her Desdemona.

Desdemona had a Saturday stall in the Portobello Road from which she sold assorted junk, mostly with beads on it. But the

---

* Soon after the divorce was absolute and the last bill had been paid, I was swapping paranoias—the standard exchange of the newly unmarried—with a British playwright who was exactly my age but extremely successful. His legal fees for an uncontested divorce were twenty times larger than mine. It was the only occasion on which I have ever been glad to be broke.

tourist season was over and the baby needed clothes for winter. For ten pounds, Desdemona told me, I could use her name; she would prefer cash.

Since the lawyer had waived the need of our being "discovered" together, we went directly to his investigator's office and made our formal statements there. We arranged to have lunch beforehand. Halfway through the meal, our diaries out on the table to pick a set of dates for the fornications we had never had, my wife walked in with a friend. That spoiled my concentration as well as my appetite. I chose the last three dates at random, then hustled poor Desdemona out, smiling sweetly at my wife.

The investigator had a one-room office at the top of a decrepit terraced house somewhere between Grays Inn Road and the Mount Pleasant Sorting Office. The office had Dickensian ledgers and mahogany furniture, and the agent, equally Dickensian, was a hunchback. "Central Casting," I murmured, "would have been more subtle about it." "What's Central Casting?" asked Desdemona loudly. But the investigator took our depositions down in a businesslike manner and shook our hands briskly when we left.

Out on the street, I gave Desdemona two five-pound notes and walked her to the bus stop. I never saw her again. It seemed a curious postscript to a Great Passion, and a long way from New Mexico.

Later, when the case came to court, my wife, who had seen the original papers, remarked to the lawyer that some of the dates were the same in the two depositions. "Your husband," he replied, "seems to have been leading a rather busy life."

I was transformed into a standard divorce bore, alternatively whining about my broken marriage and boasting about my paltry conquests to anyone who would listen. I didn't stop even when I saw their faces stiffen and their eyes begin to water with the effort not to yawn. On and on, until even my best friends stopped inviting me.

On and on, until even I began to weary of it all. Weary first of the heartache, the troubles, the wife, the German girl. Then wearier still of all the earlier miseries: my drab wartime pre-

adolescence, with the Blitz, the blackout, the meager awful food;
then the long years at a dour games-playing boarding school,
followed by an equally long and dour spell in all those libraries
while I was trying to turn myself into a respectable scholar. It
no longer seemed quite decent that my life should have been so
unremittingly strenuous, so upright, so lacking in fun. The time
had come for a little bad behavior.

It seemed the thing to do in those days when the Swinging
Sixties were getting under way. Austerity was dead at last, no
one was unemployed, there was money around. Some evenings
in the King's Road, Chelsea, I swear you could smell it, as sharp
and pervasive as the scent on all the pretty girls in their mini-
skirts. The sweet smell of social change, if not of corruption. It
was smarter to have a cockney twang than an Old Etonian tie,
and the in-people were no longer the titled sprigs of landed gen-
try but pop singers or photographers or hairstylists or improbable young men who spent a few hours each day on the telephone,
buying and selling property. "At a certain age," a friend remarked, "men talk about sex and think about money." Sex was
the only topic of conversation and, to judge by the crowded restaurants and hectic parties, the only activity most people took
seriously.

It was as if poor old England had finally mustered the energy to celebrate the end of World War II in an appropriately
vulgar and rackety way, while I and those like me—free, white
and thirty-one—responded in kind. Whatever attention was not
absorbed by chasing girls I devoted to things which before had
only been mildly intriguing pastimes: climbing, sports cars,
poker. I dropped all my academic friends and most of my literary
ones; I gave up reading "serious" books. This, too, was part of
the curious, caricaturing exchange of roles between my wife and
myself after the separation: for her, the novelists of the Great
Tradition, modern poetry and *la nouvelle vague;* for me, Ham-
mett, Chandler, Ross Macdonald and horse operas. High culture
and the intellectual life—all that print, all that effort, all that
conceit—made me slightly queasy. I suffered from cultural shock
in the same way some people suffer from shell shock. Circuits
had been blown in my head that would never be put back. For
two years I couldn't even listen to serious music—which since

adolescence had been the buttress of my emotional life, as it was
of my father's. I could see no point in all that beauty. It was all
I could do to cope with the empty, rustling silence of the blown
circuits in my skull. But there was no way of explaining this.
When I refused to listen to his new records the old man used to
shake his head and say, "I don't understand you anymore." I
think he never quite forgave me for that betrayal.

Then gradually the pieces began to go back together again,
although the shapes they formed were no longer the same. It
was less a question of recovery than of forgiveness: forgiving my
wife for the fantasies I had projected onto her, forgiving myself
for having been so perverse, so theoretical, so stupidly vulnerable. As the heartache receded, it came to seem less an affliction
than a part of being young, like marching against the Bomb or
listening to folk songs ancient and modern, to Joan Baez, as
plangent as the girl next door, or to Bob Dylan doing his nasal,
urban variations on the same old themes:

> I ain't saying you treated me unkind,
> Could have done better but I don't mind,
> You just kinda wasted my precious time,
> But don't think twice, it's all right.

I used to sing that over and over to myself as a reassurance, as
a charm for warding off the evil eye, trying to persuade myself
that I, too, wasn't thinking twice. Only when I began to realize
that I was thinking not twice, but constantly, did the mixture of
rage, regret and self-pity cease to be alluring.

Likewise the promiscuity. Once I understood that the sexual
bad times were not going to come back, I relaxed and became
more of a man, less of a liability. Women no longer seemed to me
the castrating enemy, nor the philanderer's quarry, nor the mysterious Other; they were simply different, equal but separate, to
be encountered or even loved for what they were, not for the
fantasies I could weave around them; and if I was lucky, they
sometimes responded to me in much the same way. It was the
lovely, talkative Australian who first made me see, after all
those years of expensive British education in male exclusiveness,
that women could be likable as well as lovable. But we had met

too soon after I left my wife, which meant that she became
involved in the confusions of that very confused time, above all
in my terror of being trapped once again. So after a couple of
years we split up.

A month or so later, I called in on a friend who lived just
around the corner. But he had gone abroad and lent his flat to
two girls, one of whom, a schoolteacher, I knew slightly. The
other had blue eyes, an easy smile and a terrible cold. She also
had a degree in clinical psychology, but had recently dropped the
Rorschachs and TATs and was now training to be a child psychotherapist. She was Canadian—without quite realizing it, I
seemed to have had my fill of English women—but two years in
London had not yet reconciled her to the dank climate and primitive domestic heating. Her nose was red, her hair a mess and
she was bundled up in a hideous sky blue woolen dressing gown.
But there was a glow about her and a firmness, like a tree with
fruit on it, rooted, and the fact that she was looking her worst
when we met seemed to create an odd intimacy between us. We
also discovered that we made each other laugh. I came away
thinking that domesticity might not be such a bad thing after all,
and maybe I had done enough time with my hurt.

But healing is a slow process. You grow attached to your
injuries. There is even a certain status in being one of the world's
walking wounded. It becomes a habit, an unfailing excuse for
behaving badly. So for three years we were on and off like the
lights in Piccadilly Circus, breaking up, coming together, breaking up, each time a little more weary with the perverse itch for
trouble that prevented us from accepting what was becoming
more and more inevitable. When we finally married, we had had
enough divorces to last a lifetime.

And so we lived happily ever after—as happily, that is, as
can be managed by two consenting adults, one of whom now nags
the other rather smugly about cutting the crusts off toast.

III

Lawrence
and Frieda

My youthful obsession with Lawrence, Frieda and all their works appears to me now a form of madness. Yet at the time—the moralizing, timorous fifties—there seemed to be nowhere else to turn. Today a young literary couple in the throes of a divorce could console themselves with any number of high-toned cultural precedents: plays like *Who's Afraid of Virginia Woolf?* dozens of movies, culminating in *Scenes from a Marriage*—of which Ingmar Bergman, himself a veteran of half a dozen marriages, remarked, "After it was shown in Denmark, the divorce statistics went up. That's got to be good!"—and a shelf full of serious fiction, mostly American: Bellow's *Herzog*, Roth's *My Life as a Man*, Updike's *Couples*, Cheever's stories and Herbert Gold's. The desire "to speak of the woe that is in marriage" drives characters as different as Joan Didion's Maria Wyeth and John le Carré's George Smiley. Only Norman Mailer, the most married and divorced of all contemporary novelists, seems unmoved by the topic; the nearest he gets to it, in *An American Dream*, is wife murder.

I doubt if all this cultural reinforcement would have made

divorcing any less painful for me, but it would undoubtedly have made it easier to accept. Divorce now, in the eighties, is a part of everybody's social reality, acknowledged because it's there, like Everest, beyond argument, beyond morality and even, increasingly, beyond religion. Morton and Bernice Hunt quote a Boston priest who claims, cheerfully and with pride, "Catholics have become as American as apple pie, for better or for worse, and now divorce as much as everybody else." For the novelists, this new component of the scene changes the narrative line, alters the endings.

It also robs them of what was, for over a century, a major source of tragic inspiration: adultery, a theme which transfixed European novelists from that moment late in the eighteenth century when the Romantic concept of marriage for love began to clash irreconcilably with the more beady-eyed and practical arrangements which had preceded it. When marriage was a contract based on property, name and social power, drawn up between the heads of families for the families' mutual benefit, usually without more than cursory reference to the desires of the young couple who were to be married, adultery had relatively little emotional or imaginative pull. It was simply one of the rules of the game, an acknowledged social fact, as divorce is now, and therefore a source of comedy.

At the Restoration it was the dramatic staple of the playwrights and a standing joke at court:

> In pious times, e'r Priest-craft did begin,
> Before *Polygamy* was made a sin;
> When man, on many, multiply'd his kind,
> E'r one to one was, cursedly, confind:
> When Nature prompted, and no law deny'd
> Promiscuous use of Concubine and Bride;
> Then, *Israel's* Monarch, after Heaven's own heart,
> His vigorous warmth did, variously, impart
> To Wives and Slaves: And, wide as his Command,
> Scatter'd his Maker's Image through the Land . . .

Nobody needed Dryden to tell them that "Israel's Monarch" was Charles II, and the king himself was flattered and amused, not

offended. Marriages, particularly royal marriages, may have
been indissoluble but they were also formal relationships, based
on convenience, policy and cash. A royal mistress, like Nell
Gwynne, was acknowledged, famous, deferred to, and also the
object of a good deal more feeling than the queen.

Half a century later, Gay's low-life parody of court behavior,
The Beggar's Opera, is full of elegant variations on the theme of
marriage as a girl's entrance ticket into the promiscuous and
pleasure-seeking adult world:

> A wife is like a guinea in gold,
> Stamp'd with the name of her spouse;
>   Now here, now there; is bought, or is sold;
> And is current in every house.

Marriage was also a necessary precondition of widowhood, as
Mrs. Peachum remarked when she tried to persuade her daughter to have her husband hanged for the reward: "The comfortable
estate of widowhood is the only thing that keeps up a wife's
spirits." (Two centuries later the prospect of alimony would have
the same cheering effect.) A generation after Gay, Sophie Ar-
nould, an opera singer and a famous beauty and wit, called marriage "the sacrament of adultery." For cynical polite society it
was a license for promiscuity, a secure base from which to carry
out sexual guerrilla warfare. When the heroes and heroines of
Les Liaisons Dangereuses talk of fidelity they mean the fidelity
of a husband to his mistress, a wife to her lover, but rarely, if
ever, of husband and wife to each other. The progenitor of the
nineteenth-century novel of adultery is the eighteenth-century
novel of seduction: Laclos, Fielding, Richardson.

Romanticism and what Lawrence Stone calls "the growth of
affective individualism" changed all that by injecting love into
the marital equation at the expense of more tangible and traditional benefits. Parents no longer arranged marriages for their
own practical ends and over the heads of their children. The
young couple demanded a say in the matter, their feelings were
consulted, there was a show of romance and consent. To a certain
extent. But where money, class and family name were concerned, sense continued to take its accustomed precedence over
sensibility, although more circumspectly than before. The young

couple exchanged love letters and tokens, and did their best to persuade themselves that what was happening was their decision. But when the passion and the palpitations were finally brought to a seemly conclusion the announcements read, "A marriage has been arranged . . ." And the announcements were accurate.

Even in those rare instances when they were not, married life is long and romantic love notoriously short. So for the reading public, adultery was no longer a cynical adjustment to social realities over which they had no control; instead, it became imbued with feeling, a fascinating triumph of emotion over convenience. In his classic study, *Passion and Society*, Denis de Rougemont showed that the incompatibility of love and marriage is an idea at least as old as the Provençal troubadours and that European literature is distinguished from all others by the belief that great love is always illicit, unhappy, doomed. But it was not until the end of the eighteenth century that adultery and the attendant unease of marriage were transferred from poetic myth to become the great tragic theme of the European novel: *Adolphe*, *Le Rouge et le Noir*, *Madame Bovary*, *Anna Karenina*.

The Romantic movement unsettled the balance of common sense, jangled the nerves and raised expectations of excitement even in lives as provincial as Emma Bovary's. All of which imposed an unnatural strain on marriage and the settled life. "A mind made for passion," wrote Stendhal in his treatise *On Love*, "feels in the first place that this happy life [marriage] irks him, and perhaps, also, that it only gives him a few very commonplace ideas . . . There are very few mental afflictions in life that are not rendered precious by the emotion which they excite." Adultery produces unhappiness; unhappiness is inspiring; inspiration is the ultimate good; therefore adultery is desirable. That is the Romantic syllogism. When Flaubert wrote *Madame Bovary* he was too shrewd to try to disprove it—and perhaps too involved, despite his dispassionate, exquisitely precise observation: "Emma Bovary," he said, "c'est moi." Instead, he took the syllogism to its terrible, un-Romantic conclusion: flee far enough from the commonplace and you end with the ugly convulsions of suicide by arsenic.

Lawrence's novels after *Sons and Lovers* fit into that Euro-

pean tradition in an idiosyncratic way. He wrote about marriage
in the same way as Tolstoy and the others wrote about adultery:
as a jagged, draining fight against the emotional and social odds,
as a doom, as a fate. No doubt he was provoked into this by the
fact that his own life, from the time he met Frieda, was dramatically similar to the plot of *Anna Karenina* or *Le Rouge et le
Noir*. As a result, *Lady Chatterley's Lover* reads to me like the
last kick of an exhausted tradition, despite the four-letter words,
or maybe because of them. He had originally intended to call the
book *Tenderness* and the rude words were there less to shock
than as a desperate way of emphasizing the urgency of his
theme: tenderness is tenderness no matter how it is expressed.
Seen from a certain angle, *Lady Chatterley* is a bloody-minded
answer to *Anna Karenina*. In it, Lawrence took the novel of
adultery and tried to make it, in some perverse way, *respectable*
by using the initial infidelity as the basis for what he saw as a
genuine marriage. No matter how Lawrence was construed in
his lifetime by the disciples of free love, by the time his work had
filtered down to the moralizing 1950s, he was above all the apos-
tle of true matrimony, a fierce and intolerant church, with Cambridge as its Rome and F. R. Leavis as pope.

So the spirit of Lawrence and Frieda brooded unnaturally,
as a model and as an inspiration, over my own first attempt at
marriage. They were the couple by whose teachings and standards we would all be judged. I had swallowed him whole and so
uncritically that a reaction inevitably set in. Like a youthful love
affair, it was hard to be friends after. His influence compounded
with my own stupidity to produce a disaster, and in some obscure
way I blamed him. "After such knowledge, what forgiveness?"
For years I was unable to reread any of those novels I had once
thought so marvelous. That was one of the more bizarre and
lasting side effects of my divorce, although it says more about
my derangement than about Lawrence's books.

But reading him again now, two decades after the event,
there seems an unbridgeable gap between the myth of Lawrence, as created by his books, his preaching and his followers,
and the reality of his life with Frieda. That difference says nothing about the quality of his imagination—on the contrary, it
shows how the creative imagination works—but it bears down

very hard indeed on the attitude toward love and marriage and divorce of a whole generation, now middle-aged.

For people like myself who were students in the earnest fifties, it is hard to know how much our youthful passion for Lawrence's writing was not in reality a passion for his hugely romantic life. Or rather, for what seemed hugely romantic to young literary hopefuls, since we fixed on the flow and urgency of his work and chose to ignore his rhetoric, his repetitions, his nagging, hectoring tone. We were also too young to know about the drab grind of putting pen to paper or the exhaustion of living hand to mouth or the dissatisfaction and irritation which drove him to shift continually about the globe in search of some archaic Eden he must have known he would never find. The travel seemed pure adventure and therefore purely desirable, especially to a generation which had spent its adolescence cooped up in wartime England and was only just beginning to discover the pleasures of "abroad": the alien tastes and scents and sounds and habits and languages.

Added to that, Dr. Leavis had told us that Lawrence was a great writer. And told us and told us until we could parrot how and why and wherefore automatically, in heavy critical prose, without thinking, without even looking, in one long mindless paternoster. All of which provided a marvelous excuse for hero worship of an utterly uncritical kind. But the underlying attraction was the romance of Lawrence and Frieda themselves. To the adolescent, it seemed a paradigm of the creative life: the young genius intuiting the one woman who knew his worth; the older woman, in her turn, giving up her children and a comfortable marriage in order to follow his questionable star; and behind them the usurped, elderly husband. It was a classic case in a long tradition of classics: *Oedipus Rex*, *Tristan and Iseult*, *Anna Karenina*, not to mention *Peg's Paper* and *East Lynne*.

Which is not to cheapen them, but simply to emphasize how perennial and universal is the yearning for the Great Passion, for the triumph and unhappiness of love at first sight. "Happy love has no history," wrote Denis de Rougemont. "Romance only comes into existence where love is fatal, frowned upon and doomed by life itself. What stirs lyrical poets to their finest flights is neither the delight of the senses nor the fruitful contentment of the settled couple; not the satisfaction of love, but its *passion*. And passion means suffering. There we have the fundamental fact . . . Passionate love is a misfortune. In this respect manners have undergone no change for centuries, and the community still drives passionate love in nine cases out of ten to take the form of adultery."

The power of that myth, however unreal and unrealistic, still held Frieda after Lawrence's death and all their difficult years together, when she wrote her autobiography:

> I see him before me as he entered the house. A long thin figure, quick straight legs, light, sure movements. He seemed so obviously simple. Yet he arrested my attention. There was something more than met the eye. What kind of bird was this?
>
> The half-hour before lunch the two of us talked in my room, French windows open, curtains fluttering in the spring wind, my children playing on the lawn.
>
> He said he had finished with his attempts at knowing women. I was amazed at the way he fiercely denounced them. I had never before heard anything like it . . . We talked about Oedipus and understanding leaped through our words.
>
> After leaving that night, he walked all the way to his home. It was a walk of at least five hours. Soon afterwards he wrote to me: 'You are the most wonderful woman in all England.'

The rest is famous: the elopement, the scandal, her agony for the children she had abandoned which sowed the seed of their savage fights, but all of it apparently vindicated by his work and their restless, questing and, presumably, rich life.

Dr. Leavis resisted all that strenuously. He was sniffy about their marriage, "this homeless and childless vagabondage with Frieda," and even sniffier about Frieda herself: "She had, as Lawrence's wife, no home, and, having abandoned her children, no maternal function. She was, in fact, neither maternal in type nor intellectual; she had no place in any community, and nothing much to do—the request for novels for Frieda to read is a recurrent note in Lawrence's letters."

I suppose Lawrence himself would have reacted to this view

from Cambridge in the same way he reacted to his one experience of the place: with outrage. After all, it was his obsession with Frieda and their life together which made the myth so alluring. His stormy marriage became for him a kind of profession, as engrossing and exhausting as his writing, as well as its major source. It and she reappear throughout his books persistently, like a single narrative thread holding the whole fabric together. And because the connections were always very close between his immediate experience and his art, he seems to have viewed his life as if it, too, were fiction, a novel containing the novels. What was happening to him also colored the way he read other people's books: hence his passionate defense of Hardy's passionate outcasts and his preoccupation, while he and Frieda were in Cornwall, with Tristan and Iseult.

At the start, he was a highly literary young man who saw what he was doing in terms of the great literary love stories. "Oh Lord," he wrote from Germany, immediately after he and Frieda had eloped, "it's easier to write history than make it." What others had imagined, he was acting out. It was a distinction that was to dog him all his life; whence his determination to be good at things, to cope, to see for himself, instead of remaining chained to a desk. Meanwhile, the master script was Tolstoy's. "I daren't think of Weekley . . ." he wrote, again from Germany, "I only know I love Frieda . . . I can think of nothing but Anna Karenina."

Over the years, as the romance wore off, he hardened in his determination to set Tolstoy on his head:

> Nobody in the world is anything but delighted when Vronsky gets Anna Karenina. Then what about the sin?—Why, when you look at it, all the tragedy comes from Vronsky's and Anna's fear of *society*. The monster was social, not phallic at all. They couldn't live in the pride of their sincere passion, and spit in Mother Grundy's eye. And that, that cowardice, was the real 'sin.' The novel makes it obvious, and knocks all old Leo's teeth out.

He wrote that toward the end of his life when all that was left of his own great passion was a difficult union between two embattled middle-aged warriors. Nevertheless, he was still taking the book personally, as if the need to justify himself remained, even at that absurdly late stage of the game.

In the beginning, this need was overwhelming. Lawrence, I think, was as deeply shocked by what he and Frieda were doing as was Ernest Weekley himself. As if to prove that the guilt was not all his, he insisted that Frieda go to her husband and tell him "the truth" about their marriage. According to Robert Lucas, Frieda's biographer, she confessed her other affairs—a casual one with a Nottingham neighbor, a crucially important one with a German called Otto Gross—but did not mention Lawrence. He seemed, in fact, curiously left out of the main action, a shadowy figure off to one side of the picture. Weekley did not even find out about him until after Frieda arrived in Germany. His younger daughter, Barbara Weekley Barr, says that he sent Frieda a telegram: "Believe Lawrence is with you. Please reply yes or no." Even then, Frieda wanted to prevaricate—to spare her husband's feelings, she claimed. It was Lawrence who persuaded her not to.

It was also Lawrence who refused, before they left England, to sleep with Frieda in her husband's house and who wrote her a note when they were briefly apart in Germany, saying, "I have written a letter to Ernest. You needn't, of course, send it. But you must say to him all I have said. No more dishonour, no more lies. Let them do their—silliest—but no more subterfuge, lying, dirt, fear. I feel as if it would strangle me." It was Frieda who had left her children, but it was Lawrence who was appalled and frightened by what had suddenly happened to his life.

Like Mr. Prufrock, this was not what he had meant at all. With his fierce mother and his nonconformist upbringing, he was the last person to make moral history. Up until the time he met Frieda, he seemed set on a far more conventional course: that of the young genius who in order to work well needed, as he said, "a woman behind him," to sympathize, to sustain him, to share his literary tastes and high-minded, often priggish attitudes to the world. And he seemed to have no difficulty in finding them: Jessie Chambers, Louie Burrows, Helen Corke; all of them vigorous, independent, ambitious young women, serious and dedicated, who hated superficiality and were using their talents and determination, like Lawrence himself, to move up in the world.

They were united, at least, in their belief in his overwhelming gift.

In the ways that matter, their world was similar to Ernest Weekley's, although one generation behind. Weekley had already made the jump they were attempting. For forty years his father had been the Relieving Officer of Hampstead, a very minor civil servant with the Dickensian job of distributing alms to the poor of the parish. He and his wife never lost their vestigial cockney accents and they lived conveniently next to the workhouse in New End. When they moved to John Constable's house in Well Walk, the street was still a long way from being the suburban Gold Coast it has since become; their rent was one pound a week. Ernest, the second of their nine children and oldest surviving son, got himself out of the lower-middle-class poverty trap in the same way Lawrence did: by talent and hard work. He was a scholarship boy with a flair for languages and a passion for words. He became a schoolmaster at seventeen, worked in his spare time for an external degree at London University, studied German for a year at the University of Berne, then won a scholarship to Trinity, the most prestigious of all Cambridge colleges, where he took a brilliant First in Middle English and Modern Languages. For a year he attended lectures at the Sorbonne, followed by another year as Lektor at Freiburg University. Then, when he was still only thirty-two, he was offered a professorship at the new University College in Nottingham. To celebrate he took a working holiday in the Black Forest, where he met Frieda.

He was not, in short, born into the Establishment; instead, he had won himself a place in it by virtue and achievement. As Lawrence himself might have done, with slightly different gifts and a vastly different sensibility. As his mother most certainly wished him to do. Perhaps that is why there was curiously little bad blood between the two men. Soon after the elopement, Weekley wrote to Frieda in Germany, "I bear him no ill-will and hope you will be happy with him." Even Lawrence, who could rarely resist savaging people he knew in his books, was unusually restrained with Weekley. In *The Virgin and the Gypsy* it was the Weekley family he pilloried and its suffocating effect on the children, not the cuckolded husband. "W is really *awfully* good," he wrote to his mentor, Edward Garnett: "what the English *can* be if they are hauled by the neck into it, is something rather great . . . He's rather fine—never, for one moment, denies his love for F, and never says anything against her herself, only against the previous lover, a German, who put these 'ideas' into her head. He says I am 'ehrlich' and have a great future." Weekley's gentlemanly behavior combined with the underlying similarities, and even sympathy, between the two men to fuel Lawrence's sense of shock at what he had done. Thereafter he went on to explain and justify his actions again and again throughout his work, as if his guilt could never be laid to rest. By using his life with Frieda and their grand passion so insistently as the basic material of his fiction, he turned them into a public property. (When he published a book of poems about their elopement called *Look! We Have Come Through*, Bertrand Russell remarked, "They may have come through, but why should I look?") In his social behavior at least, he became a prophet *malgré lui*, because there was no other position to occupy. Unlike Vronsky, he lacked the defenses, the indifference, which rank and income create.

Because he made so much of Frieda in his books, we tend to see her as his creation. At times she also saw herself in this way: her literary style was pastiche Lawrence, and so occasionally was her behavior. But this tends to confuse the fact that she was a lady with vivid ideas about herself before she met Lawrence. So vivid, indeed, that there seems in the end less difference between Lawrence and Weekley than between Frieda and them both. It was not a question of class. Too much has been made of her aristocratic background, particularly by Lawrence who boasted about it in their early days together when he was still keen to "get on" in ways which would have impressed his mother. In comparison, not enough has been made of Frieda's concept of herself as a new woman, an embodiment of the sexual avant garde, who did as much to create Lawrence, both as a man and an artist, as he did to create her.

This is the thesis of Martin Green's fascinating study *The von Richthofen Sisters*, which attempts to see Lawrence "as part of a European movement, and not as a purely British phenomenon." To do this, Green examines in great detail the German intellectual milieu in which the sisters flourished. There were three of them, all extraordinary women in their different ways, although Nusch, the great beauty of the family and the youngest, devoted her life to love affairs without benefit of theories, and so does not fit into Green's scheme of things. According to Barbara Barr, Baron von Richthofen once told his daughters, "I don't mind whom you marry, so long as it isn't an Englishman, a Jew or a gambler." Inevitably, they did what he told them not to: Frieda married her English professor; Elsa married Edgar Jaffe, a Jewish economist who became Finance Minister for Bavaria; Nusch's first husband was a gambler. All three marriages were disasters.

The crucial influence on the lives of both Frieda and Elsa was Otto Gross, one of the first psychoanalysts and also, in the beginning, one of the most gifted. Ernest Jones and Wilhelm Stekel thought he had genius and Freud himself said that Gross and Jung were the most original of his followers. But Gross was also a wild man, a drug addict who preached sexual libertarianism and spectacularly practiced what he preached. His behavior was altogether too volatile, provocative and compromising for Freud, who had enough abuse to cope with himself. So Gross was summarily ejected from the charmed analytic circle. He died in 1920, starving and addicted.

But in his prime he was an eloquent spokesman for all those Germans who rejected Bismarck's authoritarian Prussian rule. Against the chancellor's tyrannical patriarchy, with its cult of discipline and subservience, of "blood and iron," Gross preached the virtues of matriarchy: instinct over intellect, sensual love over political power, feeling over will, bodily knowledge over reason. He flourished in Schwabing, a bohemian suburb of Munich which, before the First World War, was the center of the international avant garde, as Montparnasse was in the 1920s or Greenwich Village in the fifties. Kandinsky, Paul Klee and Franz Marc lived there. Matisse visited. Bruno Walter played the piano at one of the cafés where Wedekind and Mühsam, the anarchist poet, sang and acted, and Hofmannstal, among others, wrote the lyrics. Gross and his colleagues in the Cosmic Circle believed they were the prophets and forerunners of a new life and a new, liberated, sensuous society. And the instrument of their rebellion was eroticism.

He had love affairs with both the older von Richthofen sisters. Elsa bore him a child and Frieda was so much under his spell when she ran off with Lawrence that she tried to explain herself to her outraged husband by sending him letters Gross had written her. In them he called her "the woman of the future," "the only person who *today* has stayed free of chastity as a moral code and Christianity and Democracy and all those heaps of nonsense." As Martin Green points out, the language of these letters, and their image of Frieda as a pagan female power and creature of the sun, is uncannily close to Lawrence's. Similarly, the theories of the Cosmic Circle, with its belief in blood knowledge, physical as opposed to mental consciousness, and *Mutterrecht*, Mother-Right, is reechoed in the confused metaphysics Lawrence later expanded in *The Crown* and *Fantasia of the Unconscious*.

The story of Frieda's affair with Gross has a depressingly familiar ring to it: the powerful and dissatisfied woman of a certain age who comes under the influence of an equally powerful and seductive guru from the psychoanalytic demimonde, and then goes on to change her life dramatically, destroying in the process the lives around her, carelessly, almost unwittingly. Half a century later, R. D. Laing had a similar effect on similar followers: emotional, unintellectual women who had brooded intensely about themselves and were waiting to be shown, by someone who had also pondered these things, what their special qualities were worth. Clearly, they constitute a potent temptation, particularly if, like Frieda, they are full of vitality and arrogance. Since she was strong, headlong, attractive and intensely ambitious to be taken seriously, it was almost inevitable that Gross should have picked her as the incarnation of all his cracked theories.

As his "woman of the future" she believed unreservedly in the gospel of free love. Hence her affairs while she was married to Weekley. Hence, too, her affairs while she was with Lawrence: "after thirteen years of confining domesticity," wrote Paul Delany in *D. H. Lawrence's Nightmare*, "she wanted to sow some wild oats with men less priggish and demanding than Lawrence: she had at least three casual affairs in the first year they were together, and made sure Lawrence knew about them." After that first flush of liberated promiscuity subsided, she continued to have intermittent affairs: with Cecil Gray, for example, and later, more seriously, with Lawrence's most passionate and ingratiating disciple, Middleton Murry—an interlude which inspired at least two of Lawrence's tales, "The Border Line" and the sardonic "Jimmy and the Desperate Woman." Later still, while he was writing *Lady Chatterley's Lover*, Frieda's lover was Angelino Ravagli, whose villa they had rented and whom she later married; which makes that notorious book cast a curiously double image. Her son Montague called her "an erotic adventuress."

She herself did not think of it that way. As Otto Gross's chosen disciple, sleeping around was as full of meaning and intention as homosexual experiment was to radical feminists half a century later. It was a political action, it showed she was serious. And when she was in her thirties she was a lady who took herself and her unique destiny very seriously indeed. Perhaps Weekley's gravest crime against her was his failure to do likewise, despite the fact that he loved her devotedly in his withheld and scholarly way. She was a high-spirited teenager when he married her, and he went on treating her like one over the years, mocking her when she strummed the piano or aired her execrable French or belatedly discovered one of the classics he had slogged through as a schoolboy. Part of the blame lay with his crushing Cambridge imperiousness—the Trinity scholarship, the First, the professorship—part with the more understandable impatience of an exceptionally well-educated man with the vagaries, enthusiasms and self-regarding naïveté of someone ebullient, uneducated and far younger. He was at fault and she was at fault, but she could not forgive him for it. Even her son, who went brilliantly through the same educational mill as his father, was unable to take her intellectual pretensions seriously, although she used to tell him repeatedly that, whatever he thought, she was a clever woman. But she did not mention that she had the great Otto Gross's word for it.

Lawrence was young enough and uncertain enough at the start to believe her claims. If Green is right, she projected onto him the concept of herself Gross had given her, which Lawrence accepted, then reinterpreted and re-created imaginatively in the heroines of his books. He not only took this mishmash of ideas seriously, he was able to use it for his own ends. It represented something he needed and was ready for after all his years of change and secret preparation; it corresponded to some element in his own genius. So although they fought bitterly and grumbled about each other incessantly to their friends, in his writing Lawrence refused to see her behavior as shabby. He swallowed her inflated idea of herself as an all-powerful demiurge of *Mutterrecht* and transformed her promiscuity into the mysterious workings of the feminine principle. It made no difference that his own adored mother had dourly endured her ghastly marriage without ever breaking out. By grafting his straight-laced noncomformist upbringing onto Frieda's free and easy selfishness, he created a paradigm of marriage no less idealized than the marriage of Levin and Kitty in *Anna Karenina*, and also no less removed than Tolstoy's from the marriage he actually had.

As for Frieda: she had a knack for seeing herself dramatically, as the figure in the spotlight at the center of the stage. Hence her taste for improbable or socially impossible men. Rayner Heppenstall has remarked, "At one time, Nottinghamshire miners were as exotic as the inhabitants of the Faubourg St. Germain." More so, perhaps, to the daughter of a minor aristocrat serving in the Prussian army. But so too was Ernest Weekley, an older man and distinguished scholar who had made it by hard work and talent from the English lower middle class. The only things not exotic about him were his sexual timidity and the dull conventionality of professorial life in Nottingham; but Frieda had no idea of that when she married him. When she finally erupted she chose Otto Gross, the most outlandish of all her lovers and practitioner of what was then considered—however improbable this now seems—a vaguely scandalous submedical discipline. The German and Italian peasants and American Indians whom she later took casually to bed were all part of the same pattern: exotics, outsiders, adjuncts to her personality. She was, determinedly, one of those women who always stoop to conquer. Gross merely provided her with high-flown excuses for a tendency to behave badly which she seems otherwise to have come by quite naturally. Just after the elopement, Lawrence wrote to Weekley, man to man: "Mrs. Weekley is afraid of being stunted and not allowed to grow, and so she must live her own life. All women in their natures are like giantesses. They will break through everything and go on with their own lives. The position is one of torture for us all . . . Mrs. Weekley must live largely and abundantly. It is her nature." Since Weekley had already read Gross's letters to Frieda, he would presumably have recognized the message. Whence, perhaps, his restraint toward Lawrence. They were both victims of an alien theory.

Even Frieda may have thought the same at first. Green quotes her as saying that she and Lawrence had no grand passion for each other when they left England together. Maybe that was why she was so casual in her farewells to her children: she thought she was simply acting out Gross's theories as she had done before, with the secret reservation that she might return to her husband when the adventure was over. At the back of her mind, she may even have had the idea of teaming up with Gross, since she took Lawrence off to Munich in their first month together and they went back there for two months the following year, before returning to England.

But she was reckoning without Lawrence's need and intensity, and without her own recognition of the overwhelming life and talent in him. He also had the advantage of being younger and more biddable than either of the other two men, more conventional than Gross and less dangerous. She must have sensed that it would be possible to make a real life with Lawrence, whereas with Gross, whatever his attractions, she could only make a disaster. Nevertheless, it was Gross who had prepared her, during their time together, for the world of serious artists, and she repaid the compliment by impregnating Lawrence with his theories. Everyone who knew them well—the Murrys, Lady Ottoline Morrell—blamed Frieda for the excesses and metaphysical confusions and sexual hysteria in Lawrence's writing.

She was also important to him in a more simple way. According to his son, Weekley was a robust man with tremendous powers of work. He didn't need any support. He just needed someone to run his home and keep an eye on things. In contrast, Lawrence was a chronic consumptive, frail and exposed, a man whose nerve ends showed, who hovered continuously on the edge of breakdown of one kind or another. Where most people fall ill occasionally, Lawrence had brief spells of good health,

remissions from the general fragility of his condition. Frieda
carried him—quite literally, toward the end—with her unsink-
able vigor and her brutal physical imperviousness to illness or
fatigue. There are endless stories of Lawrence's rising from what
had seemed to be his deathbed the moment she breezed into the
room.

In many ways Lawrence and Frieda were like the lion and
the unicorn, darkness and light, and all the other polar opposites
he celebrated in *The Crown*, the confused and hectoring statement of his philosophy. Each needed the other's strengths and
weaknesses in order to survive and flourish. For both of them,
this symbiotic dependence justified everything else:

> Frieda and Lawrence had undoubtedly a profound and passionate
> love-life [wrote Aldous Huxley]. But this did not prevent Frieda
> from having every now and then affairs with Prussian cavalry of-
> ficers and Italian peasants, whom she loved for a season without in
> any way detracting from her love for Lawrence or from her intense
> devotion to his genius. Lawrence, for his part, was aware of these
> erotic excursions, got angry about them sometimes, but never
> made the least effort to break away from her, for he realized his
> own organic dependence upon her. He felt towards her as a man
> might feel towards his own liver: the liver may give trouble from
> time to time, but it remains one of the vital organs absolutely
> necessary to survival.

No hint of Frieda's promiscuity gets into Lawrence's fic-
tional portrait of her. On the contrary, he transformed their
stormy life together into an ideal marriage: complex, adult, passionate. And this, in some underground way, helped change the
attitude toward divorce. Since Lawrence and Frieda had
brought it off so spectacularly in his books, perhaps this dangerous, scandalous act was worth it after all: worth the pain, the
trouble, the social obloquy and uproar. It is easy to make psy-
chopathic behavior appear glamorous; Lawrence also made it
seem dignified, profound and true. In the 1950s, when the Lawrence fever was at its peak in England, it was impossible to
believe that the High Priest of Marriage was also, in his fashion,
a complaisant husband. He and Frieda existed in the British
undergraduate imagination with the purity and concentration

and coherence of figures from myth. Like most of my contemporaries, I swallowed the fiction whole and chose to ignore the small, shoddy, deadly betrayals which made up the reality.

Two betrayals, however, were less easy to brush aside: Frieda's sacrifice of her children and Lawrence's violent jealousy of them, which was the initial excuse for those famously savage domestic fights, and may even have been Frieda's private excuse for her infidelities. In those days when divorce was still rare and outrageous, she had already put herself beyond the moral and social pale when she walked out on her husband. She automatically forfeited most of her legal rights, and, as the flagrantly guilty party, she forfeited all rights to her children. Weekley played this card early, in the hope of getting her back: if she chose Lawrence, she would lose her children forever. But by then Frieda and Lawrence were far off, spiritually as well as geographically, moving in what Lawrence called "the Hinterland der Seele," and the accusing voices from the world they had left behind could not get through. When Weekley realized he had really lost her, he stuck by his threat, less out of revenge—he wasn't, his son said, a spiteful man—than out of shame and anger at his public humiliation. Montague is convinced that the divorce, and the way Lawrence in his books kept the wound insidiously open, deprived his father of the professorship at Oxford or Cambridge for which his publications and international reputation so obviously qualified him. At a time when divorce was socially intolerable, even the innocent party was contaminated by the scandal, guilty by association.

He may even have believed it himself. In the Weekley family, said Montague, "there was only one cardinal virtue: respectability. My grandmother was always talking about who was respectable and who wasn't. I can still hear her saying about somebody or other, 'Bohemian sort of people.' With an emphasis on the 'o.' It was an indication of unspeakable fornications." No doubt, his adoring, implacable mother played on Weekley's rage and vanity and self-pity in order to become, once again, the dominant power in his life. It is even a natural motherly response, of a kind. What seems less natural is that Weekley himself, who was a vigorous and handsome man in his forties when Frieda walked out, should have yielded up his manhood so readily, delivering his children into the care of his devouring mother and his dreadful spinster sister, and refusing to be comforted by any of the eager, presentable ladies who clustered sympathetically around him. He may have started in shock:— scandalized, humiliated and, because he loved his wife, desperate.—but he finished stuck with a badly written, faintly outmoded role: the suffering, wronged husband of Victorian melodrama.

Melodrama: soon after Frieda left him, Weekley sent her a photograph of her two young daughters, with a letter saying, "You will never see your children again; I will be father and mother to them." When the letter arrived, Frieda, in her anguish, lay down and banged her head on the floor. Lawrence later described the scene to Barbara Barr: "There was I—a man of twenty-six—with this madwoman. I said to her, 'If that's how you feel, you must go back to him.' Frieda cried, 'You don't love me.' I said, 'You know I do, but you must do what you want fundamentally.' " When Barbara asked him, "What would have happened to you if she had gone back?" he replied, "I would have been finished."

Melodrama: Aunt Maude, Weekley's spinster sister, was religious, deaf and prone to fearful outbreaks of what Lawrence, in *The Virgin and the Gypsy*, called "green rage," particularly against the younger of her nieces. She kept house for the family, but without pleasure. The cooking was terrible, the quantities inadequate. Later the children remembered being hungry much of the time, especially during the war when Aunt Maude used to hoard their meat coupons for her own beloved father.

Melodrama: three evil spirits haunted the household: fear, respectability, scandal. The older people were clenched continually against the possibility that Frieda might at any moment reappear to see her children and infect them with her immorality; in blue spectacles, presumably, and disguised as a governess, like the last act of *East Lynne*. And they were right. When Frieda finally returned to England in 1913 she waylaid her daughters on their way to school. "Run, children, run," shrieked Aunt Maude. They ran. Later, she managed to sneak in through the back door of their new house in Chiswick and appeared in the nursery suddenly, like a ghost, at teatime. Granny and Aunt

Maude drove her out physically, aided by the terrified children. After that, a court order was taken out to restrain her. When she and the children were eventually allowed to meet, it was as strangers in the office of Weekley's solicitors.

Added to all this melodramatic sin and mystery and fear, fabricated by Weekley's mother and sister for their own devious purposes, was another ingredient, harder to pin down, more insidious and of Weekley's own making: his unfeigned misery made the children feel they were somehow to blame. "If Ernest had been childless," said Barbara, "he would have found another woman. His celibacy was a kind of reproach to us."

For the rest of their lives, two of the three children felt they must make amends in the hope of living down that unspoken reproach. Only Elsa, the middle child, had neither time nor patience for her romantic, unstable mother, and at an early stage appears to have dismissed the whole messy business from her life. Having no taste for melodrama and not much admiration for Lawrence's books, she saw her mother no more than was strictly necessary, and without enthusiasm. After Frieda's death she refused to discuss her with outsiders. She was her father's child, very much a Weekley, the Cordelia in whose house he lived out his last decade and died peacefully. She seems never to have forgiven her mother and also never to have seen the point in pretending to have done so. As a result, she survived more or less unscathed and made a calm, reasonable and successful married life for herself.

In worldly terms, Montague was also successful—he eventually became the distinguished curator of a distinguished museum—but without Elsa's assurance and single-mindedness. As the oldest child and only son, just on the edge of puberty, the loss of his mother was like a violation. Frieda was only twenty-one when he was born, still almost a girl and with a girl's high spirits and physical intensity. When he was in his late seventies he could still vividly remember "riding on her back like a dolphin" in the River Trent when the two of them went bathing from the bungalow of Will Dowson, a Nottingham lace manufacturer (who was also one of Frieda's lovers), or plunging crazily about in the sea with her during their summer holidays on the Lincolnshire coast at Chapel St. Leonard, Skegness and Sutton-on-Sea. "It was like," he said, "having a wildly exuberant wench to play with." She was an overwhelming presence in the household and her going left a terrible void in his life, particularly since his father was rarely around, always off laboring to make ends meet. His chair at Nottingham was poorly paid, so he spent each summer locked in his study, marking school examination papers and writing his own distinguished but formidably learned books.

On one side, the paradise image of the child on the dolphin and the wildly exuberant wench who, briefly and miraculously, had been his mother; on the other, the remote, overworked, obscurely grieving father. But because Montague loved and admired his father, he felt his unspoken reproach most strongly of all the three children and exhausted himself to make reparation for the damage his mother had done. Yet he was given no facts: his father first told him his mother was ill and thereafter refused to mention her at all. This sense of hidden enormity added to his adolescent bewilderment. He began to suffer from attacks of nausea and wept on Sunday evenings when his father left their London house to return to the university. In some dim way, he seems to have been more sorry for his father than for himself. At prep school in Nottingham he had been an uninterested and indifferent pupil. But in London, first at Colet Court, then at St. Paul's, he did brilliantly, winning a scholarship to St. John's, Oxford, taking a First and topping that with a Blue for athletics. All to please his father and make good the injuries his wayward mother had caused: "I wanted to cheer him up, so he would think, Well, at least Monty doesn't reveal any fearful tendencies to vice!"

In his old age he could joke about it, just as he was able to acknowledge the poignancy both of his childhood memories of Frieda and of the anguish she caused when she walked out. Yet he had no illusions about his parents' marriage or what might have been if Lawrence had not arrived on the scene: "It was a most incompatible marriage, hopeless from the start. Looking back on it now, I see there was no prospect of its lasting. Of course, the world has always been full of erotic adventuresses, like Frieda, who manage to maintain a façade. But my father had a crushing schoolmasterly manner and not much tact; he couldn't resist putting her in her place. And Frieda was a rather cock-a-hoop person who needed to be handled gently. She was always a cake eater and haver. Whatever the rights and wrongs of the case, that always loomed large with Frieda: a cake eater and haver. She wanted everything and didn't see why she shouldn't get it.

"She was one of those slightly creative people who reject any kind of mental discipline. That was brought home to me when, after well over forty years, I finally met her sister Elsa, who was one of the first women graduates from Heidelberg. The contrast with Frieda was overwhelming. Elsa's English was extraordinary; although she lived in Germany, she spoke it with a far better accent than Frieda ever acquired after all her years in England and America. But the main thing was the immediate rapport between us. We had both been brought up in the same intellectual nursery: Oxford and Heidelberg. It was as though we were in the common room together. And it made me wonder if, in fact, the whole myth of Frieda as the woman of instinct, Lawrence's Egeria and therefore somehow superior, wasn't in itself a weird perversion of the truth. Perhaps she was not, after all, particularly intelligent."

Yet none of that lessened the impact of Frieda's vivid presence. He remembered every detail of his schoolboy meetings with her after she left: "to Covent Garden to hear Beecham conduct Mozart's *Figaro*, with Frederick Ranelow, of *Beggar's Opera* fame, as Figaro, and somebody called Desirée Ellinger as Suzanna"; "tea with her and Katherine Mansfield at a place called Bancock's Dairies, which had a tea-room right up against Baron's Court station"; "tea with her and Lady Glenavey in the studio of Mark Gertler at 15 Rudolph Crescent"; "the appalling farce of our first meeting with her at the offices of my father's lawyers: Goldberg, Batherton, Newell. Why should I remember that name?"

Why? Presumably because nothing could finally eradicate the strain and exhaustion of having been the responsible eldest child in a marital disaster of such proportions. In his old age he could make a joke of his huge effort to do well at school and university in order to cheer his father up, "so he'd think, 'Well, at least Monty doesn't reveal any fearful tendencies to vice!' "

But according to his younger sister, his account of his career to
Frieda herself was altogether bleaker: "I did it to please my
father," he said, "and it all meant nothing to him." "Not strictly
true," said Barbara, meaning her father took great pride in his
son's achievements. But probably true enough so far as Montague was concerned, since he knew that nothing could finally
compensate the old man for his wife's betrayal. And because of
the fame Lawrence bestowed on Frieda through his books, the
scandal never properly died away. Instead, it seeped on through
the lives of her children and their children, like a dye coloring
everything. "It was," he said, "a terrible inheritance."

The full burden of that inheritance was borne by Barbara,
the youngest child—seven when Frieda left—and the most
imaginative, her father's darling, who nevertheless went on to
spend the most time with her scandalous mother. In her childish,
disdainful way, she disliked her spinster Aunt Maude and was
cordially disliked in return. Her memories of the cramped but
lovely Georgian house which had once belonged to Constable are
selectively bleak: "The things I remember best about Well
Walk," she wrote to me, "are the ground floor bathroom smelling
of coal tar soap; the 'leads' which extended like a platform from
the dining room at the back . . . and the lillies of the valley which
bloomed in some nether gloom of a tiny garden." She also remembered the Dickensian moral gloom which brooded over the
household:

> When Elsa and I asked my father at breakfast, "Where is Mama?"
> he became pale and went out of the room. Granny said, "You girls
> mustn't ask about Mama just now. Papa is worried. . . ."
> Elsa and I lay in bed at night and cried. . . .
> Ernest was like a man who has had a mortal blow. We children
> all felt so *sorry* for him, and I was always saying, "Poor Papa!" As
> I grew older, however, I felt that too much of my sympathy had
> been expended.

Where Montague, the responsible oldest child, accepted as his
lot the emotional exhaustion imposed by his father's grief, Barbara eventually said no. The usual adolescent awakening to the
frailties of beloved parents became, in her, open rebellion. When

she was expelled from St. Paul's Girls School for drawing male nudes in her arithmetic book, the Weekleys must have thought that all their nightmares were coming true: unlike her brother, she was displaying Frieda's "fearful tendencies to vice."

But at the same time, she was also displaying considerable talent as a painter. At art school her teachers thought her exceptional and predicted a brilliant future. It never quite materialized, although she continued to paint beautifully when the spirit moved her. Perhaps she lacked the steel, ambition and inner discipline which finally separate the true artist from those merely gifted by nature. Perhaps, that is, she was too much her mother's child, for from the time she was old enough to decide for herself, she attached herself flamboyantly to Frieda's camp. She spent increasingly more time in Italy with the Lawrences, becoming part of the family, confided in by both of them, sitting in on their spectacular quarrels:

> A few days later [she wrote in one of her memoirs] the sparks flew again when Lawrence, after inveighing bitterly against Frieda, flung his wine in her face. This time I joined in, shouting, 'She's too good for you; it's casting pearls before swine!'
>
> After Frieda had gone out of the room in anger, I asked Lawrence, 'Do you care for her?'
>
> 'It's indecent to ask,' he replied. 'Look what I've done for your mother! Haven't I just helped her with her rotten painting?'

The elegant, witty style she developed—in her life as well as in her writing—came later. At the time, she seems to have been excited, defiant, overwhelmed—and also, perhaps, since she herself was gifted and creative, a little competitive. She had been brought up to believe that Lawrence and Frieda represented some ultimate form of depravity; she found him, in fact, "a queer, unearthly creature . . . beyond being human and ordinary." He cast his extraordinary spell on her, as he cast it on nearly everyone, and, if *The Virgin and the Gypsy* is anything to go by, he in turn responded to her in a tender, sorrowing way: to her youth and vulnerability and flaring, unsteady spirit.

While he was alive this mutual affection and devotion sustained her; after his death, it almost destroyed her. Barbara had

had depressions before, but when he died she suffered a major breakdown. As Robert Lucas describes it in his biography of Frieda, it was precipitated by her mother's usual breezy callousness. When Middleton Murry arrived in Vence with condolences, Frieda promptly took him to bed—just as Lawrence had ironically predicted in "The Border Line." When Murry left, Frieda traveled across the border to Italy with Barbara and Pino Orioli, the publisher of *Lady Chatterley*, to meet Angelino Ravagli, another of her lovers. When Ravagli tried to put an end to their affair Frieda talked him out of it. It was as though Lawrence had never existed.

At this point, Barbara broke down entirely. Perhaps Frieda's brutal betrayal of Lawrence so abruptly after his death reminded her daughter of her earlier betrayal when she had walked out on the lot of them—equally abruptly. Whatever the reason, according to Barbara's own account to Robert Lucas, all the hatred, resentment and terror of her mother she had bottled up since childhood came pouring out. Frieda's idea of a cure was a monstrous parody of Lawrence's dottiest, most inflated mysticism: she sent in a peasant to make love to her daughter. "In some curious way," Lucas commented dryly, "Lawrence's phallic ecstasies seem to have become mixed in Frieda's mind with the theories of Dr. Otto Gross." It was as if she were determined to prove, single-handed, that all the dirt ever flung at Lawrence was justified.

The storm passed in time, and when it did Barbara forgave her mother. In some odd way, the episode even sealed her devotion. She became Frieda's sturdiest public champion, and after the old lady's death wrote about her lovingly, movingly and with a wry, throwaway wit, usually at her own expense: "I believe she was right to act as she did; all the boring women who have told me 'I could never leave my children' have helped convince me."

Perhaps in defending Frieda she was also defending the life she had chosen for herself as an artist, as someone ineluctably "different" from what Frieda used to call "the stuffy old show." As a child, she had clung to her belief in her romantic mother as an antidote to the drab, stifling respectability of the Weekley household. Later, she was attracted to Lawrence and Frieda because they moved in a world to which her own talents as a painter had given her an entrance ticket, and because the life they had together seemed so vivid and full of possibility—despite their violent quarrels, or maybe even because of them.

But perhaps she was also powerless to resist the myth of Lawrence and Frieda for the same reason I was a generation later: because Lawrence, by using his life with Frieda as the focus of all his writing, had made it so terribly seductive. For Barbara, this was compounded by the personal appeal of the man himself, which even someone as emotionally shut off as Aldous Huxley found impossible to resist. But for her, his seductiveness was also full of moral ambiguities. She had been brought up by the embattled and humiliated Weekley clan to believe that Frieda and Lawrence between them represented sin in its most shameless form—"Bohemian with an emphasis on the 'o' "—and that what they had done was so scandalous that it could never even be spoken about. It was years before she was told the truth about her mother's sudden departure, and her beloved father barely mentioned Frieda's name again until his death more than forty years later. Between 1912 and 1923—that is, all through her late childhood and adolescence—she saw her mother maybe half a dozen times, always chaperoned, always as a stranger, often as someone rather frightening. She wrote, for instance, of the terrible evening when Frieda crept up to the nursery of the house in Chiswick: "And while she stood at bay before our relations, we children gazed in horror at the strange woman she had then become."

Art and respectability, sin and liberation, terror and seduction. Montague suffered muted, gentlemanly heartbreak and tried to make amends to his father; Elsa, having been abandoned, responded by washing her hands of her mother; but Barbara, the youngest and the artist, let it go through her. "It was," she once said, "like a dreadful aphrodisiac."

Lawrence himself clearly understood how much his grand passion for Frieda had cost those on the edges of it. Perhaps that is why he insisted so strenuously on justifying it, again and again, in his writing. It was a way of making up to Frieda for the loss of her children. It was also a way of making the public understand that every life is owed its own fulfillment, whatever the cost. And he wrote with the authority of a man who had spent a great deal of his time close to death. But as he went on, he also became shriller, more strident and unforgiving in his preaching, as though he never finally managed to silence the accusing voice of his chapel-going mother.

As for Frieda: her children agree that for a time she was a marvelous mother. But she was also intensely, brutally selfish. So it was unlikely, as her son suggested, that she would finally have been content to settle for the compromises of conventional marriage and the undramatic sacrifices ordinary mothers make. Had Lawrence not turned up in her life, sooner or later she would have left with someone else, but with someone who would probably have cared less for what she had done and who certainly would not have had either the genius or the intense desire to make such overwhelming reparation through his art.

As for the children: for a few years, they received from her generously; for the rest of their lives, they had to pay.

On September 29, 1969, Montague Weekley unveiled a blue plaque commemorating Lawrence's stay at I Byron Villas in the Vale of Health, the tiny village which seems to have been left by oversight in the middle of Hampstead Heath. Precisely why the authorities had decided to put up a plaque was not clear, since the Lawrences had lived in the house for less than five months in 1915. Perhaps it had something to do with Hampstead's reputation as a literary suburb.

It was a brilliant early autumn morning, the air immaculate and cool, the sun strong. Out on the Heath the trees were just at the point of turning, their greens undershot with yellow, as if the colors were layered on gold leaf, like a Sienese painting. The house was small and unprepossessing, redbrick and late Victorian gables, a workingman's house now gone up-market. A dozen people were gathered outside for the occasion: two pale, plump men in baggy suits, representing the Greater London Council and the Borough of Camden, a couple of journalists, a handful of vaguely literary locals and Barbara Barr, looking particularly stylish in flowing, autumn-colored tweeds.

Montague Weekley, however, treated us as if we were a

plenary session of the Royal Society: modestly, wittily, with respect. He was a startlingly handsome old man with an aristocratic profile, strong teeth, silver hair blowing about in the wind and the nervous confidence of an English gentleman. The speech he made was graceful beyond the call of that particular duty: he got in all the facts, told a couple of amusing anecdotes, made a tender joke at the expense of Frieda's accent, then another at Lawrence's, put in some charming references to Hampstead. The little group clapped politely. Montague unveiled the plaque. More polite clapping. Then everyone drifted off about their day's business.

Afterward, Montague, Barbara and I walked back together across the Heath, then along Well Walk, past the house where Frieda had left her daughters fifty-seven years before. There didn't seem much to say. The sun had gone in and the wind was colder. The trees moved their heavy branches about anxiously, as though upset. It seemed odd how even a minor, formal occasion like this could generate such sadness: the children's muted, motherless lives, their father's loss and humiliation, and the Cambridge professorship he never, despite his achievements, received. All those books, all that vanished intensity. It should have been over and done with for more than half a century, so why did it still seem so present?

Because Lawrence himself could never let it go. And it occurred to me that beyond his famous passion for life and his cant of the dark gods there was another Lawrence nobody mentioned; the Lawrence who could at times write so exquisitely and with such restraint out of a sense of guilt and grief, in the hope of making good some of the damage; the Lawrence who, with Frieda's daughter in mind, wrote in his most beautiful love story, *The Virgin and the Gypsy*, "Be braver in your heart, or you lose your game. Be braver in your body, or your luck will leave you."

IV

⟨❦⟩

Proper
Bostonians

In 1911, the year before Frieda eloped with Lawrence, Edith
Wharton published a story, "Autres Temps . . . ," based on a
famous scandal of thirty years before. The story concerns a Mrs.
Lidcote who long ago had sacrificed a respectable marriage in
the cause of love and was brutally ostracized for her daring. For
years she has acquiesced in society's judgment, exiling herself to
Florence, but when the story begins she is returning in middle
age to help her only child, Leila, when she in turn is exposed to
the public agony of a fashionable divorce and remarriage. But
"autres temps, autres moeurs": divorce is no longer of much
consequence to the smart young things among whom Leila
moves; they take it as part of the natural process, with no hard
feelings. Mrs. Lidcote is stunned, relieved, resentful:

> Here was she, a woman not yet old, who had paid with the best
> years of her life for the theft of the happiness that her daughter's
> contemporaries were taking as their due. There was no sense, no
> sequence, in it. She had had what she wanted, but she had had to
> pay too much for it . . . Now, at the sight of the young man down-

stairs, so openly and jovially Leila's, she was overwhelmed at the
senseless waste of her own adventure, and wrung with the irony
of perceiving that the success or failure of the deepest human ex-
periences may hang on a matter of chronology.

But then she thinks, if Leila is not blamed, perhaps she too will
be forgiven after all her years of penance. She is not. Her contemporaries continue to snub her, her daughter keeps her hidden
away upstairs while older, influential people call, even the man
who wants to marry her cannot disguise either from her or from
himself the degree to which she remains a social pariah. In the
end, she returns to Florence as outcast as when she left, but now
without even the sense of being needed by her daughter.

Edith Wharton wrote "Autres Temps . . ." when she was a
couple of years away from divorcing her own wayward husband,
and appalled at the prospect. Whence the story's poignancy and
pervasive grief, its carefully modulated anger against a society
"too busy to revise its own judgments." Yet when her divorce
went through, her case was much like Leila's: nobody blamed
her, scarcely anybody seemed to notice, polite society continued
to accept her as its own, her status as a literary lioness was
undiminished. Nature, for once, failed to imitate art.

Yet the realities for the woman on whom the story was
based were as harsh and constrained as Mrs. Lidcote's, and the
reverberations from them rolled on almost a century later. I
discovered this by chance from a friend in New York, a woman
of perhaps Mrs. Lidcote's age, with all Mrs. Lidcote's subtlety
and sense of style and none of her passivity in the face of convention. Emily looks at least twenty years younger than she is:
intelligent forehead, expressive mouth, blue, amused eyes. She
is witty and hospitable and not easily put off her stride in a circle
which includes politicians and writers as well as Manhattan's
curiously elusive aristocracy. A considerable time ago she married and divorced twice in a period of half a dozen years. Since
then she has remained single, preferring life on her own terms,
although, over the years I have known her, any number of men
have tried to change her mind in their favor. But she has refused
them all with such conviction that I began to wonder if perhaps
she was initiated into some quirky secret about marriage and

divorce which America's "old" families keep hidden from the rest of us: nuances, possibilities, private codes. Yet when I finally got up the nerve to ask her, one early-winter afternoon on the Upper East Side at the end of the 1970s, over tea and imported biscuits from Fortnum & Mason, her answer was mostly about another city, another century and her beautiful and vivacious grandmother Charlotte, who was Edith Wharton's model for Mrs. Lidcote.

In 1890 Charlotte, then in her middle thirties, ran off with a man fifteen years her junior, leaving in the lurch her proper Bostonian husband and a brood of bewildered children. It was the first fashionable Boston divorce and its effect in that decorous world was seismic. "Nobody else's mother," said Emily, "had ever run away with anybody." Charlotte then compounded the scandal with recklessness. When her husband realized that she would neither come back nor be held back he swallowed his principles for the sake of appearances and did what no other Boston Brahmin had so far dared: he offered her a divorce. He was by nature an unforgiving man, famous for his atrocious temper, and the terms he offered were appropriately harsh. But at least they would have given the unsavory affair an aroma of legality. Face of a kind would be saved: his face. But Charlotte fluttered her hands, thanked him sweetly, then went off and lived openly with her lover without waiting for the formalities to grind their way through the courts. All that could be said to alleviate the family's humiliation was that she had enough sense of style to move to Paris, where these things were supposed to be common, even acceptable. Like some well-heeled Manon Lescaut, she and her lover settled into an apartment in the rue St. Honoré. They married a couple of years later, but that did not redeem them in the eyes of Boston. The young husband was blackballed from his clubs and, like Mrs. Lidcote, neither of them was ever acceptable again in polite American society. So they stayed on in the rue St. Honoré until the Germans invaded France fifty years later. Charlotte by then was in her eighties, although still a scandalous figure in certain elderly and exclusive New England circles.

In Edith Wharton's story the scandal blights one life only, Mrs. Lidcote's; her daughter lives happily ever after, forgiven and forgiving. But Mrs. Wharton knew the outraged families socially, so she handled her subject with tongs and gloved fingers. Charlotte's children were less ceremonious. They sided wholly with their father, "a tiresome, angry old man," according to Emily, "who was worshiped as a god and could do no wrong." Except in his choice of a dizzy second wife, whom they looked down on and treated badly. Since their father controlled every detail of their lives, they never saw their mother throughout their childhood. Not until they were grown up and married, with families of their own, did they begin to visit her on their annual grand tours of Europe, but briefly and on the sly, without telling their father or their children. When Charlotte, after years of penance and exile, mustered the courage to return to the States, they allowed her to visit them equally furtively: in a limousine with drawn blinds when her grandchildren were out of the house. The name of her seducer was never mentioned, although they had been married for years. He was simply referred to as "that man."

Her children had suffered when the scandal first occurred: the son was brutally teased at Groton, the daughters mysteriously lost their playmates from among the first families. Although nothing was said, they were made to feel they had been exposed to some insidiously contagious disease and they never forgave her for it. In time the infection passed, the friends became friendly again, but as they grew in years and conventionality Charlotte's children learned to cope with their troublesome mother in a proper Bostonian manner, part formal, part secretive and oblique, but with melodramatic undertones; that limousine with drawn blinds is *East Lynne* rewritten for millionaires. So far as their own children were concerned, they took propriety to its logical conclusion and omitted to mention her existence.

Emily discovered her grandmother was alive by accident when a second cousin—the grandchild of her grandmother's sister—casually mentioned his aunt Charlotte. "Who's she?" asked Emily. She was twelve years old by then and disdainful of this cousin who came from a less distinguished branch of the family. He turned on her with scorn: "Idiot! Don't you know your own grandmother?" "My grandmother's dead," she answered haughtily. "Not at all," he replied, "she's visiting my mother."

Faced with a straight question in the presence of the cousin, Emily's mother confessed grudgingly, saying she had never actually told her children their grandmother was dead. The fact that she had never led them to believe she was alive was beside the point. "My mother," Emily explained, "was not given to acknowledging error in any form." But Emily was on the edge of adolescence, vulnerable and too emotional to appreciate the decorum of her mother's evasions. She also sensed, without understanding it, the horrified and debilitating prudery of proper Boston on the rampage. She felt shocked, roused, betrayed, and she could not cope. She fled upstairs to her room, locked the door and wept for two days, refusing to eat or speak. Her mother was irritated but not impressed, and when Emily eventually emerged, tight-mouthed and still trembling, the rift between them did not close. She talks of the occasion now as if it were her fall into the real world of deceit and perfidy.

From then on her grandmother loomed unnaturally large in her life, first in her imagination, then, as she grew up, as a model. Charlotte was the one who got away, free, romantic and with no part in the treacherous propriety which swaddled Emily's childhood. On the next family pilgrimage to Europe she insisted on meeting the old lady and after that stayed passionately in touch. She is pleased to have been the first member of her branch of the family to invite her grandmother to tea, although that was not until much later, after Emily herself had married.

Their first meeting in Paris sealed her devotion. Charlotte was still charming, vivacious and disproportionately beautiful. She also had the exquisite gift of embarrassing Emily's mother by chattering away loudly in public places and making what her daughter later referred to, disapprovingly, as "very French remarks." When, for example, the latter mentioned the dull husband of a dull cousin, Charlotte threw up her hands in mock despair, turned to Emily and asked in a bright voice that carried all round the hushed dining room of the Ritz, "How, my dear, would you like to wake up with *that* head beside you on the pillow?"

Emily, who was thirteen at the time, looked at her with wide eyes. "It had never occurred to me to wake up with any head beside me on the pillow," she explained. "I had not given the matter any thought. I had yet to imagine a world where people woke up with other people beside them. The idea was completely foreign to me." She was delighted, triumphant and also a little scared.

In part she was scared of her mother's fierce disapproval, in part of the dangerous world her grandmother represented, which was personified in the shadowy figure of the lover through whom all that disgrace had been visited on the family. When Emily left Boston at seventeen to spend a winter in Paris her mother made her swear a blood oath that, no matter how much she saw of her grandmother, she would never meet "that man." Although Charlotte had been married to him for over thirty years and although Emily was young, optimistic and rebellious, she was unable to penetrate the aura of fear and scandal which surrounded that otherwise inoffensive elderly gentleman. To her shame, she kept her promise.

The last chapter was tragicomedy. When the Germans marched into Paris in 1940 Charlotte was still ensconced in the rue St. Honoré. She was in her middle eighties by then and on her own, since "that man" was in a sanitorium, chronically ill and prematurely senile. In panic, the family rallied itself and its innumerable connections in government. The U.S. State Department, which had other things on its mind, was badgered into finding a nurse and transporting the old lady and her now slightly dotty companion to Vichy, then to Portugal, then onto a boat through the German wolf packs to America. A suite was prepared for her at the family's country mansion and a place found for "that man" in a suitably remote New England sanitorium. He was mercifully too far gone for anyone to have to meet him. Half a century had passed, Europe was at war again, her husband was long dead, her lover disposable. It was time, the family decided, to forgive and forget. So they sent her a cable to the boat as it nosed its slow, dangerous way in convoy across the Atlantic. "Welcome home," they said and signed all their names. Charlotte read the cable, had a heart attack and died within the hour.

Once again, Emily was inconsolable. "I felt," she said, "the curse remained on us forever." But since by then she was a young married woman with troubles of her own, she understood that the curse on their lives, like the curse on Adam and Eve, concerned the knowledge of good and evil: "And the eyes of them both were opened, and they knew that they were naked." Emily had learned of her grandmother's existence at the time when she was beginning to feel the first stirrings of adolescence. At the same moment, she learned that her mother was not to be trusted in certain crucial ways, on certain crucial topics. To a naive, impressionable girl it seemed unthinkable that a woman could deny the existence of her own mother simply because of social shame. Only gradually did she realize that she had misunderstood her mother's motives and consternation.

As she told it over tea in New York decades later, the revelation was no revelation, mere common sense. It was a Sunday and in preparation for winter she had been digging over the dank soil around the edges of her flagstoned patch of garden. She wore jeans and a kerchief over her hair, which made her seem even younger than usual; another competent and disabused Manhattan matron doing her Sunday chores, and a long way from Boston. "As I grew in wisdom," she said, "I understood that her shame was not social at all; it was sexual. That was the true effect of Grandmother Charlotte's recklessness. However cunningly they wrapped it up, the whole family was in a state of sexual shock. For a year or two in childhood they had been taught a terrible lesson in what passion can do socially—scandal, disgrace, ostracism—and thereafter their lives were controlled by a muted terror of sex. In due course Charlotte's children married suitably and stayed married because the bonds of convention were stronger than those of emotion. But all their marriages were joyless, without pleasure, without communication, and none of them would have survived today. It is ironical that they were prevented from divorcing, even when all their friends were doing it, by the fact that their mother had pioneered divorce in Victorian Boston. Society had forgiven them, as it later silently condoned what their mother had done. But they could never forgive her and we, in our turn, were made to suffer from the constrictions of their characters."

"Perhaps that's how it always is," I said. "Divorce scars the children, the children scar the grandchildren. The miracle is that there's ever an end to it."

"If there is an end," said Emily. "Edith Wharton called it a 'dark inheritance.' There were nine grandchildren and seven of us divorced more than once, which seems a disproportionately high accident rate. The truth is, we had no chance of making a go of marriage because we were brought up to believe, consciously or unconsciously, that sex was a mortal sin. Not that the topic was ever mentioned, you understand, but the recoil from it was so absolute, the silence around it so implacable, that our sense of sin became as overwhelming as our ignorance. When we came to marry we had no idea of selection, of what would or would not do, of who was or was not compatible. It was as if we had been blindfolded and led into a ring, then reached out and took whoever was nearest to our grasp. That sexual taboo cursed my sophisticated family, for all its achievements and connections and wealth, as effectively as if it had been a primitive Amazonian tribe. Only one person might have been able to exorcise us. If Grandmother Charlotte had not died of shock on her way home, but had been received back into the household as an honored guest, all passion spent, the curse might have been lifted. From my spirit, at least."

Later I looked up Edith Wharton's story to see what she had meant by "dark inheritance." The phrase comes early in the story when Mrs. Lidcote, on the liner bringing her from Europe, has yet to discover how much the customs of the country have changed:

> Mrs. Lidcote could hear the whole of New York saying with one voice: "Yes, Leila's done just what her mother did. With such an example what could you expect?"
>
> Yet if she had been an example, poor woman, she had been an awful one; she had been, she would have supposed, of more use as a deterrent than a hundred blameless mothers as incentives. For how could any one who had seen anything of her life in the last eighteen years have had the courage to repeat so disastrous an experiment?
>
> Well, logic in such cases didn't count, example didn't count, nothing probably counted but having the same impulses in the blood; and that was the dark inheritance she had bestowed on her daughter.

Unlike Leila, Emily's mother coped with her "dark inheritance" by denying the impulses in her blood and concentrating on decorum. But that in no way lessened her private sense of doom. She, her brothers and her sisters were convinced they would never recover from the disgrace of their mother's elopement, no matter how grand the marriages they made. Like the children of a gambler, they felt their lives had been ruined by their mother's emotional profligacy, their moral and social capital squandered.

However much Emily and her mother were at odds, both believed something was wrong in their lives and, despite the trappings of privilege, that they had no real chance of happiness. For Emily's mother, who accepted Boston's rigid and complacent nineteenth-century values and found no fault in society's elephantine memory, the culprit was Charlotte and her headlong carelessness. Emily, who adored her grandmother and disliked her mother, translated the same sense of doom into the equally formal Freudian language of twentieth-century Manhattan. In their different ways, both were unreconstructed determinists.

Toward the end of the Depression, after her winter in Paris, Emily reasserted her role as the family rebel by joining a different enemy. She moved down to Washington and took a job with the New Deal. Her family were, to a man and woman, conventional Hooverite Republicans. They spoke of Roosevelt with the same dismayed intensity and in the same anonymous terms as they spoke of Charlotte's lover: he was "that man in the White House." They were dumbfounded when their daughter went to work for their foe, and even Emily was secretly shocked by her own audacity. She had been brought up to believe that private enterprise, which had settled America and given it the highest living standard in the world, was the most honorable possible pursuit for an honorable man. Yet in Washington she found herself surrounded by men as honorable and dedicated as her beloved father, who had given up the chance of earning serious money in order to help their country in its crisis. For the first time in her life she began to mix with Jews, with Catholics, with people whose accents she could not place who had made it on talent and scholarships. She was astounded by all that lay outside the confines of old Boston.

Like her grandmother, she was a beautiful young woman, lively and very shrewd under her distracted, self-mocking manner. She peers out of a portrait, now hidden away on an upper landing of her Manhattan brownstone, with a quizzical, challenging, sidelong look, the elegant rebel. Yet when it came to matrimony . . .

Her mother had been set on her making a fashionable marriage to someone from a socially acceptable family, preferably Bostonian, although Philadelphia or New York, she conceded, would do at a pinch. All that mattered was that he should be a man whose parents she and her husband "knew." Her first question when a possible suitor was mentioned was, "Who is he?" Then she would purse her lips, shake her head and announce, "I know who he is," grimly, with the finality of a hanging judge. "Definitely second drawer," her mother would add, as if describing a hereditary deformity.

Her other criterion was less specific but more loaded: "If ever my mother used the word 'nice,' she meant the girl had no sex appeal, the man posed no sexual threat. Try as I might, I found it hard to develop a taste for 'nice' men." And try as she might, when Emily finally fell in love she was unable to disguise from her mother that the interest she and the young man took in each other was—electrically, treasonably—not nice at all. Her mother pronounced judgment as usual: "His family is not in the Social Register; he doesn't belong to a Harvard final club. And between you and me, my dear, he is not really . . . nice. In the last analysis, not in the least . . . nice." But when Emily took no notice she panicked, imagining Charlotte's ghost riding again at each sullen exchange with her daughter. Then she remembered that Charlotte was placidly minding her own business in the rue St. Honoré, so she packed Emily off on an extended trip to Europe with an aunt and uncle, saying, "Talk it over with your grandmother, if you must."

"But four months," said Emily, "is too long at that age. When I got back he was involved with someone else." And she acquiesced in that as she had acquiesced to the trip. Perhaps her time in Washington had used up her fund of rebelliousness. Or perhaps she was still overwhelmed by the secret guilty equation, sex equals sin, and was bowing to her determined fate. "You were not," she remarked, "sexually happy with a husband. To be so did not accord with the way the world was arranged."

So she made a marriage which did accord, a fashionable

disaster. The man was ten years older than herself, which seemed a lot at the time: stolid, worthy, dignified, paternal, "and paralyzingly dull, my dear"—she drew the words out in mock horror—"of a dullness you cannot conceive." She made a helpless, fluttering movement with her hands to indicate the enormity both of his rectitude and her innocence.

"Then why . . . ?"

Her hands moved sharply inward, cutting off the past. "Out of pique and because I was on the rebound. I came back from Washington one weekend to be a bridesmaid for a friend who was marrying up in Maine, and he was delegated to drive me there. We spent the entire day together in his car and he was so difficult to talk to I was outraged. So I made up my mind to get him. It was a matter of pride. And get him I did. To the altar, for better or for worse. He had never discovered anyone he could talk to before, and now I know why: he was incapable of talking. So I exerted myself out of a kind of childish ambition and by the time I realized what was happening, it was too late. It was like trying to shift some enormous boulder: you heave and strain out of bravado, then it rolls back down and crushes you. Once I had awakened him out of his Kraken sleep, there was no stopping him. He bullied me into marriage, chided me like an impatient father, scolded me for not being able to make up my mind. And my parents, in their wisdom, went along with it, perhaps because they had so recently been busy breaking up my relationship with a man I really wanted. I was on the rebound, and that is a condition which provokes stupidity."

She brooded a moment in the dull afternoon light. The tall windows of her library were obscured by potted plants brought indoors to protect them from the New York winter. There were books stacked on the floor beside her chair, and a pile of newspapers, cryptically marked, waiting to be clipped. It seemed a long, busy way from Edith Wharton. Then she shrugged and gave me her quizzical, sidelong smile, like the girl in the portrait upstairs. "So there I was. As Jane Eyre said, 'Reader, I married him.' " Her smile faded. "On the eighteenth of February at three o'clock in the afternoon, to be precise. I can still remember coming out of the church and finding myself with an absolute stranger in a Boston snowstorm, knowing my life was over be-

fore it had properly begun. All my friends had implored me not
to marry him, and even I knew it was all wrong. So much for the
arrogance of youth."

Another silence. When she continued her voice was amused,
faintly whimsical. "The honeymoon was a disaster. I was a virgin
—such a waste of human endeavor—and he was not much further on. He had never been involved with anyone but 'babes.' He
had not had any 'nice' girls, as far as I can determine. He was,
therefore, very unskillful." A faint shudder, then again the
amused glint. "Apparently these things show—to everyone, that
is, except the poor principals in the drama. Bets were taken by
the other guests at the hotel; there was a kind of sweepstakes on
the private beach. Had I known about it, I'd have taken wagers
myself. The only thing that stopped me filing for a divorce immediately after we got back from those ghastly six weeks was I
found I was pregnant."

She picked up her cup, surveyed the cold tea in it and put it
down again. "When I think of him now I feel sorry for him. He
had all the stolid New England virtues; he was honest, he wasn't
mean, he wasn't a philanderer. I think he was just bewildered to
find himself shut up with a person who took no interest in what
he considered normal pursuits: golf, business, the stock market,
small talk."

From the street outside came a screech of tires and the blast
of a car horn, then angry voices exchanging insults. She glanced
briefly at the window. "It didn't seem like that at the time. I was
too busy feeling sorry for myself. I came back numb. When my
parents saw me they were appalled. Guilty too, although it was
not their style to admit it. But I knew it couldn't go on and told
them so. My father was very upset. He told me later that I was
like a bird in a cage, fluttering miserably at the bars. A sweet
Victorian image.

"Whenever I saw him, the expression in his eyes was . . .
well, stricken. As if something had stopped short in him. He
made me go around and talk to one of his oldest friends, who was
also a doctor. And the doctor heard me out patiently, then said
to my father, 'There are some things, like the weather, you can't
do anything about. There is no solution. For reasons best known
to herself your daughter has chosen someone totally alien to her,

hostile almost, with whom she will always be a stranger. There
is nothing to be done.' Now once my father had satisfied himself
of this fact, the question of divorce became, in his view, academic. It was inevitable, so he would endure it."

The ugly voices faded in the street, the light thickened.

"My mother endured it, too," said Emily, "but with less
grace. Needless to say, she worried about what people would
say. Although divorce was common enough by then, the older
generation in Boston still frowned upon it. And my mother was,
if nothing else, older generation. As usual, she made me feel a
failure; once again I had let her down. But since my father was
on my side, she refrained from saying so to my face. She sent
her sister to pay me a solemn call in the country. This aunt of
mine sat and listened and nibbled her underlip and said, 'You're
behaving about this marriage like a child with an arithmetic
book: you're just staring at it; you refuse to turn the pages or
learn a thing.' All very wise and disapproving, you understand.
I was suitably impressed, suitably put in my place. But it occurs
to me now that my aunt had made a dreary marriage and stayed
with it. So she had a point, although that made no difference to
me at the time. But when she duly reported back that the situation was hopeless, my mother gritted her teeth and prepared for
another family scandal."

She leaned over and switched on the reading light beside
her. The corners of the room filled with shadows.

"It didn't happen. Times had changed. Nevertheless, it was
a painful process. But then, I suppose it always is, however grim
the marriage, however much you both want out. That wrenching
of the fabric—'You take the silver, I'll take the dinner service'
—breaking up the *lares* and *penates* of the household, taking a
child away from its father. *Partir, c'est mourir en peu.* I guess I
died a bit in order to get my life back."

"What sort of life?"

"Different. At least from the Boston point of view. For me,
it had a certain gloomy continuity, but my mother and her circle
thought otherwise. I suppose my divorce scandalized her more
than she cared to admit. Maybe it reminded her of the family
curse. Or maybe it reminded her that I had always, by choice,
been more her mother's ally than hers. She began to brood about

me. Whatever she said, whatever the occasion, she couldn't keep the glint of doom and disapproval off her face. In the end, there seemed nothing to do but go along with this fallen image she had of me. I moved to New York."

"Fallen?" I made a movement with my hand to take in the high, shadowy library and the rest of the house above us and below: the family portraits and Baccarat vases in the drawing room, the family silver on the Sheraton table in the dining room downstairs; a sedate, rich house in a row of sedate, rich houses, with Park Avenue a few steps away. "I don't understand," I said.

"My mother," Emily replied, "was a proper Bostonian. To her, New York was the sink of iniquity, the original city of dreadful night. I would become a fallen woman here: done to love and truth, lost to hope and honor." She shook her head sadly. "She belonged to another world, and she refused to change. I can't even blame her."

"And you, were you still part of that world?"

"In some ways. But as I've said, I was the rebel of the family. And Washington had given me a taste of *out there:* clever people, politics, literature, a life without barriers. I'd lost my patience with the narrow society I'd been brought up in. In Manhattan I felt I had come into my rightful kingdom."

Out in the street the car horns were at it again. She smiled vaguely toward the window where snowflakes were beginning to drift in the dark. "See what I mean?"

"Your grandmother Charlotte would have approved."

She nodded soberly at this. "Perhaps I *am* my grandmother Charlotte. After all, I came here because I'd fallen in love. But the man was married, more or less happily, and with children, so there was no question of divorce. I hadn't really expected it to be otherwise, however miserable I felt at the time. It was the family curse: you were not happy with a husband."

"You still believe that?"

She shook her head. "Edith Wharton got it wrong. Poor Charlotte: the real curse was not hers, it was my mother's overpowering sense of sin. My father never shared it, but she was the stronger force in our lives. She dominated the household, swept all before her, brooked no opposition. The only way to

survive was to give in to her. Which he did for sixty years. But
just once, not long ago, I had a glimpse of how it might have
been. The October before my father died I took him for a drive
to see the fall colors. Somehow the name came up of a man I was
involved with at the time and my father suddenly asked, 'Do you
like to touch him?' I almost drove off the road. He was ninety
years old by then, my mother was long dead and I was sixty, but
it was the first time in my life he had made any reference to the
forbidden subject. I thought, What a tragedy for all of us. Perhaps if I had been able to speak openly to him about my troubles,
my whole life would have been different. 'Do you like to touch
him?' If that's a curse, then yes, I believe in it."

"A terrible burden."

"Here in New York I did my best to shed it. I worked,
cultivated other people, organized my life, even went to a psychiatrist. But it's not easy to change beliefs."

The snow was heavier now, edging the base of each window-
pane, muffling the passing cars and footsteps into unnatural
quiet.

"So what did you do?" I asked.

She raised her hands in mock horror. "I married somebody
else."

"In the circumstances, wasn't that rather rash?"

"Oh, in the circumstances. The circumstances were the mixture as before: I was on the rebound and the man was impossible.
But at the time it didn't look that way. He was full of charm,
easy, amusing, voluble, intellectual. He was also a liar. My first
husband, for all his faults, was full of character; my second husband had no character at all. Once more everybody seemed to
see it except myself, and everybody warned me against him.
Which only stiffened my resolve. So we married and there was
nothing there, nothing between us at all. A couple of years later
we were divorced. The identical dance with a different partner, except that this time I was subjected to the shabbiest dupli-
city."

"You might have gone on like that forever."

"But that's the miracle: I didn't. Most of my family did;
marriage after marriage after marriage, Boston or no Boston.
Come to think of it, most of Boston did. Likewise New York,

Philadelphia, Washington and points west. My second husband is on number five now. Or is it number six?"

"How did you escape?"

"I'd learned my lesson. I'd finally turned the pages of the arithmetic book and taken it all in. And the lesson was: I am not the marrying kind."

She gave a little snort of amusement, but her voice was flat, categorical, as if she were announcing a fact I could not possibly deny, like the snow outside or the time of day.

"I seem to recall an unreasonable number of admirers who were eager to marry you. Are eager still."

"The problem," said Emily carefully, "is not the admirers, it's matrimony: the bells ringing, the snow coming down and that total stranger holding your arm just above the elbow, like a policeman. The bar of matrimony drops and you are no longer at liberty to associate with anyone. I don't mean sleeping with people other than your husband. In my marrying days, the idea had scarcely crossed my mind. I mean everything has to be doubled-checked: lunch with X, shopping with Y, cocktails with Z. You're expected to report in. It's like working for the FBI." Again the little snort of amusement, the dismissive, downward movement of the hands. "Maybe that is what my father meant when he said I was like a bird fluttering against the bars of its cage. A Victorian image, but accurate."

"How did your twentieth-century psychiatrist describe it?"

"He heard me out at great length and even greater expense, then explained to me in broken English that I married men with whom it was impossible for me to fall in love and fell in love with men whom it was impossible for me to marry. But he dressed it up in Greek mythology."

"Impossible? But your grandmother did the impossible long ago."

Emily shook her head fretfully. "There are occasions when divorce doesn't come into the reckoning. Believe it nor not, I am not stupid enough always to fall in love with happily married men. If they were *happily* married there would be no love affair. The impossibility is the children, or the wife who can't be left because she's too ill or too helpless or too rich. There is a difference between being happily married and being heavily married."

"And as far as you are concerned, all marriages are heavy marriages?"

"I have only my own experience to draw on. For me there is love, happiness and the independent life. Then there is duty."

"Edith Wharton," I said, "wouldn't have believed you. She once said to a friend: 'Ah, the poverty, the miserable poverty, of any love that lies outside marriage, of any love that is not a living together, a sharing of all.' "

Emily shrugged. "What a pity. I've always thought she would have understood."

V

The History

1. ANTECEDENTS

"Divorce," said Voltaire, "is an institution only a few weeks later in origin than marriage." Although he was speaking cynically and in exasperation, as a rationalist and a reformer, the experts have subsequently proved him right. When Edward Westermarck wrote his monumental *History of Human Marriage*, tracing it back into remote prehistory, he could muster only a handful of primitive tribes among whom divorce was unknown. Yet to Voltaire's contemporaries his aphorism was probably as outrageous as he intended, since divorce in Christian Europe, even in the sensible and sophisticated eighteenth century, was virtually impossible.

Even now this seems a normal and proper attitude to anyone born before World War II. Easy divorce—without fuss, without social stigma, without too much recrimination—seems a recent invention, as modern and mysterious as the digital computer. It is in fact no more modern than the wheel, which the Sumerians invented about 3000 B.C.; a few years later the same Sumerians instituted laws which allowed women to seek divorce, as well as men. As for our new liberalism: all that has happened in the last couple of decades is that laws, customs and attitudes to divorce which were universal until the sixth century A.D. have grudgingly been restored. Historically speaking, it is the taboo on divorce that is the recent phenomenon, and one not easily explained. It has more to do with Christian idealism and ascetic fanaticism than with the institution of marriage.

In its remotest beginnings, say the anthropologists, the family existed solely for the protection of the young. Thus birds have families, reptiles do not, although both breed by laying eggs. But the embryo crocodile is developed by the heat of the sun and emerges armed and ready, while the embryo bird has to be kept warm by its parents before it can hatch, then comes into the world helpless, needing to be fed and protected. With the human infant, this period of helplessness extends for years, not weeks. Without a mother to take care of it and a father to protect them both, the human child would never survive. It may be that the family will in time become obsolete as the state gradually takes the place of our hunting fathers as provider and protector; the new attitudes to marriage and divorce may even be preliminary steps toward this dubious Utopia. But in their origins marriage and the family were means to survival. "It is for the benefit of the young that the male and female continue to live together," wrote Westermarck. "Marriage is therefore rooted in the family, rather than the family in marriage."

This was the original realpolitik of matrimony. The earliest families, like the earliest tribes, were dominated by their male providers and protectors who took wives and disposed of them more or less as they pleased. Later, in the early agricultural and pastoral communities, a man's wives and children were both the symbols of his economic power and his means to it. "Slave labor was, for most people, unavailable," Bertrand Russell remarked, "and therefore the easiest way to acquire laborers was to breed them." This concept of the wife as the property of her husband —bartered for like a prize heifer and without rights of her own—was the basis of the earliest Roman and Hebrew marriage laws. Since social stability depends partly on stable marriages, the state intervened swiftly to protect defenseless wives from the whims of their husbands. As early as the time of Romulus, a law was passed forbidding the repudiation of wives unless they were guilty of adultery or drinking wine. A Roman who wished to get rid of a faithful, sober wife forfeited her dowry. Similarly, the laws in Deuteronomy provided a minimal protection for innocent wives: divorce was easy—a husband had only to present his wife with a formal bill of dismissal (a *git*)—but he was forbidden to do so if he had committed a crime against her before marriage or falsely accused her of adultery.

The original intention of both the Roman and Mosaic laws was to prevent a man from killing his wife when he was tired of her. Later, as manners improved, they discouraged him from divorcing her for utterly frivolous reasons—although, then as now, frivolity was in the eye of the beholder. The Book of Esther records approvingly that the Persian king Ahasuerus divorced Vashti when he was "merry with wine" at a feast because she refused to display her beauty to his guests. His councillors advised him to get rid of her in order to demonstrate the then self-evident truth "that every man should bear rule in his own house."

"If thy wife go not as thou wouldst have her," said Jesus, the son of Sirach, "give her a bill of divorce and let her go." In Mosaic and Roman law, divorce existed for the sake of a one-sided domestic peace: the prospect of it kept the wife in her place, curbing her pride or disobedience or obstreperousness, as well as her more obviously vicious behavior (the punishment for adultery was death). It also spared the husband the indignity of losing his temper. "Maimonides tells us," wrote Milton, "divorce was permitted by Moses to preserve peace in marriage and quiet in the family."

The theory was simple, although its clarity was continually muddied by the psychopathology of everyday life, as the Book of Proverbs eloquently testifies:

> There be three things which are too wonderful for me, yea, four which I know not:
> The way of an eagle in the air; the way of a serpent upon a rock; the way of a ship in the midst of the sea; and the way of a man with a maid.

> Such is the way of an adulterous woman; she eateth, and wipeth her mouth, and saith, I have done no wickedness.

Neither patriarchy nor polygamy was a defense against the hurt and ambiguities of marriage. Manners change but not the confusions, and the paean of praise for "the virtuous woman" whose "price is far above rubies" with which Proverbs ends seems, in context, more wistful than convinced.

2. ROMAN DIVORCE

The Romans boasted that in the five hundred years of the Republic no husband took advantage of the laws' bias in his favor to get rid of a troublesome wife. The women seem to have been correspondingly serious and devoted; the constancy of Roman wives, such as Lucretia and Paulina, was legendary. Pliny even believed that women demonstrated their inherently superior purity when they drowned by floating modestly facedown, while drowned men floated on their backs. In its essence, therefore, Roman marriage was a union between equals. A jurisconcult aptly named Modestinus defined it as "a lifelong fellowship of all divine and human rights."

This tradition continued even when other traditional virtues were eroded by the wealth and luxury of the empire. By about the time of Christ, Roman marriage was thought of as a civil contract between two equal partners for their mutual benefit. When the affection on which the contract was based broke down, the marriage could be dissolved, like any other civil partnership, by mutual consent. All the law required was a certain formality in the process of divorce—greater formality and ceremony than was needed for a marriage. According to the *Lex Julia de adulteriis*, the husband or wife had to serve a bill of divorce in the presence of seven witnesses, all of them adult citizens of Rome. Once that was properly done, the marriage was over. But since marriage also exists for the benefit of children—and through them, indirectly, for the state—casual divorce was discouraged by financial penalties and by limiting the power of remarriage.

The inhibitions gradually disappeared until, by the fifth century A.D., the laws were so relaxed that a wife could divorce her husband for any of twelve reasons, ranging from treason and murder to "introducing immoral women into his house." As though to emphasize that women were still not altogether equal in the eyes of the law, a husband had fifteen grounds for divorce, including her "going to dine with men other than her relations without the knowledge of or against the wish of her husband" and "frequenting the circus, theater or amphitheater after being forbidden by her husband."

In other words, the legal excuses covered any reasonable eventuality. Roman divorce was as free as Roman marriage and almost as common: Pompey married five times, Caesar and Mark Antony four, Augustus three, although his final marriage lasted forty-three years. Juvenal mentions a woman who had eight husbands in five years, and Martial capped that with one who had had ten. Seneca spoke with distaste of those noblewomen who "count their age, not by the number of consuls, but by the number of their husbands." Saint Jerome claimed to have heard of a Roman matron who married her twenty-third husband and was herself his twenty-first wife.

But if divorce was abused and trivialized when the empire was running heavily to seed, it was because of the reasonableness of Roman laws, not because of their hypocrisy. Both in law and out, divorce was a firmly domestic affair to be settled in private between the partners. Like Robert Graves, the Romans believed that "the hazards of their love-bed were none of our damn business," and the whole process of law was designed to keep out the public. In the early days of divorce by mutual consent, any dispute about property or the care of the children—to whose maintenance and education both parents had to contribute —was settled by family council. Later, when it began to seem unlikely that any family meeting would ever be impartial in an argument about cash, these questions were settled by a judge at a public inquiry. His business was not to pry into family secrets but to decide if there was enough moral blame on either side to influence the practical financial arrangements. If both parties seemed equally guilty, he refused to intervene; if they divorced without wrangling, he was not consulted. Either way, an unhappily married couple was not inhibited from divorce by fear of their dirty linen being washed in public.

Roman divorce set standards of fairness and common sense that we are now slowly regaining. Reforms which have been introduced with difficulty in Britain, the United States and Scandinavia within the last decade were standard practice in Rome two thousand years ago: divorce without the need of a guilty party and therefore without public scandal, available equally to husband and wife, the reasons for it their own, the court concerned only with the well-being of the children and with settling, as cleanly as possible, the inevitable quarrels about property. Like the breakup of a business partnership, divorce was a civil action and everything was done to arrange it as civilly as possible. It was also based on an equally reasonable attitude to marriage: as a civil union, for their mutual benefit, pleasure and support, between two people who loved each other. "If marriages are made by mutual affection," wrote the emperor Justin, "it is only right that when that mutual affection no longer exists they should be dissoluble by mutual consent."

3. JESUS AND DIVORCE

Since it seems so obvious and so sane, where did it all go wrong? Even the law of Moses, which was altogether less tender toward women than Roman law, was careful not to turn "the blessing of matrimony," as Milton put it, "into a familiar and cohabiting mischiefe; at least into a drooping and disconsolate houshold captivitie, without refuge or redemption." In Jewish law a marriage was indissoluble only when the husband had committed a crime against his wife or faked the grounds for divorcing her. The ancient Hebrews, like the Romans, believed divorce was something every household should have and the restrictions on it existed solely to protect a wronged wife.

Christianity changed all that by transforming a civil arrangement into a spiritual condition. "Christianity has had no greater practical effect on the life of mankind," says the *Encyclopædia Britannica*, "than in its belief that marriage is no mere civil contract, but a vow in the sight of God binding the parties

by obligations of conscience above and beyond those of civil law."
Although marriages did not have to be formally celebrated in
church until the Renaissance,* the institution became a symbolic act, a model in miniature of the eternal marriage of the
Church with Christ.

The symbolism is elegant, ingenious and convincing, but it
is also a relatively late rationalization of beliefs founded less on
what Jesus said than on the psychological eccentricities of the
Early Fathers of the Church. Jesus' teaching itself was ambiguous enough to become the source of, literally, endless squabbling
and interpretation:

> The Pharisees also came unto him, tempting him, and saying
> unto him, Is it lawful for a man to put away his wife for every
> cause?
>
> And he answered and said unto them, Have ye not read, that
> he which made them at the beginning made them male and female.
>
> And said, For this cause shall a man leave father and mother,
> and shall cleave to his wife: and they twain shall be one flesh?
>
> Wherefore they are no more twain but one flesh. What there-
> fore God hath joined together, let not man put asunder.
>
> They say unto him, Why did Moses then command to give a
> writing of divorcement, and to put her away?
>
> He saith unto them, Moses because of the hardness of your
> hearts suffered you to put away your wives: but from the beginning
> it was not so.
>
> And I say unto you, Whosoever shall put away his wife, except
> it be for fornication, and shall marry another, committeth adultery:
> and whoso marrieth her which is put away doth commit adultery.†

* The Greek Orthodox Church demanded formal religious celebration of marriage as early as the eighth century, but it was not until 1563 that the Council of
Trent laid down that the presence of a priest was necessary for a valid marriage
between Roman Catholics. In England it was another two centuries before Parliament declared, in 1753, that all marriages, except those of Jews and Quakers,
not contracted before an ordained minister in a parish church should be "null and
void." Curiously enough, the state took the initiative and the Church merely
acquiesced. Less than a century later, in 1836, the law was changed again for the
benefit of nonconformists and non-Christians; civil marriages before a secular
official once more became valid.

† Matthew 19: 3–9. There are also different versions in Mark 10: 2–12 and
Luke 16: 18; also in the Sermon on the Mount, Matthew 5: 31–32.

The context is important. At the time of Jesus' ministry, a rabbinical quarrel was raging concerning divorce laws as set out in Deuteronomy 24:1:

> When a man hath taken a wife, and married her, and it come to pass that she find no favor in his eyes, because he hath found some uncleanness in her: then let him write her a bill of divorcement, and give it in her hand, and send her out of his house.

According to Rabbi Shammai and his followers, "uncleanness" meant sexual immodesty, even something as mild as a wife's going into the street with her hair down. The opposing group, led by Rabbi Hillel, interpreted the phrase as a male chauvinist's charter: any source of displeasure on the part of the husband was excuse enough to dispose of his wife.

The purpose of the question was to embroil Jesus in an already heated religious-political squabble. As usual, he sidestepped the trap by shifting Mosaic law back to its origins in Genesis and God's reasons for instituting marriage. He even seemed to imply that God's purpose in distinguishing between the sexes was in order to bring them together again in marriage as "one flesh." By these ideal standards, the Mosaic laws of divorce are nothing more than a sop to the frailty of human nature, an acknowledgment of "the hardness of your hearts."

In both Matthew and Mark the disciples seem so surprised by the rigor of Jesus' attitude to divorce that they question him afterward in private. In Mark, the earliest of the Gospels, he draws strict conclusions from what he has already said: "Whosoever shall put away his wife, and marry another, committeth adultery against her. And if a woman shall put away her husband, and be married to another, she committeth adultery." The scholars think this is an interpolation for the benefit of the Gentile Church in Rome, where Mark's Gospel was written, since in Jewish law it was not possible for a woman to "put away" her husband. Similarly, Matthew's qualification, "except it be for fornication," seems to have been inserted for the benefit of the Jewish Christian Church. In Matthew's Greek the word is *porneia*, which most biblical scholars now believe means "sexual immorality." Matthew, in short, was doing what Jesus tried to avoid: coming down squarely on the side of Rabbi Shammai. This casual muddying of the text for temporary political ends was to become a source of intense theological wrangling for the next two thousand years.

But in Matthew there is also a further private explanation to the disciples which set the tone for the subsequent attitude of the Early Church to marriage:

> His disciples say unto him, If the case of the man be so with his wife, it is not good to marry.
> But he said unto them, All men cannot receive this saying, save they to whom it is given.
> For there are some eunuchs, which were so born from their mother's womb: and there are some eunuchs, which were made eunuchs of men: and there be eunuchs, which have made themselves eunuchs for the kingdom of heaven's sake. He that is able to receive it, let him receive it.

As usual, the disciples speak up for human fallibility: if marriage is final and mistakes can never be recouped, surely it is better not to marry at all? Jesus does not answer this question directly; his teaching, he says, is too stern for fallen humanity. He then goes on to imply that true holiness lies with those who "have made themselves eunuchs for the kingdom of heaven's sake"— that is, with those who are not only beyond divorce, but beyond marriage as well. The purity he preaches is not compatible with physical desire.

Perhaps this is why he creates a mystery from the simple folk narrative of Genesis: God fashioned Eve from Adam's rib, but by making them husband and wife he turned them again into "one flesh"; any subsequent liaison is a violation of that divinely ordained union, adultery by any other name. It is a theological variation on the paradox of love, like Shakespeare's beautiful and mysterious poem, "The Phoenix and the Turtle," in which reason, identity and all the philosophical absolutes are made nonsense of by perfected pure love, "married chastitie." It is also like Plato's more playful and worldly allegory of love in the *Symposium:* man was once a perfect sphere whom an angry and jealous Zeus cut in two "like a sorb apple which is halved for pickling, or as you might divide an egg with a hair." After which, each half spent its life searching for its other perfect half. Once it is found, if ever, "there is not a man of them who . . . would not acknowledge that this meeting and melting into one another, this becoming one instead of two, was the very expression of his ancient need. And the reason is that human nature was originally one and we were a whole, and the desire and pursuit of the whole is called love." Although Plato gives the speech to the comic poet Aristophanes, the language is strangely similar to that of Genesis. Each in its different way is concerned with a perennial yearning which existed long before Christ and has outlasted the decay of religion: a desire to give meaning to our existential choices and endow them with dignity, a belief that happiness lies in joining together once and for all with what the psychoanalysts would now call "the ideal object," that one person who embodies all the confused images and wishes—the special temperament, tastes, coloring, shape, smell and intellectual style—which we bundle together under the name of love and for which, when we think we have found it, we are willing to make extraordinary compromises with our own temperament, tastes, habits and style. Love: "the desire and pursuit of the whole"; "they twain shall be one flesh." The language changes, the impulse remains the same. The polytheistic Greeks instituted monogamy and the polygamous ancient Hebrews instituted monotheism. Christianity brought the two principles together: one God, one wife.

4. SAINT PAUL AND THE EARLY FATHERS

Whatever Jesus meant when he spoke of marriage, the way was now clear for the self-made eunuchs of the spirit, the fanatics, the body haters. What he suggested in private to his disciples as a counsel of perfection—"he that is able to receive it, let him receive it"—Saint Paul proceeded to write large:

> Now the body is not for fornication, but for the Lord; and the Lord for the body. . . .
> Know ye not that your bodies are the members of Christ? shall I then take the members of Christ, and make them the members of an harlot? God forbid.

What? know ye not that he which is joined to an harlot is one body? for two, saith he, shall be one flesh.

But he that is joined unto the Lord is one spirit.

Flee fornication. Every sin that a man doeth is without the body; but he that committeth fornication sinneth against his own body.

What? know ye not that body is the temple of the Holy Ghost which is in you, which ye have of God, and ye are not your own? . . .

. . . It is good for a man not to touch a woman.

Nevertheless, to avoid fornication, let every man have his own wife, and let every woman have her own husband.

Let the husband render unto the wife due benevolence: and likewise also the wife unto the husband.

The wife hath not power of her own body, but the husband: and likewise also the husband hath not power of his own body, but the wife.

Defraud ye not one the other, except it be with consent for a time, that ye may give yourselves to fasting and prayer; and come together again, that Satan tempt you not for your incontinency.

But I speak this by permission, and not of commandment.

For I would that all men were even as I myself. But every man hath his proper gift of God, one after this manner, and another after that.

I say therefore to the unmarried and widows, It is good for them if they abide even as I.

But if they cannot contain, let them marry: for it is better to marry than to burn.

And unto the married I command, yet not I, but the Lord, Let not the wife depart from her husband:

But and if she depart, let her remain unmarried, or be reconciled to her husband: and let not the husband put away his wife.

I Corinthians 6: 13, 15–19; 7: 1–11

Where Jesus was concerned with what God intended by the institution of marriage, Saint Paul harped remorselessly on sin and lust and the perils of the flesh. The ideal he yearned for was not the "one flesh" for which "a man shall leave his father and mother, and shall cleave unto his wife," but Adam's earlier restless isolation, of which God Himself said, "It is not good that the man should be alone." To this merciful and supremely sensible judgment, Saint Paul could only grudgingly reply, "It is better to marry than to burn."

In time, this became the charter by which the patients took over the asylum. For three centuries after Christ the Roman laws of divorce were essentially unchanged. But when Emperor Constantine inaugurated the alliance between the Church and the State at the beginning of the fourth century, other influences began to prevail. Above all, those of Jerome, Augustine, Tertullian, Origen, who, in their attitude to desire and love and marriage, were more Saint Paul's men than Jesus'.

Their horror of the body was absolute, like the virulence with which they expressed it. Saint Jerome, whose sexual temptations in the desert were such a boon to the painters of the quattrocento, called a woman who remarried after her husband died, "a dog returning to its vomit and a washed sow returning to its wallowing place." The language is like that of the teenage crazies of China's Cultural Revolution, but with this difference: the influence of the early Christian "Gang of Four" grew steadily more powerful. Because of their hysterical intolerance of the flesh, marriage itself became the abhorred *porneia* of Matthew's Gospel, and chastity the one true virtue.

It follows that where marriage was regarded as a sinful weakness, divorce was a sign of total depravity. Tertullian dismissed it curtly as "the fruit of marriage." "It was for many ages," wrote Milton, "that marriage lay in disgrace with most of the ancient Doctors, as a work of the flesh, almost a defilement, wholly deny'd to Priests, and the second time disswaded to all, as he that reads *Tertullian* or *Jerome* may see at large."

Since those who read Tertullian are now hard to find, here is a relatively balanced example to prove Milton's point:

> The Lord Himself said, 'Whoever has seen a woman with a view to concupiscence has already violated her in his heart.' But has he who has seen her with a view to marriage done so less or more? . . . It is laws which seem to make the difference between marriage and fornication; through the diversity of illicitness, not through the nature of the thing itself. Besides, what is the thing which takes place in all men and women to produce marriage and fornication? Conmixture of the flesh, of course; the concupiscence

whereof the Lord put on the same footing with fornication . . .
Accordingly, the best thing for a man is not to touch a woman; and,
accordingly, the virgin's is the principal sanctity, because it is free
from affinity with fornication.

Origen, Tertullian's contemporary, took this fierce belief in
the absolute value of chastity to its logical conclusion: he cas-
trated himself. He was not canonized, because the Church condemned him for his allegorical interpretations of the Scriptures,
but his essential sanctity, like his place on the demented margin
of history, has hardly been in question.

The cult of chastity brought with it excess, shrillness, intolerance, a denial of all the values Jesus taught when he preached
the supreme virtue of charity. Perhaps that is why it proved so
compelling. It is one of the truisms of history—which the terrorists are at present demonstrating all over again—that liberal
virtues, like tolerance, are vulnerable to the fanatic's single
mind, closed to everything except its own obsession. They seem,
in comparison, unconvinced and unconvincing. Even the subtle
and persuasive Augustine was not immune; he repented of his
marriage more than of his youthful excesses with prostitutes.
"Fornication," said Clement of Alexandria, "is a lapse from one
marriage into many." Conversely, even the most loving
and faithful marriage was incompatible with the saintly life.
W. E. H. Lecky illustrated this vividly in his *History of
European Morals:*

> St. Gregory the Great describes the virtue of a priest who, through
> motives of piety, had deserted his wife. As he lay dying, she has-
> tened to him to watch the bed which for forty years she had not
> been allowed to share, and, bending over what seemed the inani-
> mate form of her husband, she tried to ascertain if any breath still
> remained, when the dying saint, collecting his last energies, ex-
> claimed: "Woman, begone; take away the straw, there is fire yet."

The borderline between chastity and satyromania, between
sanctity and farce, was shadowy but impossible to recognize at
the time. And because this perverted, unnatural lust for sexual
purity was a qualification for sainthood, it produced a permanent
deformation in European morality, splitting body from soul and

goodness from desire, changing marriage from a blessing into a
grudging concession which would spare those incapable of holy
chastity from the sin of fornication, and surfacing in the belief—
brilliantly analyzed by Denis de Rougemont—that true passion
is always doomed and tragic. On a more practical level, the
Canon Law which dominated Europe for fifteen hundred years
was built specifically on this psychotic no-man's-land.

5. CANON LAW

The history of divorce in Rome in the first millennium A.D.
is like the inscription reputed to have been carved above the
Great Gate of Agra, the city of the Taj Mahal:

> In the first year of the reign of King Gulef, 2,000 voluntary sepa-
> rations between husbands and wives were pronounced by magis-
> trates. The Emperor was indignant and abolished divorce. In the
> course of the following year there were, at Agra, 3,000 fewer mar-
> riages than in previous years and 7,000 more cases of adultery.
> 3,000 women were burnt alive for having murdered their husbands
> and 75 men were burnt alive for having murdered their wives. The
> value of the furniture destroyed in the course of domestic brawls
> amounted to 3,000,000 rupees. The Emperor then re-established
> divorce.

In Rome there was a similar running battle between Church and
State, priests and citizens. In 416 Augustine took part in a
Church council which tried to abolish divorce, condemning the
discontented husband and wife to be reconciled or remain celibate. It did not succeed. A century later, the emperor Justinian
instituted a Novel (law) forbidding divorce by mutual consent;
the penalty for the unfortunate couple was to be confined for life
in monasteries and to forfeit all their property. This lasted until
565 when Justinian was succeeded by his nephew Justin who,
like King Gulef of Agra, immediately repealed the prohibition:
"He yielded to the prayers of his unhappy subjects," wrote Gib-
bon, "and restored the liberty of divorce by mutual consent; the
citizens were unanimous, the theologians were divided, and the

ambiguous word which contains the precept of Christ is flexible to any interpretation that the wisdom of a legislature can demand."

Despite the objections of the clergy, Roman emperors and civil lawyers continued to protect the domestic rights of their citizens. As late as the beginning of the tenth century, Emperor Leo was still concerned with "the benediction of marriage" and the need for each partner to be able to escape from an intolerable union. But when the popes assumed complete power, civil law was replaced by papal decretals, which were eventually systematized into Canon Law, which in turn became absolute throughout the Holy Roman Empire—that is, in all the courts of law in Christian Europe.

As a result, temporal affairs came under the control of an essentially spiritual code. Well-being and decent conduct in this world became subservient to laws which would ensure immortality in the next. In its beginnings, Christianity had been a religion of the poor and the underdog, justifying their present sufferings with the promise of bliss in the hereafter. When the Church took over the machinery of the State this strategy was intensified. The law codified the teachings of Christ, as set out in the Gospels and interpreted by successive popes, and thus became an instrument for salvation.

At one stroke, marriage ceased to be a civil contract which could be dissolved, like any other contract, when it became inconvenient to the partners. It became a vow in the sight of God, a sacrament, a small-scale embodiment of the eternal marriage of the Church with Christ, indissoluble by definition. For the faithful, there was only one God and one Church; therefore there could be only one marriage. QED. By that simple equation the ecclesiastical bureaucracy assumed jurisdiction over the most intimate details of every Christian's domestic life.

Canon Law decreed that there could be no divorce *a vinculo matrimonii* (from the bond of marriage), only a separation *a mensa et thoro* (from bed and board). Divorce in the Roman or modern sense, which sets the partners free to marry again, was theoretically impossible. The best that could be hoped for was a separation or annulment obtainable for any of six reasons: adultery or unnatural offenses; impotence; cruelty; infidelity; enter-

ing into religion, i.e., retiring into a monastery or nunnery;
consanguinity.*

"God never dies," said the theologians, and the sacrament of
marriage was similarly immortal. Since "one flesh" could never
again become two, a second marriage was necessarily a form of
adultery. Even after a formally sanctioned separation, remarriage was not permitted.

The effect of all this was to make marriage not only indissoluble but penitential. The ecclesiastical laws were not passed for
the benefit of the marrying kind but for the satisfaction of a
nominally celibate clergy, themselves inspired by the Church's
founding fathers whose "favorite doctrine," said Lecky, was that
"concupiscence or the sensual passion was 'the original sin' of
human nature." Prohibiting divorce was a rationalization of the
priestly aversion to marriage itself.

The irony went unnoticed, like all the other ironies in the
history of this touchy subject. For example, the first temporal
ruler to declare marriage indissoluble and divorce a crime was
Charlemagne, the most married monarch in Christendom. His
sexual career was summed up by a Dr. Arsène Drouet during a
debate on divorce in the French Parliament in 1876: "Charlemagne, whom a historian has described as 'a little inclined to be
too fond of women,' married nine times, had several mistresses,
and was even intimate with his daughters. He was canonized."
He also set an example for what was to follow.

For the largest irony of all was the sexual morality of the
nominally celibate clergy during the Dark and Middle Ages.
Lecky quotes contemporary accounts of nunneries "like broth-
els" where "multitudes of infanticides" took place, of homosexual
orgies in the monasteries and of the "inveterate prevalence of
incest among the clergy." He cites a pope who was condemned
for crimes which included incest and adultery; an abbot-elect of
Saint Augustine, Canterbury, who had seventeen illegitimate
children in a single village; a Spanish abbot who had seventy

* The Orthodox Eastern Church interpreted the teaching of Jesus in a broader
way than the Church of Rome and allowed complete divorce with the right to
remarry for the cause of adultery. It also permitted the clergy to marry. For
these two heresies it was formally excommunicated by Pope Gregory VII in the
eleventh century.

concubines; and Henry III, bishop of Liège, who was deposed in 1274 for having sixty-five illegitimate children. Lecky summarizes the whole shabby scene by quoting a tenth-century Italian bishop, Ratherius, who declared "that if he were to enforce the canons against unchaste people administering ecclesiastical rites, no one would be left in the Church except the boys; and if he were to observe the canons against bastards, these also must be excluded."

"Humor saves a few steps," said Marianne Moore, "it saves years." Likewise honest depravity in an age devoted to chastity. Desire did not fail when the clergy was declared celibate, bad marriages did not cease when the institution became a sacrament, and divorce did not disappear when it was prohibited. No sooner had the canons concerning divorce been enacted than they became, like any other laws, a challenge to the ingenuity of the lawyers. And since both the lawyers and the courts were ecclesiastical, divorce—disguised as annulment or separation—became a substantial source of Church income, like the sale of pardons and indulgences which so provoked Chaucer.

The most commonly cited canons concerned consanguinity, marriage between those related by blood. And in the reckoning of the Church, blood was spread very thin indeed: marriage was originally forbidden between couples as remotely related as the seventh degree. (According to Canon Law, second cousins are related only in the third degree; in civil law, they are related in the sixth degree.) This was complicated by relationships which had nothing whatever to do with blood ties. "Affinity," for example, or relationship by marriage: when the Earl of Bothwell wanted to marry Mary Queen of Scots, he divorced his wife on the grounds that one of his ancestors had married into her family nearly a century before. There was also "spiritual" relationship by baptism, through which the family of the godparent who sponsored a child at baptism and that of the priest who officiated were drawn into the forbidden network. This meant that in a village or small town it was almost impossible *not* to marry within one of the prohibited degrees. To do so, it was necessary to pay the Church for a dispensation, and if the marriage turned out to be a disaster, to pay again for the ecclesiastical legal machinery to be put into reverse.

The other canons could also be interpreted, at a price, in an equally flexible way. Despite the doctrine of marriage as a sacrament, canon lawyers treated it, like the Roman lawyers before them, as a contract based on consent and followed by a consummation which made the two partners one flesh. Without that, the marriage was declared null. This could be arranged even when a couple had lived together for years, if the husband was willing to pretend to be impotent and so make his children illegitimate. To save face, impotence was usually blamed on witchcraft.

The more subtle the canons, the more intricate the legal maneuvering and the greater the expense. Some were so refined as to be virtually royal prerogatives. Henry VIII divorced Anne of Cleves, for instance, on the grounds of his "lack of inward consent" to the marriage. Two and a half centuries later, Napoleon divorced Josephine for the same reason, pleading the example of thirteen French kings.

According to S. B. Kitchin's comprehensive legal *History of Divorce*, it was even possible to interpret as adultery the act of love between a married couple, if one of them was thinking about someone else at the time. Similarly, heresy or religious differences became "spiritual adultery," and during the Inquisition legal expense could be saved by denouncing an unwanted partner as a heretic or a witch or a sorcerer. In *A History of the Inquisition*, H. C. Lea gives a chilling example of a man who was burned at the stake for heresy, although the main witness against him was his wife who was already living with another man and had openly "wished her husband dead that she might marry a certain Pug Oler, declaring 'that she would willingly become a leper if that would bring it about.'"

But in general divorce could be obtained by less bloodthirsty means. As in all legal matters, it was a question of money and language. The loopholes existed and their size was directly proportional to the power and wealth of the plaintiffs. The sophistry of the canon lawyers was equal to the famous sophistry of the medieval theologians, but at least it could be made to work for practical, domestic ends. So, too, the corruption of the medieval Church and the cynicism of its dignitaries; because most of them were worldly, sensual, venal men, they were willing to take a correspondingly worldly, sensual, venal attitude to the sacrament of marriage. Their cynicism was humanizing; it helped make a theoretically rigid institution flexible—despite the laws, despite the antisexual fanaticism of the Early Fathers.

6. THE REFORMATION

When Luther publicly burned the books of Canon Law at Wittenberg in 1520—proclaiming, "Because thou hast vexed the Holy One of God, let the everlasting fire consume thee"—he was expressing in the most dramatic possible way a growing general outrage with the chop logic of what John Donne called the "wrangling schools," and also with the corruption and cupidity of the Church. His aim was to restore to Christianity its founder's original purity of spirit, but the incidental result was to slam the door shut on divorce and turn bad marriages into prisons.

After the Reformation, said the British Royal Commission on Divorce of 1853, "the doctrine of indissolubility was . . . not only re-established, but it operated in this country with a rigour unknown in Roman Catholic times; the various fictions and devices in the shape of canonical degrees and alleged pre-contracts, which then afforded so many loop-holes of escape from its severity, having, each and all, been put an end to at the Reformation." Instead of basing their interpretations on papal decretals so intricate that they were permeable as latticework, the Reformers went back to the Scriptures themselves for final authority. These turned out to be altogether less amenable to sophistry, particularly when interpreted in the new, strict Reformist spirit by Lutheran, Calvinist and Puritan legal theologians.

In their eyes, nothing less than a crime was sufficient reason for breaking up a marriage. So to the traditional, biblical grounds of adultery they added a single invention of their own, malicious desertion. This was derived not from the Gospels but from Saint Paul: "But if the unbelieving depart, let him depart. A brother or a sister is not under bondage in such cases: but God hath called us to peace." Desertion had always been considered reasonable grounds for divorce, by canon lawyers as well as by Roman, but as Kitchin says, "it was the crowning achievement of the Reformers to treat it as 'malicious' and make it into a

crime." It shows a curious, autocratic confusion between private
failing and civil offense, despite the fact that the Reformers were
otherwise so determined to separate Church from State that
they rejected the Roman Catholic conception of marriage as a
sacrament and made it once again a civil contract which could be
validated by a magistrate. Although the Puritans idealized "holy
matrimony" as fervently as the Catholics idealized virginity—
marriage, said the preacher William Perkins, is "a state in itself
far more excellent than the condition of a single life"—they continued to think of it, like Saint Paul, as a channel for lusts which
might otherwise be satisfied indiscriminately: "It is better to
marry than to burn." In this obsessed Pauline spirit, "malicious
desertion" was interpreted in Dutch law as a refusal of either
partner to pay his or her "carnal debt"—that is, it could take
place without ever leaving home.

A new restrictive spirit was abroad and a new literalism.
Lawyers began seriously to argue that adultery should be pun-
ishable by death, as in the Old Testament. One of them solemnly
proposed that an act to this effect should be put before the Tudor
Houses of Parliament. They even preferred polygamy to divorce,
since it had been practiced by the biblical patriarchs. Luther,
Melanchthon and Bucer, who were among the two hundred
learned authorities consulted by Henry VIII when the pope refused to divorce him from Catherine of Aragon, all agreed that
what had been permitted Abraham could not be forbidden by
God. (Saint Augustine had held the same opinion, as had the
pope who advised Henry IV of Castile.)

These absurdities were esoteric, almost theoretical conclusions, exclusively for royal consumption. The nobility contented
themselves with a liberal interpretation of the laws on adultery
for their continuing frequent divorces. But for those less fortu-
nate, wealthy and well-placed, the law was like iron. Even Milton, the foremost polemicist of his day, as well as the greatest
poet, was unable to shift them and hurt himself in the attempt.

He married late, inspired by the Puritan ideal of matrimony
as the God-given remedy for loneliness. But the girl he chose
was half his age, frivolous and uneducated, the daughter of an
Oxfordshire squire who owed Milton's father money: "His first
wife (Mrs. Powell, a Royalist)," wrote John Aubrey, "was

brought up and lived where there was a greate deale of company
and merriment, dancing, etc. And when she came to live with
her husband, in St. Bride's Church-yard, she found it very solitary; no company came to her; oftimes heard his Nephews beaten
and cry. This life was irkesome to her . . ." A couple of months
after the wedding she went back to visit her family and refused
to return. It was three years before friends engineered a reunion
between the estranged couple.

Milton did not divorce her for desertion or adultery, although he could have done so without much trouble. Instead, he
channeled his outrage and hurt into a series of four powerful,
learned tracts on the iniquity of the divorce laws and the misery
of failed marriages:

> What thing more instituted to the solace and delight of man then
> marriage, and yet the mis-interpreting of some Scripture directed
> mainly against the abuses of the Law for divorce giv'n by *Moses*,
> hath chang'd the blessing of matrimony not seldome into a familiar
> and co-habiting mischiefe; at least into a drooping and disconsolate
> houshold captivitie, without refuge or redemption.

Marriage, he argued, was designed by God not primarily for
sexual relief or the procreation of children but for "the apt and
cheerful conversation of man with woman." Where that did not
exist "there can be nothing left of wedlock but the empty husk of
outside matrimony." This was the Puritan conception of marriage taken to its logical conclusion and Milton, as a skilled and
exceptionally learned debater, made his case in elaborate detail.
But now, when all that vast ecclesiastical and legal scholarship
no longer means much, what still moves us is his eloquence on
the pain and disillusion engendered by bad marriages.

He had gone to the altar gravely, as a Puritan, not as a
romantic with impossible expectations of unending love, but for
a kind of divine completion, so that he could continue in his
vocation as a poet with help and sympathy, just as in his youth
he had considered celibacy as a sacrificial dedication of his talents
to God. Instead, he found himself lonelier than before and baffled, as millions of others have been, by the paradox that his
loneliness was intensified by the presence of an unloving and

unloved wife, continually reminding him of his folly, his rashness, his inexperience:

> The solitarines of man, which God hath namely and principally
> ordered to prevent by marriage, hath no remedy, but lies under a
> worse condition then the loneliest single life; for in single life the
> absence and remotenes of a helper might inure him to expect his
> own comforts out of himself, or to seeke with hope; but here the
> continuall sight of his deluded thoughts without cure must needs
> be to him, if especially his complexion incline him to melancholy, a
> daily trouble and paine of loss like that which Reprobates feel.

For a man imprisoned in a loveless marriage, the only alternatives are adultery or despair; both endanger his salvation, both
contradict the basic Christian belief that the Creator has the
well-being of His creation at heart. To condemn the innocent to
misery of this order, he argued, goes against charity, Jesus'
"supreme dictate."

Milton was the first English writer "so speak of the woe that
is in marriage" so passionately and so directly. He was also,
according to Edward Westermarck, the "first protagonist in
Christendom" of incompatibility as grounds for divorce.* His
contemporaries hounded him for it from every side: the Puritans,
he complained, "railed at the book as injurious and licentious, if
not worse," while the Cavaliers—"the brood of Belial, the draffe
of men"—used it as an excuse for debauchery. His reputation
never entirely recovered during his lifetime and it was another
three hundred years before the divorce laws caught up with him.

In the meantime, the judges of the Reformation, like the
Catholic bishops before them, were instructed to do everything

---

* This is not strictly true. Sir Thomas More, a Catholic so devout that he was
martyred for his faith and later canonized, guardedly proposed divorce by mutual
consent as early as 1516 in his *Utopia:* "And matrymoneie is there never broken,
but by death; except adulterye breake the bonde, or els the intollerable waye-
ward maners of either partye . . . But nowe and then it chaunceth, where as the
man and the woman cannot well agree betweene themselves, both of them fynd-
inge other, with whome they hope to lyve more quietlye and merylye, that they
by the fulle consente of them bothe be divorsed asonder and married againe to
other. But that not without the authoritie of the counsell. Which agreeth to no
divorses, before they and their wyfes have diligently tried and examyned the
matter. Yea and then also they be lothe to consent to it, because they know this
to be the next way to break love betwene man and wyfe, to be in easye hope of a
new marriage."

they could to keep marriages together, despite the wishes or
well-being of the blighted couples who came before them. Any
hint of collusion or connivance—which would have been evidence
of mutual consent to the Romans—became in itself criminal and
made divorce impossible. In other words, the unhappier the couple and the more desperate to part, the less chance they had. If
they finally took matters into their own hands and split up, despite the law, this too became a criminal act. In seventeenth-
century Amsterdam they were fined one hundred florins for
every month they lived apart and were sent to prison if they
failed to pay.

7. THE LAW AND THE PUBLIC

The intolerance of the Reformation in allowing divorce for
nothing less than a crime had two lasting side effects. First, it
meant that in every divorce there was always *by law* a guilty
party and an innocent one, a wrongdoer and someone wronged.
Because this attitude is so remote from the realities of both
marriage and the human temperament, it established a habit of
distrust between lawyers and those forced to use them, a paranoid conviction that, in its dealings with domestic misery, the
law was not impartial; on the contrary, it was positively at odds
with the welfare of each and every unhappily married couple.

For the devout who believed Canon Law to be an instrument of salvation and Christian virtue, this attitude may even
have made a strained and contradictory moral sense. But long
after most people ceased to think of marriage as a sacrament or
as a social device to contain the sexual drives of those who lacked
the ambiguous gift of chastity, public disgrace remained as a
powerful disincentive. So long as divorce was impossible Roman-
style—by mutual consent and with no guilt on either side—the
law decreed that the intimate details of every marital disaster
should be aired in court. "Whom God hath joined let no man put
asunder," and those whom the fear of the wrath of God no longer
bothered were kept from sundering by fear of scandal. Until the
early years of this century, the terror of excommunication from
society was as great as that of excommunication from the
Church.

The other side effect followed from the first: an equally pervasive and paranoid belief in the secret connection between politics and divorce, between the state of the nation and the state of marriage. Both the major revolutions of modern history were, literally, celebrated by reinstituting the Roman practice of divorce by mutual consent. This was one of the first actions of the French lawyers after 1789 and of the Russians after 1917. In France it provoked such an epidemic of divorce that by 1806 the framers of the Code Civile felt obliged to bring back the traditional grounds—adultery, crime, cruelty—so that "the most sacred of contracts should not become the toy of caprice." It was Napoleon, at that point working up to his divorce from Josephine and anxious to spare himself unsavory publicity, who insisted they keep "mutual consent" and "incompatibility." For political reasons, he was also forced to consult Catholic priests as well as Republican lawyers, so his Code Civile lacks that first, fierce revolutionary determination to sweep away dead social conventions which had fired the lawmakers of 1789 and their Soviet counterparts who drew up the 1926 code. As if to demonstrate their total rejection of religion, the Russians went on to introduce the concept of unregistered marriage and divorce: a marriage was recognized legally if a couple could prove *orally* that they were living together, and a divorce could be registered on the request of only one party, if he or she could produce proof that the marital relationship was over.

From the revolutionary standpoint, the relationship between the divorce laws and society is direct and symbolic: marriage is the symbol of social repression, divorce of liberty. The French lawyers were perfectly clear about this in their preamble to the new divorce laws: "Considering how important it is that all Frenchmen should enjoy the right to divorce, as a corollary of that individual liberty which would be nullified by any indissoluble engagement . . ." That is the Catholic symbolism of human marriage—as the model in miniature of the eternal marriage of the Church with Christ—turned upside down. The revolution proves its sincerity by making a political gesture in an impenetrably private area. Citizens may or may not be taken in by political rhetoric, but when the rulers change the divorce laws they mean business.

As though to illustrate the principle that history repeats

itself, first as tragedy, then as farce: in 1968 European and American students went to the barricades spouting Marx and Mao and Marcuse, and came away with "the sexual revolution" and the establishment of the "no-fault" system of divorce. They had revolutionized society and enlarged individual liberty in ways which were incalculable, but not what they had in mind.

The symbolism holds for both sides: the first gesture of the reaction which invariably follows revolution is to raise the drawbridge on the fortress of marriage and bar all the gates. After the fall of Napoleon in 1816, the Catholic Bourbons abolished divorce and restored Canon Law (this lasted until 1884), and Stalin remorselessly tightened Soviet marriage laws until, by 1944, the courts once again had sole jurisdiction over divorce. This law, which provoked great hostility, was finally modified in 1968, and Russia now has one of the highest divorce rates in the world.*

8. ENGLAND

It is ironic that England, which later did as much to hinder divorce as the Roman Catholic Church, was the one country

---

* With some variations, the other countries of the Soviet bloc have followed the prim Stalinist line on marriage and divorce: too casual an attitude is thought to be bad for social stability. Nevertheless, divorce remains cheap in Eastern Europe, and alimony to the wife—as distinct from maintenance for the children—is rarely allowed since it is assumed that women work. Only the Chinese Communists followed the early Soviet example of unrestrained divorce for anyone and everyone, although under Mao there was probably less danger of flippant divorce than of no one having time or opportunity to find a mate; according to Western journalists, one of the first stunning indications of change after the fall of the Gang of Four was the sight of young people walking hand in hand in the streets. But the Chinese attitude to marriage and divorce was influenced by an utterly different cultural tradition. In pre-Communist times divorce was the concern of the family, not the state. Secondary wives were permitted and incompatibility was a sufficient ground for divorce, provided the wife's family was willing to have her back. There was also a wealth of more exotic excuses. For example, a wife could be divorced because she was a chatterbox or for conduct displeasing to her husband's parents, though not if she had carried out proper mourning for their death. If a husband was ill-used by his wife, he could hand her over to justice, or even sell her. A deserted wife could file a complaint with a magistrate and apply for permission to remarry. Within this family-oriented culture, the traditional Chinese attitudes to divorce were measured and reasonable. The question of love—in the romantic, European sense—seems scarcely to have arisen.

where the connection with politics was once obvious and dramatic. The Church of England broke away from Rome not because Henry VIII supported the Reformation—on the contrary, the Vatican awarded him the title of "Defender of the Faith" for his refutation of Luther—but because the pope, for political reasons, was afraid to dissolve his marriage to Catherine of Aragon. This should have been simple since Catherine was his sister-in-law, his brother's widow, and the marriage, made to preserve an alliance with Spain, had originally required questionable papal dispensation. But Catherine was unable to provide a son to secure the Tudor succession, so in time Henry—who had fallen in love with Anne Boleyn—began to fret about his spiritual health: had God refused to grant him a male heir because he was living in sin with Catherine, despite the pope's dispensation? He put this question to the legal and theological experts of all the universities of Europe, in order to be told what he wanted to hear. Two hundred learned doctors duly agreed that, because of the couple's close relationship, the marriage had never properly taken place. But the pope, who was afraid of Catherine's nephew, Emperor Charles V, still refused to grant a dissolution. After five years of wrangling, Henry lost patience; he set up a commission of bishops who tried the case, granted him a divorce and pronounced the surviving child of his marriage to Catherine illegitimate. Henry then declared himself head of the Church of England, in place of the pope, an obedient Parliament passed the necessary legislation, the pope excommunicated him and England seceded from Rome.* In other words, England's national independence began with a royal divorce.

But with Puritanism on the rise, what was good for the king and his nobles was not deemed good for the country. Like Charlemagne, Henry eventually reacted against the liberties he had

---

* Henry's impatience had been exacerbated by the fact that Anne Boleyn was pregnant. But she, too, bore him a daughter, so he divorced her—alleging precontract between her and the Earl of Northumberland—then beheaded her for adultery. His next wife, Jane Seymour, died within a year of giving birth to the longed-for son, the future Edward VI. Henry then made a diplomatic marriage to Anne of Cleves, but divorced her six months later when the diplomatic reasons were, as they now say, "no longer operative," claiming that he had never "inwardly consented" to the marriage. Immediately afterward, he married Catherine Howard, who, like Anne Boleyn, was a niece of the Duke of Norfolk and whom, also like Anne, he beheaded for infidelity within a couple of years. His last wife, Catherine Parr, managed to survive him.

strenuously pursued in his youth and drew up an act declaring marriage indissoluble. Later still, he had second thoughts and appointed a commission, headed by the Archbishop of Canterbury, to "rough hew" Canon Law to conform to England's new religious independence. The commission's recommendations were not original—more a shrewd mixture of Canonical and Reformist practice—except in one detail: for the first time since the Roman Empire, the wife was not to be discriminated against; she and her husband were to have equal rights before the law. Unfortunately for England, this astonishingly modern piece of legislation died with Henry. Edward VI ratified it but lacked the clout to push it through Parliament; it went into abeyance during the reign of the Catholic Bloody Mary—its originator, Archbishop Cranmer, was burned at the stake—and was never taken up again by Elizabeth, the unmarried Virgin Queen. Instead, just before her death the Court of the Star Chamber reaffirmed Henry's declaration that marriage was indissoluble. The law remained that way—despite Milton, despite Selden, despite public resentment and private misery—until after the Restoration when divorce by private Act of Parliament, a method used by both Henry and by his contemporary, the Earl of Northampton, was grudgingly reintroduced.

In the whole history of long-winded and expensive legal machination, this was the longest-winded and most expensive. The aggrieved husband had first to obtain from an ecclesiastical court a judicial separation *a mensa et thoro*. Then he had to go to a civil court and bring a successful common-law action for damages against the wife's lover for trespass to the husband in his marital property. (As property, the wife was naturally excluded from taking part in this action.) He then had to bring a private act before the reverend bishops in the House of Lords, who finally handed the act down to the House of Commons for ratification.

Only the wealthiest could afford this intricate, lengthy charade, and in almost two hundred years—from 1669 to 1850—a mere 291 of these acts were passed. Even then, the process was effectively closed to women. In the same period, only four managed to obtain a divorce by private Act of Parliament, all of them from husbands who compounded simple adultéry with bigamy or incest.

For those poor enough to be socially invisible, there were other ways out: "In a society without a national police force," writes Lawrence Stone, "it was all too easy simply to run away and never be heard of again . . . The second alternative was bigamy, which seems to have been both easy and common." Stone also mentions a third alternative, the medieval folk-custom of "wife-sale," by which the husband put a halter around his wife's neck, led her to market like a brood mare and auctioned her to the highest bidder. Thomas Hardy began *The Mayor of Caster-bridge* with a toned-down version of this ritual and the last recorded instance was in 1887.

In fact, the law had begun to come to terms with domestic reality thirty years earlier, although the Divorce Act of 1857 was precipitated, in the best British fashion, not by an outburst of popular discontent but by the irony of a High Court judge. He was trying the case of a poor but respectable man whose wife had run off with a lover years before and never reappeared. Eventually, the unfortunate man remarried, was indicted for bigamy and found guilty. Mr. Justice Maule sentenced him as follows:

> "Prisoner at the bar: You have been convicted of the offense of bigamy, that is to say, of marrying a woman while you had a wife still alive, though it is true she has deserted you and is living in adultery with another man. You have, therefore, committed a crime against the laws of your country, and you have also acted under a very serious misapprehension of the course which you ought to have pursued. You should have gone to the ecclesiastical court and there obtained against your wife a decree *a mensa et thoro*. You should then have brought an action in the courts of common law and recovered, as no doubt you would have recovered, damages against your wife's paramour. Armed with these decrees, you should have approached the legislature and obtained an act of parliament which would have rendered you free and legally competent to marry the person whom you have taken on yourself to marry with no such sanction. It is quite true that these proceedings would have cost you many hundreds of pounds, whereas you probably have not as many pence. But the law knows no distinctions between rich and poor. The sentence of the court upon you, therefore, is that you be imprisoned for one day, which period has al-

ready been exceeded, as you have been in custody since the commencement of the assizes."

The Establishment—in the person of a High Court judge—had formally and literally pronounced sentence on its own privileges and the way was open for divorce to be debated in Parliament as a preliminary to long overdue reform. It is one of the few recorded cases in history when irony, that last infirmity of the legal mind, not merely helped change the law of the land but actively contributed to human happiness.

Yet it was more than another century before the Divorce Reform Act of 1969—put into effect in 1971—made British divorce cheap, easy, nondiscriminating, democratic, rational and, in a word, Roman. During that interval, Great Britain still lagged behind most of Protestant Europe. Frederick the Great of Prussia, influenced by Voltaire and the Encyclopaedists, had introduced divorce by mutual consent by 1784. Norway and Sweden had allowed divorce for "incompatibility of temper" and "mutual detestation" since 1810, and soon after that the Norwegians extended the law to allow divorce by mutual consent after one year's separation without stating the grounds and with the husband and wife equal before the law—a form of legal sanity that Great Britain has barely achieved in the last decade. Even Catholic Poland was once more advanced than England. When in the late eighteenth century King Stanislas Augustus, like Henry VIII, preempted the pope's right to grant divorces, his loyal subjects went enthusiastically to his aid by deliberately celebrating their marriages in ways which made them canonically invalid: parents would ritually box the bride's ears before the ceremony to indicate coercion, or the husband would allege impotence in the marriage contract.

But unlike Prussia or Scandinavia or Poland, Britain had a global empire through which to spread its word: Australia, Canada, New Zealand, South Africa and the white populations of the colonies all held rigidly to the old English belief that marriage was an irreversible condition, like terminal cancer. Even the United States continued to follow British practice long after 1776. South Carolina, for instance, still had no divorce laws in 1912, and one of its judges announced with pride that "in South

Carolina, to her unfading glory, a divorce has not been granted since the Revolution." Social rectitude, apparently, had replaced religious belief, or was masquerading as it. The unfading honor of Old Dixie notwithstanding, had the judge not existed, Dickens might have invented him: his style of hypocrisy was peculiarly Victorian, the obverse of the missionary earnestness with which the empire builders went out to face "the lesser breeds without the law." Decency and parliamentary democracy on one side, blind propriety on the other. It was that combination of imperviousness and self-assurance which enabled them to stick by their convictions in the teeth of hostile experience. Perhaps this explains the paradox by which, in Kitchin's words, "one of the greatest of Protestant nations has been mainly instrumental in perpetuating and spreading all over the world the Catholic Canon Law made by the monks of the Middle Ages."

9. THE PRESENT

In 1890, in a book called *News From Nowhere*, William Morris peered over the battlements of Victorian morality and disapproval and saw a Utopia with no divorce courts:

I know that there used to be such lunatic affairs as divorce courts. But just consider; all the cases that came into them were matters of property quarrels: and I think, dear guest . . . that though you do come from another planet, you can see from the mere outside look of our world that quarrels about private property could not go on amongst us in our days . . . Well, then, property quarrels being no longer possible, what remains in these matters that a court of law could deal with? Fancy a court for enforcing a contract of passion or sentiment! If such a thing were needed as a *reductio ad absurdum* of the enforcement of contract, such a folly would do that for us . . . We do not deceive ourselves, indeed, or believe that we can get rid of all the trouble that besets the dealings between the sexes. We know that we must face the unhappiness that comes of man and woman, confusing the relations between natural passion, and sentiment, and the friendship which, when things go well, softens the awakening from passing illusions: but we are not so mad as to pile up degradation on that unhappiness by engaging in sordid squabbles about livelihood and position, and the power of tyrannising over the children who have been the result of

love or lust . . . If there must be a sundering betwixt those who
never meant to sunder, so it must be: but there need be no pretext
of unity when the reality of it is gone: nor do we drive those who
well know that they are incapable of it to profess an undying sentiment which they cannot really feel . . . You did not seem shocked
when I told you that there were no law-courts to enforce contracts
of sentiment or passion; but so curiously are men made, that perhaps you will be shocked when I tell you that there is no code of
public opinion which takes the place of such courts, and which
might be as tyrannical and unreasonable as they were. I do not say
that people don't judge their neighbors' conduct, sometimes,
doubtless, unfairly. But I do say that there is no unvarying conventional set of rules by which people are judged . . . no hypocritical
excommunication which people are *forced* to pronounce, either by
unconsidered habit, or by the unexpressed threat of the lesser
interdict if they are lax in their hypocrisy.

Morris thought it would take another two centuries to achieve
this sweet reasonableness. Although he overestimated the stam-
ina of Victorian prudery, divorce was still the last bastion to fall
in England. Long after everyone had lost the dubious privilege
of starving in a wealthy country or being unable to afford proper
medical care, divorce remained difficult, expensive and shameful.

It took the explosion of scandal in high places and plain bad
behavior everywhere else in the Swinging Sixties to change public opinion radically enough to affect the laws. The sixties, said
Richard Rovere, were "a slum of a decade," but at least they
marked the end of a certain style of smugness and hypocrisy.
The young began to flaunt their sexuality as aggressively as
their elders had concealed theirs and, whatever their private
confusions and uncertainties, seemed determined not to be taken
in by the old humbug. So they went to bed together ostenta-
tiously, often promiscuously, and without bothering with the
cleansing, purgative ritual of marriage. Meanwhile, the big public scandals of the time, like the Profumo Affair, demonstrated
for all to see that the kids were merely following in the footsteps
of father—or grandfather. Those in between—the earnest
young marrieds of the 1950s—took their cue and went through
with the breakup of marriages which, ten years before, they
would probably have been shamed into maintaining. Despite the

student revolutions and the universal proliferation of what Jean-François Revel labeled "Pidgin Marxism," it was the middle class and middle-aged who emerged from the sixties with their liberties enlarged.

So, too, did the majority of women. In his brilliant book, *The Making of the Modern Family*, Edward Shorter suggests that what took place in the sixties was a "historic change of mind" which amounted to a sexual revolution: "People of all ages —but adolescents in particular—began to strip away the sentimental layers from the romantic experience to get at its hard sexual core, thinking eroticism most precious in what human relationships have to offer us and impatient with the delays that feeling once imposed." But this erotic realism was only made possible by dramatic advances in contraception which freed women at last from the fear of unwanted pregnancies. Like equality of opportunity or equality before the law, equality before and after sex is a major liberty, the precondition, I suspect, of the political reforms feminists subsequently demanded. The ability to make love for the pleasure of it, without anxiety, as casually or fastidiously as men, was like a new theory of relativity for women, reordering their moral universe. "You cannot seduce anyone," wrote Elizabeth Hardwick, "when innocence is not a value. Technology annihilates consequence." But in this instance technology has moral consequences which outlast fashions. The full frontal life-style of the Swinging Sixties went the way of the miniskirt without affecting the "historic change of mind."

In the matter of divorce the change has not been in behavior but in the attitude to behavior. In 1936 Edward VIII chose to abdicate from the throne rather than go back on his decision to marry a woman who had been twice divorced. (He had no choice: as King he was Supreme Governor of the Church of England which still regards matrimony as a bond for life.) The Royal Family never forgave him, and twenty years later the young Princess Margaret renounced Peter Townsend, the divorced man she had fallen in love with, rather than abdicate as princess. Yet in 1978 she divorced the Earl of Snowdon with remarkably little fuss. Her case was simply one on a list that day, one of some 170,000 other divorces in England that year. In short, nothing out of the ordinary, and she used what had by then become the standard procedure: automatic divorce after two years' separation, requiring no judicial investigation into the "facts"—the new neutral term into what used to be called the "grounds for divorce," that is, who was guilty of what. No arguments, if both partners are agreed, not much expense and no invasion of privacy. "It is reassuring," remarked a woman whose divorce had gone through in the same batch as the princess's, "finally to do something the Royal Family approves of."

It was a long and unruffled way from the shrillness with which the Divorce Reform Act had been debated in Parliament a decade before, when its defenders talked piously of "buttressing the institution of marriage" by providing a way for "dead marriages" to be "dissolved with dignity," while its detractors prophesied doom.* Yet when the act became law in 1971, morality of the country did not crumble instantly to ash, young people continued to marry as recklessly as ever, and divorced people continued, even more recklessly, to marry again. All that had happened was that a great number of confused couples were spared a great deal of gratuitous torment.

After more than a thousand years, we are back to the reasonable attitude toward divorce that prevailed everywhere until Saint Paul and the demented ascetics who followed him turned the Book of Genesis on its head by proposing celibacy, rather than marriage, as the ultimate perfection in an imperfect world. But instead of a new wave of immorality, there is its opposite: an altogether moral refusal to go along the conventional hypocrisy, coupled with an equally moral desire for happiness in the present in place of misery now and justification in the hereafter. By these lights, divorce is not a sin but an aid to virtue, a means of preserving, in Milton's words, "peace in marriage, and quiet in the family." As it always was. "There is no use speculating on that subject," said Oscar Wilde. "Divorces are made in heaven."

---

* For example, the clause which allowed one partner to divorce the other unilaterally after five years' separation was ringingly denounced by Baroness Summerskill as "a Casanova's charter." She feared that heartless, bored husbands would use it to trade in aging wives for newer models. In the event, the reverse has happened: it is the women who have taken greater advantage of the legislation, the aging husbands who have found themselves indignantly in the knacker's yard.

VI

The Patriarch

Wife and Children are a kind of Discipline of Humanity.

FRANCIS BACON

Neither a sexual revolution nor enlightened legislation can eliminate overnight more than a thousand years of divorce taboo. It lives on like a ghost, chilly and half-perceived, generating a kind of moral shudder even in those to whom religion no longer means much and society does not accuse. Pride, or the superego, takes over where the Church and community leave off, and no amount of acceptance or understanding or social indifference lessens the sense of personal failure. It is possible that the next generation will become immunized even to that vertigo, but for those who have lived as adults through the last quarter of a century of changes the story is different.

We met first at a New England women's college in the days when women's colleges were still only for women. Leo was their bright young philosopher who, unlike most of his colleagues, also applied his mind to subjects outside his field: to history and sociology, even to the arts. I had read one of his articles in *Partisan* or *Kenyon*—I don't remember which—and wanted to meet him. So a mutual friend took me over to his house one Sunday morning. It was a gray March day with a nagging wind and low clouds scurrying over the Victorian Gothic, the lawns still streaked with dirty snow, the roads whitish and crusty with what was left of the salt.

The house was as bleak as the weather outside and furnished mostly with books, as if by someone who didn't much care for the comforts of life. Leo, too, seemed bleak and preoccupied: a large presence, six foot something, with the broad Germanic bottom and hips that often afflict Americans, but muscular in a sleepy way, his ample belly balanced by the span of his shoulders. Even now, when he is over fifty and living the Manhattan life, he keeps in shape, jogging in Central Park and working out once a week in a downtown gymnasium. But in those days there was a glow about him, an aura of physical well-being and power which showed through despite the gloom. His dark face—heavy mouth, melancholy eyes—was faintly exotic, a throwback to the Odessa of his grandparents, with its tight-knit community of soulful, quarrelsome Jews. His voice was low and resonant, at odds with his tough New York talk and the even tougher career he had already carved himself in the academic jungle, where the knives are sharp, and among the East Coast intellectuals, where they are sharper.

But that day the romantic vibrato of his voice was muted and his mind elsewhere. He kept lapsing into silence, staring at the rush matting on the floor, his head cocked as though listening for something. After half an hour of broken, desultory talk I raised my eyebrows to the friend who had brought me. He shrugged and shook his head. We both looked at our watches.

At that moment the door was opened abruptly by a thin, bristling girl who might have been pretty had her cheeks been less sallow, her jaw less set, her mouth less spoiled. But even by my standards of all those years ago she seemed disproportionately young: narrow hips, childish hands, curly reddish hair no one had ever done anything with. The baby-sitter, I thought.

She stood in the doorway, a suitcase on either side of her, and made no move to come in. She merely eyed us coldly and said to Leo, "I'm off."

He shifted uneasily from ham to ham and did not reply.

"You know where to reach me." Her voice was precise and matter-of-fact, as if she were giving instructions to the answering service.

He nodded.

"Well, then . . ." She bent to her suitcases.

He made no move to help her. "Where's Jake?" he said.

Her jaw tightened, the corners of her mouth turned down for battle. She opened her mouth to say something, then snapped it shut, lifted the suitcases and answered, "Asleep."

"Good."

"Well . . ." She shrugged. "See you."

"Yeah. See you."

She closed the door behind her.

Leo slumped in his chair, eyes half closed. We heard the sound of the front door shutting firmly, then the noise of a receding taxi.

"That was Marilyn," Leo explained, and lapsed back into silence.

We tried to get the conversation going again, but he answered in monosyllables, shifting about morosely in his armchair and staring even more fixedly at the floor. After ten minutes of this the door suddenly opened again and a small boy came in, trailing a blanket and rubbing his face sleepily. He was a beautiful little child, a couple of years old, with his father's dark eyes and a shock of black curls.

"Where's Momma?" he asked.

Leo jumped up and lifted him into his arms. "Gone," he answered.

The boy looked at him, puzzled, his head to one side. But when Leo smiled encouragingly the child smiled back. Then, without warning, both of them were laughing.

A couple of days later my friend telephoned to say that "Momma" had, in fact, gone for good, and what we had witnessed was the end of a marriage.

Later, when I got to know Leo well, he dismissed the whole episode: "Sixties stuff," he called it, "theater of the absurd." Not only could he no longer remember anything of the upset I had witnessed, he could scarcely even recall the girl. There had been a ten-year marriage before her and an eight-year marriage after. Marilyn, in comparison, was like the British idea of a sandwich: a wafer-thin slice of something with no particular taste but slightly contrasting color, which does not quite succeed in taking your mind off the bread. And by the time of Leo's third divorce he was exclusively preoccupied with the bread of marriage— wholesome, sustaining but bafflingly indigestible. The only reality Marilyn had for him was that she had brought Jake into the world.

"It was a kind of nothing," he said. "Like two guys in advertising who decide to pool their resources and open an agency. But after a couple of years the accounts haven't come in and somehow it's not working out too well, so they split up and go their own ways with no hard feelings."

"None at all?"

"None that I can remember."

"Then why did you ever marry?"

"She had gotten pregnant, what else?" He looked at me with his dark, emotional eyes. "My ma, God rest her, had an abortion once and, because I was her eldest, she made me her confidant. Since then it's not been a subject I could ever handle. Anyway, Marilyn wanted to have a child. Or so she imagined. At least, she liked the idea of a child. And I thought, Why should I impose on her? She should be allowed her freedom. I should have said, 'The kid's got nothing to do with it. What matters is, we're not a couple.' But I didn't. I just went along with it. I guess you could say I chickened out."

He grinned at me disarmingly, knowing that the effect he creates is not of a man who is chicken, but also knowing, since he does not miss these nuances, that the tone was not right.

Perhaps the remark about being made to bear his mother's confidences was too glib and too well used, the sort of comment that
elicits a satisfied sigh from a certain style of old-fashioned psy-
choanalyst but is not quite proper for a friend. I wondered if the
disarming smile itself was nearer the truth: with some women in
some situations he really is disarmed. The fact of a girl carrying
his child undercuts all his presuppositions, strengths and defenses. No matter how much younger and less experienced she may
be, pregnancy makes her his superior. It was a mystery he resented but which was, nevertheless, beyond his control.

Was and is.

Yet with or without his overwhelming mother, he believed
in women, in their power and vulnerability, their otherness. He
had felt it as a sensitive elder son, anxious to please, and continued to feel it long after he had graduated into an altogether less
sensitive and placating middle age. He was on the side of
women's liberation before it even existed, not out of a sense of
social justice but because he believed women were on to truths
he himself would never arrive at, not even when he took his
confused yearnings to the consulting room and dutifully worked
on what his analyst called "the feminine parts of his nature." So
he cared for his children and helped with the housework out of
desire, because, for him, motherliness was part of being a father.

In the end, he came to hate the women's movement more
intensely than any macho bully. Where the machos were disbe-
lieving and contemptuous, he hated it because he had been there.
The female impersonations which passed for womanliness in the
radical phase of the movement outraged not only his sensibility
but his belief in the way the moral world was ordered.

He had married his first wife in 1950, when they were both
students, and their union became, on reflection, a paradigm of
that solemn decade. Leo and Myra: young, priggish, ambitious,
united against the world—however divided between themselves
—using their marriage as a way through to what their beloved
Henry James called the "tragic sense of life." There were times,
God knew, when late-night shopping at the A & P for diapers,
Johnson's Baby Powder and Gerber's pap seemed a long way
from what they had imagined, when they started out, a tragic
sense of life might entail. But then, the Master had also said,

"It's a complex fate, being an American," and complexity was what they were after. So they had done their growing up together through their marriage and the uncompromising drudgery of rearing their two children. And it had exhausted them. The longed-for maturities they finally achieved turned out to be different and mutually incompatible. That they should have put in all that hard work in order to drift apart became, for Leo, a source of considerable bitterness, a grievance he never properly forgave, although he and Myra continued to see each other for the sake of the children. His grievance, anyway, was not against her; it was against the state of marriage itself and his impossible expectations of it. He began to think of himself as a victim of the ideology of a decade which had led him, in his innocence, to believe that marriage and responsibility and maturity were the only true goals for the serious man. He wrote a brilliant and much quoted paper on "cultural determination"; in private he called it "being suckered."

Then came Marilyn, who had been his student, and after that interlude his attitude changed. He had three children now, which seemed more than enough compensation for his failure as a husband, and he devoted himself to their well-being. He rearranged his work so they could stay with him not just alternate weekends, which was standard practice, but for weeks at a time. He cooked for them, washed their clothes, listened to their troubles and tried to make sure that the women who dropped by in the evenings were gone before the kids woke up the next morning. Since the women were mostly his students, young and flattered to be invited, they complied, however grudgingly.

"*Si la jeunesse savait, si la vieillesse pouvait.*" Leo, now in his middle thirties, both knew and could, and profited accordingly. To have his children with him while he led what was beginning to be called a "swinging life" was an elegantly satisfying way of reconciling responsibility and pleasure, the ideology of the fifties with that of the more knowing decade that followed.

Elegant but not cynical, since he had—still has—an extraordinary way with the young, who flock to him as much for his understanding as for his renown as a philosopher. They not only look up to him, they bring him their troubles, their confidences, their ambitions. To all of which he is unflaggingly sympathetic, shrewd and alert. He had a genuine feeling for talent, pure and disinterested, and can recognize it in a student without feeling threatened, without trying to enlist it in his own cause. He loves the discipline he teaches not for the glory it brings him but for its own sake: for the light it can shed on our lives and how we live them, for its intellectual clarity, stringency and finesse. Because of all this he respects excellence wherever he finds it and will do his best to help. His students know this and are grateful. The clever ones adore him, the less clever do not last long. They are disconcerted by his sudden objectivity about their work; it seems at odds with his *gemütlich* manner and his plangent, intimate voice.

Soon after Marilyn walked out, the call came, as he had always known it would, from the New York college from which he himself had graduated summa cum laude. Once installed in a glamorous professorship, he became a figure on the swarming metropolitan scene, courted by editors, conference organizers and the producers of better-class television chat shows. His lectures were always crowded and in private there seemed no end to the admiring, willing girls, whose company he enjoyed precisely because there was so little at stake between them. They sought him out because he was a subtle talker, a surprisingly tender lover and famous in an exclusive way. As for Leo, his natural sensuality, released at last from the moral earnestness which had dogged him for so long, widened and deepened. That awe he had always felt for women in their capacity as bearers of children slowly evolved into an obsession with the female body in itself: with its softness, ripeness and musky scents, its curves, declivities, excitement, otherness. When I saw him at this time, his face was smoother, all the harshness gone. He seemed at peace with himself, as sleek and self-contained as a sated animal. The well-tempered sensualist.

It was at this point that Emma Devenish drifted into his life. She was one of those tawny-haired, forthright English girls who suddenly appeared, as if from hiding, up and down the King's Road, Chelsea, during the brief booming period between the postwar gloom and the post–OPEC recession. It was as if the Swinging Sixties had invented them, along with the Beatles and the Stones, out of sheer generosity of spirit, to compensate

for the drab years of shortages, bad cooking and overtaxation
when the only outlet for youthful energy was in dispirited pro-
test marches against everything from the Bomb and the gran-
deurs of empire to South African grapefruit. Until then, Emma
and her kind had been hidden away like an urban guerrilla army,
camouflaged by twin sets, permanent waves and sensible shoes,
waiting for the miniskirt and the pill to release their specifically
English charms: fresh complexions, long legs made strong by
horseback riding and hockey, plump but dazzling figures and
expensively cared-for teeth. Her self-confidence and plummy
county accent were as exotic to Leo as his Odessa ancestry was
to her. She also had other exotic traits: above all, a certain def-
erence for the man of the house which she had learned from her
tweedy mother and stockbroker father. She brought Leo tea in
bed in the morning, cooked beautifully, ran up curtains for his
apartment and made love with a frankness and appetite which
overwhelmed him.

She also overwhelmed his children when he finally decided
it was time for them to meet her. She played with them, read
them stories and listened more patiently than Leo, for all his
devotion, ever quite managed. They fell for her, at first, en-
tranced by her accent and her youth, just like their father.

She, too, fell heavily enough, in her reserved British way,
for this imposing, clever, rather famous man with his adored and
adoring children whose black curls, deep brown eyes and cocki-
ness were so foreign to her. She had had one of those English
upper-middle-class childhoods that chill the blood: brought up in
the nursery by a brown-suited Norland nanny and led down to
the drawing room every evening at six o'clock sharp, bathed and
in her nightie, to be exhibited to parents whose glamour seemed
inextricably bound up with their remoteness. So the sight of Leo
playing with his children for hours on end and talking to them as
though they were his equals astonished her as much as her first
glimpse of the Manhattan skyline shimmering like a mirage just
above the horizon. She felt that in every way she had joined the
future and, against all the odds, the future was worth having.

On their own, she and Leo talked philosophy together, long
intricate Socratic dialogues, master to pupil. He criticized her
papers, no holds barred, and made love to her incessantly, also

with no holds barred. If he wasn't altogether faithful, at least he admitted it, told her it meant nothing and blamed it on the booze, the loneliness of a lecture tour, a passing fancy. He also told her she was free to come and go as she wished. She noted this fact, although not as gratefully as he intended, but did not act on it for the time being.

During her final year at college she spent more and more time in Leo's apartment and gradually moved in more and more of her things—first the toothbrush, then the change of under-clothes, then the dresses—without either of them quite noticing it. She brought over a casserole she couldn't do without, a second reading lamp for the evenings when they were both working, a couple of prints she was particularly fond of. She rearranged the furniture, bought flowers and vases to put them in, stocked up the icebox. But she went on paying the rent on the little apart-ment near Gramercy Park which she shared with two other girls.

As she and Leo moved slowly together, the balance of power between them began to shift. Also without either of them quite noticing it. She got her degree, found a job on a magazine and gave up the idea of going back to England. But as her accent became more Americanized, she found herself feeling more En-glish. At least, in certain areas. At least, so far as Leo's children were concerned. All that lovely freedom and frankness began to grate on her terribly. The kids argued about everything, talked back, sulked, then insisted on being treated as equals. Even at the beginning she had considered Leo's solemn attention to their opinions a charming aberration, lovable but not quite serious. "If something's bothering them," he used to say, "I like them to feel they can come to me and talk it out." She looked at him, from under her long blond eyelashes, nodded and held her peace, won-dering what her parents would have thought of the idea of "talk-ing it out" with her. Their own jargon was more curt and traditional: "Children should be seen and not heard."

Then history began to repeat itself. History, that is, of a certain kind and with certain undeniable references: "And Leo knew Emma, and Emma conceived, so Leo married her. And Jacob, the son of Marilyn, came to live with them."

Whereupon Emma changed the rules of the game.

Jake was the youngest of Leo's three children and the most

possessive. Before the marriage he and his father had lived in freewheeling intimacy like two old friends, sharing jokes, going to the movies, watching television until all hours. He bitterly resented the intrusion of this pretty outsider with a funny accent who shared his father's bed and began to order their lives.

The crunch came when Emma announced that from now on he had to be in bed every evening by seven, which was, she added, one hour later than her bedtime at his age.

"Won't."

"You will."

"Why should I?"

"Because I say so."

He pursed his mouth and glared at her, although his big dark eyes were already brimming with tears. Then, to salvage his dignity, he parroted something he had heard his father say about family life: "I have rights in this matter, too."

Perhaps he had hoped the grown-up phrase would work its usual magic: she would be charmed by his cuteness and all would be forgiven.

Instead, she took him by the shoulders and yelled like a witch, "You have *shit!*" Also one of Leo's sayings and a long way from her Norland nanny.

Jake burst into tears.

Leo had been watching from the other side of the room, slumped despondently in his armchair. Now he lumbered to his feet and swept the weeping child into his arms, murmuring, fondling his curls. He calmed him down, fed him his supper, helped him undress and wash and brush his teeth, then carried him to his bedroom and sang to him mournfully. All the time he was thinking, It's my fault. What have I done to him? But it was still only seven fifteen when he closed the bedroom door.

Emma eyed him truculently as he poured a drink. "We have to have *some* time alone together, you know."

"Give the kid a chance. He's jealous."

She nodded sourly. "Don't tell me. Oedipus-schmoedipus. I've heard it before." She paused, then added in her no longer quite British accent, "I do wish you wouldn't *psychoanalyze* everything."

For the rest of that evening the air between them was sharp

with resentment and, although they did their inventive best to make it up in bed, a chilly mutual wariness had entered their lives to stay.

"I do not see why," she used to say whenever the same quarrel rose again in a different disguise, "I should come down to his level. He's not my *peer*, as you both seem to think. He's just a bloody five-year-old." She made it sound as if she were objecting to some subtle cultural difference. Which was true, up to a point. But the other truth was—another of Leo's words—more "representative." When she had married "for better or for worse" she had imagined that "worse" meant poverty, illness and the indignities of old age, not other women's uppity and demanding children who were always there, working away like undercover agents to subvert her relationship with her husband.

For Leo, the subversion came from both sides: them against her, her against them, with him in the middle as referee, trying to keep the peace. He played the part, but tentatively and with distaste. He knew he should defend this new life with Emma, and support her authority over them. But he couldn't. Their misery—particularly little Jake's—wrung his heart. Rationally, he could not deny that what this exasperated new wife was saying to them—and demanding of him—was right and true and justified. But he loathed her for it, loathed her for her reasonableness, then loathed her *and* the children for the guilt they made him feel.

The more he hesitated, the worse things became. They sensed his indecision and sharpened the battle until the household vibrated continuously, like an overstrung harp, with the tension between them. Emma was first baffled, then angered by his refusal to come down firmly on her side. She felt contemptuous of his wavering and betrayed. And as her resentment grew, her demands became more stringent. He reacted by siding increasingly with the children. They had always demanded his love without any doubt about that strange and rare commodity, and he had responded spontaneously, gratefully, with a whole heart. But he hesitated to share that overflowing heart with his new wife. She had reason to feel betrayed. The silences between them grew more profound, the distance more unbridgeable.

Only the sex remained unchanged. "We screwed," he once

told me, "more than we talked. It was our form of communication." For him, this resolved most of the problems, but Emma was less easily satisfied. Maybe she had not landed such a great catch, after all. So she watched her weight during her pregnancy, and after it did the Canadian Air Force exercises each morning. She tended her complexion and wardrobe lovingly and was alert as a gundog to the way other men responded to her. She was keeping her options open.

Leo's reaction was more philosophical. He began to brood on the truism, "character is fate," and on how the failure of one marriage infected the next through the children. He called it "predictive," as though that solved something, but otherwise resisted the rhetoric of the time. The scorn poured by his trendy Marxist colleagues on "the nuclear family" left him cold. To him, the family seemed an abiding source of strength and stability, endlessly desirable. The fact that he was now into his third unhappy marriage baffled him, since at heart he felt a sturdy Jewish patriarch whose destiny was to father a tribe of children. Slowly and unwillingly he began to understand that wives, so far as he was concerned, were incidental to this fate.

Emma, in particular. What was he doing married to a girl who had been to Roedean, Commem. Balls, Annabelle's? She might as well have come of age in Samoa for all he knew or cared. Even the approach of motherhood worked on her incomprehensibly. In his first marriage he and Myra had treated her pregnancy as a sign of grace, a large and shaking natural phenomenon which would transform their innocence into the terrible maturity they lusted after. They were filled with wonder by the prospect of this unknown creature who would take them at a stroke from inexperience to premature middle age. Even nervous little Marilyn had glowed with health, becoming more cheerful and placid as her belly swelled and her childish body filled out. Emma simply became more demanding of Leo and less tolerant of Jake.

Finally, she rounded on them both in their own words: "I've got rights in this, too," she said. And stalked off into the bedroom.

Leo followed her, closing the door behind him. "What the fuck . . ." He kept his voice down, for Jake's sake.

She glared at him without blinking. "I don't like your kids."
She enunciated each word carefully and did not bother to lower
her voice. "And I don't want to deal with them as much as I've
had to. Got it?"

Leo walked out of the apartment.

They did not speak to each other for twenty-four hours. He
was appalled by the speed with which the sweet young thing he
had married had developed into a shrew. The intensity of her
resentment lengthened the perfect oval of her face and drew
lines he had never seen before round her succulent mouth. He
was also outraged by her timing. If their life together was unjust, she should have said so before getting pregnant. Then he
realized he had the sequence wrong: it was a case of strength
through motherhood; now she was pregnant she knew as well as
he did there was no easy way to end their relationship. She must
have reckoned on that, he thought, when she came off the pill.

After he walked out he spent the evening riotously with an
old girlfriend, then promptly confessed when Emma accused
him. But even that brought no satisfaction. He sensed that the
marriage was already doomed, although the child was still four
months away. But he shied away from the thought as not being
one he could live with. Make it work, he told himself. You have
these children whom you love, so you need a wife. It's up to you.

The four months passed and Emma had her baby. Once
again it was a boy and once again Leo insisted on a biblical name:
Samuel. David, Absalom, Jacob, Samuel. Just like a patriarch.
But Dave and Abe had gone back to their mother in Chicago and
even loving and beloved Jake opted for long periods with Marilyn, who had remarried and was living in Baltimore. So he consoled himself with Sam, "the half-breed," he called him, with his
mother's blond hair and his father's black-brown eyes, an easy
baby who slept well and ate with relish.

Leo did most of the feeding, since Emma, to her own
mother's dismay, had decided not to breast-feed. "I think we
should share this," she announced. "There's a lot of work, so why
shouldn't you take some of the responsibilities."

"You mean, I've got rights in this, too?"

Emma was not amused.

The lines which had appeared around her mouth on the night

of their quarrel were now there to stay, and her body, once the pregnancy was over, lost its delectable, curving softness. It became stringy and muscular, like an athlete's. When Leo suggested that maybe she was taking off too much weight, she replied curtly, "I like it this way. It makes me feel my body is all my own."

He did not bother to argue, knowing now from experience that he would not win. He didn't even want to argue, since her changed appearance was having intriguing effects on their always strenuous sex life. They seemed to undergo a curious reversal of roles. She became more active, inventive, demanding, greedy, while he lay back and let things happen.

He discussed this at length with his analyst, who was not impressed. "Surely I don't have to tell you," he said, "there is a large female component in every healthy male. Why should you think yourself an exception?"

Leo heard the faint, familiar rustle of Dr. Spellman settling in his chair, then the sigh as he pressed together his well-manicured fingertips.

"So go with the flow, eh?"

"The vocabulary of youth," the good doctor replied from behind Leo's right ear. "But if that is how you choose to put it, then yes."

Emma, meanwhile, was in the process of discovering what her analyst might have called her male components, if she had had an analyst. But she didn't. Instead, she had a generation on her side. Little Sam went from the bottle to solids to nursery school and Emma went back to work, while across the country the ghettoes and campuses exploded. Black power, women's rights and the Weathermen, hard rock and the drug culture: all of them held together by a common hatred of the Vietnam War, to which the young were vulnerable because of conscription. Johnson resigned, Nixon became president and the sixties limped to their shabby, confused end.

While Leo, with the help of Dr. Spellman, went on probing his unconscious, Emma was beginning to raise her consciousness, or have it raised for her by women she came in contact with at work. She was not attracted to the harsher, more radical aspects of the women's movement, having no taste for Marxism or lesbianism or the combination of the two which was what "sexual politics" often meant in those days. But the competence and independence of some of the women she worked with were something else again: a revelation at first, then an inspiration, finally a comfort. Capable women with careers, who had come out of the other side of marriages into lives of their own, sometimes with husbands, sometimes without them; or women who had had children without marrying and considered themselves stronger for it: to Emma, they seemed like some new and healthy mutation, an indication that the human race was taking a turn for the better.

She herself had been brought up in a household where a broken marriage was considered shocking. Her closest friend at school had taken two years to confess that her mother was divorced, not widowed, and thereafter Emma had regarded her as mysterious and a little shady, a girl whom boys, when they found out about her, would assume to be promiscuous. Emma had assumed so too, and the friendship died. She also assumed that her own identity, like her mother's, would be formed by marriage and her husband's work. They would share responsibilities, but hers would be feminine and special: he would provide the money while she administered the home, the children, the sex. Her teachers at school had been fond of quoting *Paradise Lost:* "He for God only, she for God in him."

So what these new friends told her and their response to what she told them broke down the conditioning of a lifetime. When she first mentioned the possibility of leaving Leo—hesitantly over lunch, as though confiding a terrible secret—she expected to be argued out of it, as her mother had tried to do on her most recent visit to New York: "Think of the stigma, darling, the burden of being a divorced woman. And what would we tell Grandpa?" But the friend merely shrugged and said, "If it happens, it happens. You have your own life to consider." And went on eating salad.

At first Emma was offended by her indifference. But then, as the word went round and more of her colleagues got into the act, she realized that their lack of shock was a form of support. "You gotta explore the alternatives," said one. "Think of the roads not taken," said another, more literary. "It's a man's world," said a third. "We have to band together to make our own way." "What the hell," said her best friend, "divorce is a liberating experience."

There were moments when Emma wondered if all these resolute young women who were suddenly taking such an interest were as much custodians of the conventional morality as her mother was. Maybe that, ultimately, was the woman's role. But if conventional morality had changed so radically in her favor, who was she to argue? She also wondered what was in it for them, since two of her most vociferous supporters were heavily married and showed no sign of moving on. She realized that it was easier to explore the options in someone else's life than in one's own. Liberation by proxy, she thought, then dismissed the idea as paranoid—as Leo's paranoia—and was ashamed of herself. And after all these years in her husband's shadow, it was invigorating to become a kind of culture heroine, if only to her friends.

Yet she worried at first about the problem of survival and the ethics of alimony. She could not reconcile it with the fiery talk of independence and liberation. "Call it maintenance, honey," she was told, "plus a little bit extra to redress the balance. Why should the bastard get off scot-free?" Put this way the problem seemed to evaporate. By now she was earning a respectable salary and Leo was not the kind of man to argue about money for his children. Suddenly, she lost the nagging fear of who would support her; she would support herself. And that in itself was a liberating idea: a life of her own, no longer guaranteed by a man.

And no longer at the beck and call of her child. She knew Leo was strong on shared custody. Whence the troublesome presence of Jake all through their first years together. So this time he could have his shared custody in spades: all the responsibilities—cooking, cleaning, caring, worrying—two weeks on, two weeks off. Then he would find out what it was really like.

But she mentioned none of this to Leo. She was simply preparing herself for the time she knew was coming, determined not to be caught off guard. When the marriage broke, she would be the one who did the breaking, and at a moment of her own choosing. So she began—discreetly and more out of curiosity than desire—to "explore the options" with men she met at work. Sex in the afternoon: instead of lunch, instead of cocktails. Paradoxically, it made her fonder of Leo, and more appreciative. She also let herself be seduced by a tall, pale girl from Iowa who shared her office. But she did not care for the experience. Leo mentioned that later, but only as a cultural oddity, a fragment of anthropological evidence of dubious importance. "I guess it's just one of those things young women try these days," he said, "like a junior year in Paris. It doesn't seem to make them any less heterosexual."

At the time, all he knew was that she seemed increasingly far off and independent. Although they went on making love as often as before, she was casual in her attitude to it, as though she were simply taking her pleasure, like the villain in a nineteenth-century novel. More and more, he found himself cast in the traditional womanly role: working to hold the relationship together, placating, trying not to make waves, pretending not to notice. He also found himself becoming wifely in practical ways. He spent more time than ever cooking, cleaning the apartment and looking after Sam. "It's time you made certain adjustments in the name of parity," said Emma, whose fluency in American jargon was now absolute. Leo, for once, did not argue. "OK," he said, and went back to the dishes, thinking, OK, she's got a professional life, too. OK, I'm further along in my career than she is, so why shouldn't I lend a hand? And OK, OK, I don't want this marriage to go the way of the others. How many times can you strike out?

So he worked at it, swallowing his pride and buckling down in the name of parity and a dogged faith in survival. We're going through a valley, he told himself. She's got all that pressure at work. It exhausts her. And that exhausts the relationship. Just hang in there.

Exhaustion had also become a permanent element in his own life. That morning in New England when he had opened the letter offering him the New York professorship, it seemed as if the heavens were raining money on him. From then on he would be more than comfortable, he would be almost rich, despite the burden of the two A's—alimony and analysis—which he, like most of his friends, had to bear. So he had settled into a roomy

West Side apartment and, without his quite intending it, his
standard of living had risen. He began to eat out more often,
kept his drinks cupboard well stocked, bought clothes and records when he fancied them and improved his hi-fi. The French
call this process *embourgeoisisement;* like going gray, which
often accompanies it, it is hard to notice at the time, harder to
reverse. One morning you wake up, look in the mirror and find it
has happened. By some freak of nature, Leo kept his black hair
but lost his spare time. When he wasn't doing his official work he
was moonlighting: churning out highly paid articles on subjects
that bored him, going on lecture tours, making guest appearances, reading manuscripts, advising publishers. He was caught
in what he called "the grave hassle simply to keep up, to keep
going." And this put a further strain on his marriage, for when
he lost his spare time he also discovered that he had lost his
friends. There were no more long coffee breaks and lunches and
boozy evenings, no more talking shop with his colleagues, no
more gossip. And he realized that not only had these interludes
been pleasurable and stimulating, they had also provided a mutual life support system. Without quite knowing it, he and his
friends had helped to keep up each other's morale. Now all he
had was Emma and she had other priorities. So he blamed his
troubles on the place. "New York," he used to repeat, as though
explaining some profound existentialist mystery, "works on marriages like an acid."

Perhaps he was right. Perhaps he and Emma would still be
together had they been living in some less driven and driving
community. As it was, the estrangement between them
deepened day by day. With his professional interest in the phe-
nomena of our times, he tried to interpret her resentment and
remoteness as symptoms of a larger discontent. He persuaded
himself that he was not just dealing with one woman and her
dissatisfactions but with the whole ideology of feminism which
was carrying her off at a tangent from their marriage. He
brooded about the way she and her liberated colleagues discussed her problems behind his back. One thing he was certain
of: he had been cast, without appeal, in the role of the heavy.

It was an irony he found particularly bitter, since he spent
a great deal of time and money discussing with Dr. Spellman the

benefits he might gain from refusing—God knew with what effort—the macho role. "So finally," said the doctor, "the female side of your nature is being made to work. Painful work, I grant. But different, no? And rich too, in the end, believe me." Leo nodded and gritted his teeth and kept at it. "Rich" seemed an exaggeration, though "painful" was not. But whatever else, it was humanizing, and as a specialist in the humanities, how could he knock that?

But there were other times, particularly over long weekends or when his analyst was on holiday, when the subtleties of the situation and the possible benefits they might or might not confer no longer seemed worthwhile. Emma may have had her rights, but he had his pride. He did not, however, discuss this with the good doctor, perhaps because he felt he would not get a straight answer.

He also brooded on a straight question his father had asked him years before when Leo had announced he was marrying Emma: "Isn't she a bit young for you?" "Trust me," he had answered. At which his father shrugged, "It's your life," and hadn't mentioned it again. Now Leo tried to recall the sweet young thing with the charming accent and blond hair falling around her face who had seemed so eager to devote her life to pleasing him. Who could have guessed the dove would sprout such wings, such claws? His father, apparently.

Emma also remembered their early days together and the way Leo had loomed over her, knowing all the answers, forestalling all the questions, having seen everything and been everywhere before her. So she nurtured the distance which had grown between them out of fear; if she let him come too close, he would somehow take over the new life she was making for herself, as he had taken over everything else. So she distrusted everything, even his docility. Particularly his docility. The sight of his large and impressive presence bent over a sinkful of dirty dishes or vacuuming the bedroom or tenderly dressing their small son had puzzled her at first, then elated her and finally filled her with foreboding. It couldn't be this easy; he must be up to something. So she pushed her luck, searching for some issue on which his forebearance would crack and his grim fifties' morality come roaring to the surface. Without success. If she rolled a joint after dinner, he puffed away and seemed to enjoy it more than she did. When she dropped acid he tripped amiably along with her and afterward talked wth all his old brilliance about what he had seen and felt. He was so compliant and unshockable that she was certain he was up to something.

So she raised the stakes in the hope of calling his bluff. Late one evening, when they were sitting at opposite ends of the living room, sipping brandy and reading under their separate lamps, she started to confess her affairs—quietly, casually, selectively—just as he had once done to her. He let her talk for a while, then got up so suddenly that his drink slopped out of the glass. He marched across the room to her, licking the brandy slowly from the back of his hand. She braced herself, certain that this time he was going to hit her and feeling, to her surprise, a quick stir of excitement. All he said was, "Come to bed." She did not argue.

Later, when they were lying together in their sweat, he said meditatively, talking to himself more than to her, "You know what the women's movement has given us? Equality in infidelity. I guess it's not a position any reasonable man could argue with."

She shifted a little so she could see his lugubrious face. His expression was thoughtful and without malice and she understood that she had lost that round.

He was dissimulating, but could see no alternative. The idea of losing another wife, another child, another way of life literally immobilized him. He would come back in the afternoons when the apartment was empty and sit for an hour or two at a time staring at the wall of familiar books, unable to move, his mind as blank as new paper. Eventually he would rouse a little and try to convince himself that his case was not special, that marriage was always like this: an unnatural condition, compounded of too much intimacy, too much closeness, not enough privacy; two people jammed together into a single pocket, each forced to endure the other's ups and downs, changes, misunderstandings, turnings away. Habit will hold them together, or inertia, or fear. But to make it work there has also to be goodwill, which is another, unromantic word for love. Goodwill first, then humor, then a limitless capacity to tolerate the ambiguities of daily living. You're a big boy now, he told himself. Time to stand on your own two feet.

But he was not convinced. In the end, it was simple: she had his number, he no longer had hers. It occurred to him that when love failed, all that endured in marriage was the sense of betrayal. He had woken to it the morning after her first confession and he woke up to it again, undiminished, every morning thereafter, as though it too had grown fresh and vigorous with sleep. Not just her betrayal of him with other men, but her betrayal of *them:* their child, their good times, the trouble they had been through together. In the name of all that, he fought to keep the marriage going.

But he could not get over the sense of having, once again, been suckered. First Myra and the graceless fifties, then Marilyn and the politics of swinging, now Emma moving off down the liberation trail in order to become a heroine to the sisterhood. He reread his essay on cultural determinism and wondered about bringing it up to date. It irked him to think that his life was so much at the mercy of intellectual fashions. He had thought, read and lectured to packed audiences on the subject of free will— from Aristotle to the Situationists, via Freud, Marx and Heidegger—yet none of that had prevented his three marriages from foundering "predictively" on ideologies which, he suspected, would barely rate footnotes when the cultural history of the time came to be written in the next century. Where had it all gone wrong?

He couldn't even console himself with the thought that he had lost his wives to any of the great historical causes, like his uncle Max who had been swallowed by the Communist party in 1935, or his skinny cousin Dora who was now a Little Sister of the Poor in Cleveland. He had lost them because he had lost them. Maybe he wasn't cut out for marriage.

Emma, meanwhile, no longer had any idea of heroism or even liberation. She was simply grateful that the women she worked with were on her side and refrained from gloating over her troubles. When they tried to egg her on for their own mixed motives she ignored them, as she ignored her parents, whose querulous letters she no longer answered, as she even ignored her child. She had cut loose from her old ties and was drifting, isolated and bad-tempered, waiting for some change to come.

But Leo hung on and would not let go, while the other men she met—some of whom she bedded, some she did not—seemed not to amount to much. She began to wish Leo amounted to less, so she could find a way around him. His determination to sit still for whatever she cared to dish out was out of character, but it made her helpless.

Finally, help came in a shape she had not expected: short-haired, athletic, Midwestern and Philistine, an engineer by profession and good at fixing things. (She had met him at the office when her coffee percolator broke; he had stripped it down and mended it in twenty minutes flat.) He liked junk food and read junk books—though only on airplanes; back on earth he watched television and read no books at all. He also seemed indifferent to her feminism; neither for it nor against it, simply uninterested. But he made her laugh and the sex was good.

Then one afternoon when it had been particularly good he told her he had once been impotent.

"I bet you say that to all the girls."

"No way." He grinned at her smugly. "I've been treated."

"Oh, no, not you." Her eyes widened with disappointment, her heart sank. "You mean you've been shrunk, too? Who would've guessed?"

"Guess again, baby. I'm a scientist so I went to a scientist. Behavior therapy they call it. None of that superego-ego-id jazz for me. I mean, who needs it? You are what you do."

"What did *he* do, this scientist you went to?"

"Operant conditioning is the name. Positive reinforcement plus imaginal desensitivization. It's all in Masters and Johnson."

"In plain English?"

"In plain English, dirty pictures. They find out what turns you on, then they find out what turns you off and proceed accordingly. It's cheap, it's quick and it works."

"So I gather," she said, kissing him.

His vulgarity was a relief, like everything else about him. But the elation she felt was different, pure and unshadowed, like the elation the prisoner feels when the cell door opens wide. She had been living with Leo's psychoanalysis as long as she had been living with Leo, waiting more or less patiently while he "worked through" this problem and that anxiety, knowing it was only a matter of time before she, too, was conscripted into the cause. In the name of the marriage, and in the hope that she, like him, would "work through" her problems concerning it. The pressure had been on her even before the marriage went sour. Psychoanalysis was second nature to Leo, a way of talking, like a lisp or a stutter. Whenever they quarreled he rounded on her with the same old accusation, "You need *help*," and when she savaged him back he would shrug and say, "You're proving my point." She hated his self-righteous assumption that he was privy to a wisdom she was excluded from and was suspicious of psychoanalysis in a primitive British way: to seek "help" when not in total despair seemed to her shameful and self-indulgent. "What do you do with that shrink of yours?" she once asked, then answered for him: "You just talk about yourself, don't you?" "You know, honey," he looked at her with loathing, "you think language is a plot invented by the Jews to get you." For Emma, Leo and Dr. Spellman embodied all the confusions and ambiguities that were bringing her down. They made her yearn for the comfortable, unintellectual world she had been brought up in, where moral certainties still flourished and there was, in the end, an order to things. She also resented the presence of a secret sharer in her life with Leo, the analyst with whom it was all discussed, whose advice she imagined was followed and through whose eyes her own husband's image of her was, she was convinced, filtered.

So when the engineer said, "It's a machine, this nice little body of yours, a machine that feels good and smells good. I do this—you feel pleasure. I do that—you feel pain. The mind's just one of the parts," she listened gratefully, then went home to Leo and talked in the same terms. But with conviction now, not despair: "That superego you're always on about: you ever seen it?"

Leo did not answer.

"Anyway," she went on, "what's so super about it? Perhaps you feel guilty because you've got plenty to feel guilty about. All those girls of yours, for instance."

"There aren't any girls, anymore."

"That's your story. And even if it's true, maybe you feel guilty because it saves you feeling anything else. It's something to theorize about, something to talk about to your shrink."

"You have no idea what we talk about."

"I have an idea it has nothing much to do with reality."

"Maybe you've got no idea of reality, either."

"I have an idea it may be simpler than you think, not more complicated."

"You're reverting to type. Next time round you'll vote for Nixon."

"Reagan," she said. "He reminds me of Daddy."

"Yeah, and Dr. Spellman reminds me of Adlai Stevenson. But he was before your time."

"That's funny," said Emma, "I'd always pictured him as Henry Kissinger. Particularly the accent."

For the first time since the marriage started to slide, Leo lost his cool. She was attacking him where it hurt most, taking advantage of a secret only he and she knew. He felt betrayed. He also felt torn, just as he had when she and Jake were battling it out. Who was more important to him, his wife or his analyst? There was no doubt about who was more on his side. When Emma attacked his analysis she was attacking not just him and his unseen ally, but also everything he believed in: how he lived, how he felt, his whole professional commitment to abstraction and inwardness.

Once again, it was a question of priorities: first his wife or his children, now his marriage or his analysis. He no longer thought of it as "treatment." The reasons he went to Spellman had vanished years ago; it was the way he lived. Maybe he had more of a marriage with the doctor than with Emma. Had it always been like that? All those women who had once been so important to him seemed, in perspective, curiously diminished.

Yet the *idea* of marriage remained as potent as ever. He was a man who loved children. He was also unable to talk back to any woman whom he was foolish enough to make pregnant. He explained it to Spellman as "a kind of crazy moral idealism."

The doctor was not impressed. "You flatter yourself," he said. "It has nothing to do with moral idealism. You are just one of those men who needs to be a father. That's how you are; nothing moral about it. That is why you are so good with young students. Being a father is something you do well. What I find odd is your inability to pick the right women for the role. If you want to set yourself up as a patriarch, you need a woman with the necessary strengths: a womanly woman, not a shrill feminist."

"Emma isn't a shrill feminist."

"Perhaps not." Dr. Spellman pursed his lips. His attitude to Emma had cooled considerably since she blew his cover. "But she is perhaps susceptible to shrill feminism, no?"

"There are a lot of *shoulds* in this," Leo countered, "and *shoulds* don't describe realities."

"It is for you to describe the realities as you see them, me to interpret what you see. And what I see is not only do you marry women who are impossible for your particular needs, you also don't marry them until you know they are really impossible. This Emma, for instance: you didn't marry her because you thought you'd found someone you could live with; you married her in order to stick together a relationship that was already falling apart."

"I married her because she was pregnant. I wanted to commit myself to that. OK, so there was a kind of looseness between us. Marriage would brace the foundations."

"That, if I may say, is a somewhat feckless attitude to your own well-being."

"How was I to know it would prove to be the opposite?"

"How? Because you had already been married twice. But," said Dr. Spellman wearily, "we have been through all this before."

The last time I saw Leo the divorce from Emma was final and he had just turned fifty. It should have been a bad season, but his four sons had redeemed it by gathering for a surprise birthday party: Dave, the scientist, from his job in Silicon Valley, Abe from Bloomington, Indiana, where he was majoring in music, Jake from school in Baltimore and Sam from the apartment twelve blocks north where Emma and her engineer were now living in liberated, unmarried bliss. "Four beautiful kids," said Leo, "and all of them intact. I felt it was the climax of my career. Fathering them, I thought, that's my destiny. Like Jacob in the Bible: he didn't want that fucking Leah, but he got her and out of their unsatisfactory union came the twelve tribes of Israel."

He really means it, I thought, about the twelve tribes. He's found his role at last.

Yet he didn't look vindicated.

He didn't even look comfortable. His new West Side apartment is small, with paper-thin walls through which filter other people's music and other people's quarrels. The living room is bleak without Emma's prints and vases of flowers. A table, four chairs and a couch. One wall lined with books, the others bare. The bits of furniture are tasteful but tatty. The unvarnished pine is flimsy, the imitation leather looks like what it is: plastic. His one gesture toward stylishness is a huge standing lamp which arches and droops like another, more hostile planet's reconstruction of a giraffe. He has become a citizen of Habitatland, Conran's design for living for the new underclass, the nonunionized professionals with some taste but not enough money.

Yet his salary remains large, even allowing for the now heavier load of the dreaded two A's. So if he lives like a student, it is by choice, just as he chooses to dress the part in jeans, frayed sport shirt, sloppy pullover. He retains his generation's Veblenesque distaste for conspicuous consumption, conceived in his pinched childhood during the Depression and annealed in the fifties by his equally pinched years in graduate school. He distrusts good food, good drink and elegance as symptoms of hidden triviality, not proper to the serious life. Perhaps that is why his students continue to trust him in a way that baffles his colleagues. He is on their side and proves it by his way of life. They, too, are part of his "destiny," an unending supply of children whose hearts and minds he can influence for the better.

"I've got my life back again," he said. Meaning, it was no longer being bled away by another lousy marriage. Meaning, he was no longer required to subjugate his own abilities so Emma could "have her rights, too." Meaning, he had recovered, more or less, from the humiliation of striking out a third time.

"But it's not all that terrific," he added.

Exactly what is missing still eludes him. Dr. Spellman once accused him of being a closet Romantic and, in a triumph of one-upmanship, dug out a quotation from the philosopher Fichte, which Leo failed to recognize: "Love is a desire for something altogether unknown, the existence of which is disclosed only by the need of it, by a discomfort, and by a void in search of whatever will fill it, but which remains unaware of whence fulfillment may come."

"That's all very well," Leo replied irritably, "but at my age who needs romantic love? I'm a family man."

"Just so." Dr. Spellman nodded contentedly. "And serial polygamy is no substitute for the polygamy of the patriarchs."

"Right."

"You agree? That is already a beginning," said the doctor.

The two of them are now working through his most precious delusion: Leo the Hebrew philosopher-king, subtle, sensual, fatherly, wise. They call it "the Solomon syndrome" and both of them are writing essays about it.

VII

Mourning

(i)

A century ago, Emma might have figured in a folktale or fairy story like "Snow White" or "Cinderella," not as the heroine but as the wicked stepmother. When death was the commonest way out of marriage the world of children was dominated by usurpers, new husbands and new wives who appeared with offspring of their own to upset the family balance and deprive rightful heirs of their patrimony. Their continued presence in the stories of the Brothers Grimm and Hans Christian Andersen shows how powerfully they loomed in the imagination of childhood as an evil force.

The memory lingers on, despite the domestic changes of the last hundred years. Divorce has produced a new form of extended family. Instead of grandparents, parents, children, spinster aunts and bachelor uncles bundled loosely together under one roof, there is now a single couple with no relatives to speak of—or to—and a bewildering assortment of children: children of

their own, children by previous marriages, children of affairs, all
of them battling it out like the United Nations. They call their
parents by their first names, instead of "Mother" and "Father,"
not out of false democratic jollity but to preserve their sanity.
One principle is unchanged in this chaos: the stepparent is always
wrong.

Although the children may suffer from the confusion, in
other ways their lives have become dramatically easier. When
Anna Karenina lost her beloved Serioja she lost him for good,
just as Frieda Lawrence forfeited the rights to her children when
she eloped: "Until 1934," wrote Brenda Maddox in *The Observer*
(London), "divorced mothers usually were not permitted access
to their children. Especially if they had committed adultery, the
courts felt that it was in the interests of public morality to keep
them and their children apart." So Tolstoy's portrait of Anna and
her torment for her son was against the moral grain of the period, as jolting to the complacency of his readers as Flaubert's
icy diagnosis of Emma Bovary was to the latter-day Romantics.
Although Tolstoy turned on Anna in the end and made her die
for her sins, while the insipid Kitty and Levin flourished, her
passion for Serioja was redemptive and prophetic. She is the
first modern mother in literature, a heroine from the now explod-
ing nuclear family.

Anna Karenina was published in 1877. A century earlier
her anguish would have been unthinkable and inexplicable. "In
marital separations in the diocese of Cambrai during the 18th
century," writes Edward Shorter, "there were almost no squabbles over the custody of children: women were quite happy to
surrender them to the husband. To persuade his wife Marie to
agree to a divorce, Abraham Pluchart, a merchant of Valen-
ciennes, offered to 'take on the child and care for him to permit
her to live more tranquilly.' " Before the nuclear family, the ties
of affection between parents and children were fragile, often
nonexistent, and always weaker than the ties that bound the
individual to the community. Among the wealthy, babies were
farmed out to wet nurses for the first couple of years of life, then
separated from their parents by phalanxes of servants; Emma's
Norland nanny was the last of a long tradition. Among the poor,
children were less a blessing than an unfortunate occupational

hazard of married life; whence the overflowing foundling hospitals and orphanages for children abandoned without hesitation
by parents too poor to provide for them. As Professor Shorter
describes it—on the evidence of the records of doctors, hospitals
and local historians—domestic Europe until at least the middle
of the last century was as much a battleground as the modern
divorce courts, though with a difference: husbands, wives and
children were all fighting separately for their individual survival.*

Milton, with his Puritan belief in holy matrimony, wrote
vehemently about the misery of the incompatibly married,
though with the assumption that the grief was all on the husband's side; the duty of the good wife was to make her master
happy. So far as children were concerned, he was interested only
in the effect of marital discord on their spiritual health. "Why
should we not think them more holy," he wrote of the children of
a happy second marriage, "than the offspring of a former ill-
twisted wedlock, begott'n only out of a bestiall necessitie without
any true love or contentment, or joy to their parents, so that in
some sense we may call them the *children of wrath* and anguish
which will as little conduce to their sanctifying, as they had been
bastards." Milton would have derived a grim satisfaction from
the price Flaubert makes Madame Bovary pay for her remorseless narcissism, but Anna Karenina's heartbreak for her son
would have been beyond his comprehension.

In modern literature these values are reversed. Like Milton,
Saul Bellow's Herzog detests his wife, although he is also scared
of her—not a reaction the poet would easily have understood.
But his real and dislocating grief is for the loss of his daughter,
not for the failure of his marriage. Moses Herzog, intellectual-
in-residence, ladies' man, dandy, obsessional writer of letters to
the famous dead and exemplary modern man, holds in his passionate and convoluted way to the transformed values of the
nuclear family which was founded, according to Professor
Shorter, on

* Professor Lawrence Stone, working mainly from written evidence of the
middle and upper classes, dates the rise of the nuclear family earlier than Professor Shorter, who is concerned with reconstructing the social lives of the great
mass of largely illiterate poor. The changes took time to sift downward.

the mother-infant relationship. The *prise de conscience* of infant welfare had first occurred among the middle classes, and domesticity would follow in its train. The emotional web that was spun between mother and baby would reach out to envelop older children and the husband: a sense that the preciousness of infant life required an equally delicate setting for its preservation.

When Herzog watches his baby daughter being bathed by Gersbach, his wife's crippled lover, he ruminates:

> I seem to think that because June looks like a Herzog, she is nearer to me than to them. But how is she near to me if I have no share in her life? Those two grotesque love-actors have it all. And I apparently believe that if the child does not have a life resembling mine, educated according to the Herzog standards of "heart," and all the rest of it, she will fail to become a human being. This is sheer irrationality, and yet some part of my mind takes it as self-evident.

What was self-evident to Herzog would have been as strange to Milton and his contemporaries as that other theory of relativity, formulated by Einstein: for the twentieth-century father the true world exists only through intimacy, proximity and the interplay of emotion, the parent enveloping the child like a broody hen its egg.

The safe domestic nest came in time to exclude whatever was outside and the universe dwindled until all that was left was the father, the mother, the kids and the television set. Beyond that lay danger and distraction. As the experts have pointed out, links to the community were broken and even friendship became a threat to the balance of nuclear family power. When the lines were drawn up for domestic quarrels the new battle cry was "Why is it always *your* friends?" Meanwhile, the children moved to the center of the stage. Intolerance of the world outside the front door went hand in hand with increasing tolerance within the family circle until, during the 1950s, Dr. Spock's gospel of permissiveness was distorted by anxious young parents into a doctrine of total indulgence. This was the absurd logical end of the nuclear family: not a marriage between two adults but a unit existing exclusively for the benefit of the children, and ruled by them.*

Yet that, too, was a sign of a larger change of heart which had been taking place in Europe since the Renaissance. In the sixteenth and early seventeenth centuries, says Professor Stone,

> a majority of . . . individuals . . . found it very difficult to establish close emotional ties to any person. Children were often neglected, brutally treated, and even killed; many adults treated each other with suspicion and hostility; affect was low, and hard to find . . . The lack of a unique mother figure in the first two years of life, the constant loss of close relations, siblings, parents, nurses and friends through premature death, the physical imprisonment of the infant in tight swaddling clothes in the early months, and the deliberate breaking of the child's will all contributed to a "psychic numbing" which created many adults whose primary responses to others were at best a calculating indifference and at worst a mixture of suspicion and hostility, tyranny and submission, alienation and rage.

This coldness at the heart thawed slowly, to be replaced by what Professor Stone calls "affective individualism," which culminated first in the Romantic Movement, then was followed, a century later, by the development of psychoanalysis: "The poets and philosophers before me discovered the unconscious," said Freud. "What I discovered was the scientific method by which the unconscious can be studied." But introspection mattered less than what Flaubert called "sentimental education," a willingness to feel for other people, a growing tenderness toward the world in general and one's family in particular: social conscience and parental love. As the heart grew less constricted and defended, the need for love increased until the frozen, selfish life which was once the norm came to seem a strange perversion.

* Although he later recanted, I suspect Dr. Spock had more to do with the wild antiauthoritarianism of the 1960s than Mao or Marcuse or any other of the fashionable gurus. Behind every student revolutionary and dropout was a guilty parent saying, "Yes, darling, yes." It was as though the middle-class terrorists —Weathermen, Baader-Meinhof, the Red Brigades—felt driven to violence in order to provoke someone—anyone—into saying, "No." It is no accident that Israel, the cradle of patriarchy, should have dealt with them most effectively.

Children have been the chief beneficiaries of this change. Love of them, as Leo discovered, is a great deal easier and less devious than love of one's chosen mate. It has outlasted even that great outburst of self-love Professor Shorter called "the sexual revolution," and it has changed the rules of divorce. The extent of this change is mirrored in newspapers that specialize in "human interest"—that is, in scandal and crime. Before the reform of the divorce laws, when guilt was still a legal necessity, papers boosted their circulation with gloating details of dirty linen washed in open court. When the laws changed, the headlines changed with them, from sex to money; the more outrageous and vindictive the settlement, the bigger the splash. Now the latest news is the custody fight and searing photographs of bereaved mothers or fathers whose children have been kidnapped and hurried out of the country by a fugitive spouse. The contemporary instance is *Kramer* v. *Kramer*, not *Astor* v. *Astor*.

"The desires of the heart are as crooked as corkscrews," wrote Auden. Two Swedish experts on the psychopathology of divorce, Bente and Gunnar Öberg, agree but put it differently: "Parents struggle over their children because they haven't said good-bye to each other; they even go to court in a desperate attempt to maintain contact." This terrible vindictiveness is not just bad blood and revenge; it is also part of the process of mourning every couple goes through during a divorce.

Yet mourning for a marriage is uneasier and more ambiguous than mourning for a real death, since on the surface the feelings seem a long way from grief. When a husband dies, the bereaved wife can forget the fatal tics that once drove her crazy —the way he cleared his throat or cracked his knuckles or forgot to wipe the basin after he shaved—and is free at last to idealize him as her one true irreplaceable love. But when he walks out and leaves her for another woman, she feels obliged to work herself up to a conventional pitch of hatred, however much she wants him back, dirty basin and all. Hatred and idealization are equally false, equally misleading, equally inappropriate, and both get in the way of grief. But of the two, there is no doubt which is the less confusing and painful: easier to hate than to suffer.

Yet when a marriage breaks that has been intolerable to

both partners, the mourning may be little more than regret for
the passing of a way of life and for whatever hopes and happiness
were shared at the beginning: for their youth perhaps, and for
the waste of their youth. After that, they return to the real
world unbelievingly and with relief, knowing they have been
reprieved. Unless they have children. To leave a husband or a
wife whom one no longer loves may be sane and natural, but
there is no easy way to divorce a child and, until shared custody
becomes the standard practice, no marriage counseling or social
reform or enlightened legislation to cure the breaking of the
heart. Two hearts, in fact, since children blame themselves for
the waywardness of their parents, thinking, It must have been
something *I* did. They, too, take years to recover.

Katherine, for example, had survived years of loveless
wrangling by concentrating on her child and getting on with her
work. She designed furniture, had done so successfully in New
York before she moved to London with her touchy English husband, then went on doing so when she settled again in her native
Manhattan after the divorce. The husband was in market research and he left her for a younger woman who was willing to
devote herself single-mindedly to his flamboyant career. Because
of this, Katherine was given custody of the child—which was all
she had ever wanted. But she also wished her daughter to flourish, so she made sure the father kept in touch, although at first
he was not much interested.

Meanwhile, Katherine and Debbie set up house together in
a large apartment in the East Sixties, high up, full of light and
with a view of the river. Katherine kept her drawing board in
her bedroom, by the window, and gave the rest of the place over
to the child. There was a gigantic dolls' house in the sitting room
and a Victorian rocking horse, both imported from London; the
walls were hung with paintings Debbie had done at school and
enlargements of the photographs Katherine was always taking
—she had a gift for that, too—Debbie laughing in close up with
ice cream around her mouth, Debbie in long shot against a flat
glittering sea, Debbie riding the rocking horse, Debbie thoughtful, with a doll. The place was like a shrine to a child saint, hung
with votive offerings in black and white.

Mother and daughter lived together like an old married couple, sharing jokes and confidences, going to movies and theaters, reading side by side on the big brown leather sofa designed by Katherine, tending the plants, sharing the chores in this airy temple with a *House & Garden* interior. Katherine's numerous admirers came and wondered at them and were moved. Those who lasted understood that it was a package deal: love one, love both. But Katherine married none of them, since not even the best seemed good enough to intrude on the intimacy between her and the child. That was her real marriage; her ex-husband was merely an accessory before the fact, the one who had made it possible. For that, she even forgave him his dreadful behavior.

Eventually, the husband married again, an even younger and more adoring girl than the one he had left Katherine for. He bought a large house in the Home Counties, settled into the weekend squirearchy and began to show an interest in his daughter. "A fortnight at Christmas and Easter, and a month in the summer. That's what the court stipulated," he announced defensively, as if Katherine were trying to deny him. She did not bother to reply that she had been reminding him of his legal rights for years and he had been too busy to listen. So Debbie went off to England three times a year to stay with this new figure in her life, a father who behaved like a romantic, indulgent uncle and his young, pretty and equally indulgent wife. She was dazzled by them both and by their graceful Georgian house with its lawn sweeping down to a duck pond and by the cozy, domestic countryside all around. She came back talking about her pony and hung her bedroom with rosettes won at local gymkhanas. Horses were not Katherine's scene but she made the appropriate noises and arranged for the child to ride in Central Park on Sundays.

Then late one August she went out to Kennedy Airport as usual to meet her daughter's flight from London, but the child was not on the plane and the airline had no trace of her. "The ticket was canceled two weeks ago," they said. After a series of frantic telephone calls, Katherine managed to reach her ex-husband at his London office. "I hope it's serious," he said, "you've got me out of an important meeting." "Debbie wasn't on the plane. Where is she?" "Oh," he said in a bored voice, "didn't you get my letter? I'm keeping her here. It's time she had a proper home and a proper family life. That bachelor-girl existence the two of you have in New York is not on, is it? Not in the long run. Anyway, an English girl should be educated in England." "But that's not . . ." "Talk to your solicitor. I'm in conference." He hung up.

"It's illegal," Katherine's lawyer told her. "Make her a ward of court." But when he sent her the papers to sign her nerve failed. There was no way she could turn her beloved daughter into a battleground for adults. Both of them would lose, since her ex-husband was too rich for her to fight through the courts. So she let it go, to her lawyer's chagrin. Better, she thought, to exploit the advantages of being free-lance and self-employed. So she reorganized her life in order to spend part of each year in England. She found herself a pokey little flat in Pimlico, made over one room into a bedroom for Deborah, which she furnished with great care, festooned the rest of the place with the usual photographs and waited for the occasional weekends when her ex-husband would allow the child to come up to town. But the strain of those weekends—the false excitement and jollity, the exhaustion, the farewells—and the blank intervals between wrung her out. She got no work done and began having casual affairs with less and less presentable men.

She was glad to get back to New York, where at least she had friends and serious admirers. But her liveliness did not return, nor her interest in her work. Although she spent hours each day sitting over her drawing board, she stared out at the tugs and barges on the river and could not concentrate. She began to swallow pep pills in the morning to get herself going, then sleeping pills at night to calm herself down. She became forgetful and uncertain. She missed business appointments and dates with men she liked, until the commissions stopped coming and even her most persistent admirers fell away, and she found herself isolated, distracted, uninterested. The dust formed on the white and glass expanses of her apartment and the dirty dishes piled up in the sink.

She had always been a clever talker, with a sly, sideways-on view of the world and its ways. Now words began to fail her. She stumbled over them, stuttered, lost track, her mind off elsewhere with the child. When her doctor suggested a long rest and recommended a clinic in Vermont, she shook her head and said she had to get back to London for the school holidays. And she was right. What he thought of as symptoms of a nervous break-down seemed to her natural and inevitable. She had suffered a mutilation and was in shock, like the victim of a terrorist outrage: part of herself had been blown away and nothing was going to sew it back on again. All she could hope for was to come to terms with her diminished way of life.

There is no happy ending to the story. She lives now like a ghost between London and New York, and works just enough to get by. Tacked to her drawing board is a stanza from a poem by W. D. Snodgrass, copied out in her spiky hand:

> The window's turning white.
> The world moves like a diseased heart
>   packed with ice and snow.
> Three months now we have been apart
> less than a mile. I cannot fight
>   or let you go.

But she keeps such sentiments from Debbie who has been transformed into a brusque and horsey English teenager. Katherine's stumbling speech and forgetfulness embarrass the girl—"She drinks," her father has explained, and she believes him—but she feels sorry for her and somewhere, perhaps, still remembers how close they were years ago in New York. But Debbie is never allowed to go back to Manhattan, since her father is afraid that Katherine will do to him what he once did to her. He is wrong and the poem is right: the fight has gone out of her. But his new wife resents the intensity of his hatred for her shambling, middle-aged predecessor, so she encourages his paranoia. As for Katherine: "You wouldn't recognize her," her old friends tell each other. "A bright woman like that. Such a pity." She has not remarried.

Perhaps the Öbergs would say that the ex-husband was using the child to keep in contact with Katherine, although the contact he sought was malicious and perverse. Not mourning but revenge: revenge for the fact that she was more likable and intelligent than he ever managed to be, and even as successful in her own fashion; revenge for the ease with which she had accepted his departure from her life and for the happiness she had organized after it. He was outraged by the thought that anyone could be less than heartbroken by his going. In order to break her heart properly, he divorced her all over again through the child.

They had made a compact based on weakness: his vanity, her passivity and despair. As his second wife obscurely recognized, no court of law could terminate it. Snodgrass described that, too, in another stanza of the poem Katherine has adopted as her own:

> with horns locked in tall heather,
> two great Olympian elk stand bound,
>   fixed in their lasting hate
> till hunger brings them both to ground.
> Whom equal weakness binds together
>   none shall separate.

(ii)

Divorce and suicide have many characteristics in common and one crucial difference: although both are devastatingly public admissions of failure, divorce, unlike suicide, has to be lived through. So once it is over people tend to downgrade their misery because they find it intolerable to think they have ever been so vulnerable, so obsessed, so boring to their friends. They then downgrade it further because divorce is the one situation in which, sooner or later, private emotions are translated into terms of money and things. Which is another way of saying pain is reduced to farce. There is a certain shifty glamour about a broken heart, and when you talk about it people will listen sympathetically—up to a certain point. But there is none at all about a picture or a table inadvertently left behind after the fight, and if you moan about them you look foolish and petty-minded.

Yet things have their own significance and a desire to hold on to them is not always contemptible. Objects brought into a marriage not only belong to you, they are also obscurely part of you: visible links with your earlier life, properties you have worked for and cherished. For that reason, the Öbergs urge their clients to fight for the things they value instead of letting them go listlessly, out of guilt. A final confrontation about possessions, they say, is part of the psychological process of divorce, a necessary step to the freedom of a separate life, since objects left behind represent a line of retreat or an obstruction to prevent someone else coming in. The least flattering of all perspectives for a new wife is when she is sitting in the old wife's favorite chair, under her favorite painting, drinking out of her favorite cup.

Coming to terms about property, in short, is another aspect of mourning. "Possessions," said the Danish author Suzanne Brøgger, "are the objective battleground of divorce. Because you did not get what you wanted emotionally, you will therefore take the cutlery, the chairs, the things. You forget that in reality you got a great deal from the marriage—though not necessarily what you expected." The Scandinavians talk about things rather than money because alimony is now more or less obsolete in their countries, where most women work. The husbands pay their share of child maintenance and sometimes a little brief alimony while the wife retrains for a new job, but punitive alimony settlements, American-style, are unknown and regarded by feminists with contempt as being disguised obeisance to male superiority. In Stockholm, Copenhagen or Oslo, Emma would be looked down on as a latter-day remittance woman.

Even in the United States, there are signs that opinion is beginning to shift slowly against alimony, thanks to a combination of the women's movement, the no-fault system of divorce and the community property arrangements of some states, which stipulate that the parties share equally whatever possessions they have accumulated during the marriage. There are also "prenuptial agreements" which lawyers of the wealthy sometimes draw up as a precaution against stormy weather ahead. These set out the assets each brings into the marriage, which they can then take out again without argument if the marriage breaks up, everything else to be divided equally.

All these are small, tacit recognitions of the growing equality of women in society, just as punitive alimony settlements were equally tacit recognitions of their subservience. Philip Roth, who had his own dire experience of marriage and wrote one of his best and most savage books on the subject, *My Life as a Man*, put it to me this way:

> Before the women's movement, the courts recognized that there were inequalities in the system having to do with gender. But no one paid any attention to those injustices until the marriage was dissolved; at which point it became apparent to the judges that women were not paid equal wages for equal work. But rather than trying to rectify this in social or political terms, they did it individually: men took over the role of the state. The judge would say, "That woman can't be on the dole. Her husband earns a hundred dollars a week, but she could only earn fifty dollars in the same job. It's not fair. The husband must therefore offset that, so that they both make seventy-five dollars a week." It did no good to reply, "But I didn't make the system, your Honor." They were trying to introduce the notion of equality after a marriage that did not exist in society. But that in itself was also an injustice, both to husbands and to single women. Why was a childless thirty-two-year-old woman who had been married entitled to make as much as a man when a thirty-two-year-old woman who was not married could make only half as much? The sexual inequalities accepted in society at that time were dramatized only in the courtroom. Out of the tradition of the court and perhaps out of his own sympathies, the judge would temporarily stop being a male chauvinist pig and come down on the side of the woman. Or rather, he would express his male chauvinist piggery in another way: "This poor little thing," he would imply, "can't support herself. I must come to her rescue."

Out of these inequalities has grown a whole folklore of American horror stories: husbands made more or less destitute by alimony, changing their lives and sometimes their identities in order to avoid it, or even imprisoned for nonpayment, since unlike ordinary debts, a man who refused to pay alimony could be sent to jail for contempt of court. But neither these nor the injustices engineered by clever lawyers are my concern in this book. My business is with the emotional content, texture and doublethink of divorce, not with the details of famous financial outrages: Edward G. Robinson forced to sell the Impressionist paintings he had collected over a lifetime, not as investments but out of love; the millions paid out by assorted Rockefellers and Astors, by Bob Dylan and Mick Jagger. The cost of unhappiness and the ransom paid for their freedom by the very rich are interesting only in the way freaks are interesting: as evidence of life elsewhere, beyond the run of normal experience and largely beyond the imagination. Like freaks too, they are becoming rarer, despite the law's natural conservatism and the equally natural anxiety of lawyers to protect their special interests. Before the end of this century, I suspect punitive alimony settlements will seem as remote and barbaric as hanging, drawing and quartering, burning at the stake or any of the other atrocities once blithely handed down as just punishments by courts of law.

"Divorce," said Len Deighton, whose own took place before any of the recent reforms, "is a system whereby two people make a mistake and one of them goes on paying for it." Like other divorced people, he knows that wit is the best way out of indignity. Money, that is, is the starkest form of retribution, the most demeaning, the most resented; it is also a way of expressing all the other unfinished business of marriage. It is both power and guilt, a way of keeping hold, a way of getting free. For the husband and wife alike, the monthly alimony payments are a constant reminder of each other's existence and each other's claims, a means of staying on in the home from which one has been banished or a means of saying good-bye. They become unnaturally laden with significance and feeling: with the taker's rage and fear of abandonment, with the contempt of the giver, with the malice of both. And also with bitterness, unending and unrelenting, like that of the character in one of Saul Bellow's novels who says of an ex-wife, "If she could, she'd put a meter on his nose and charge him for breathing." I'm not sure where in Bellow's work this outburst occurs, nor if I am quoting it correctly, but the image has stayed with me; it is the poetry of resentment.

The motives concerning money are infinitely impure, rarely examined and, to the sufferers, compulsively interesting. And no one is immune, however rich, however famous. I once met a woman at a party whose face was so well known that I thought the host, as a joke, had invited her look-alike, the one they used for long shots and setups. Even after I had been introduced to her, shaken her hand, confirmed she was real, I found it hard to believe that anyone so hemmed in by paparazzi and gossip columnists could have enough private life left to mention. Months before, I had read in the papers about her divorce and her ex-husband's subsequent remarriage, but it was just one more item of news, like a take-over battle between multinational conglomerates. The sums involved, the properties, the manpower had no relation to the ordinary world: mere ciphers, abstractions, extravagant figures on paper. I was prepared for the diamonds as big as the Ritz around her neck and wrists, but not for her passion or venom, still less for her eagerness to talk about it.

"Vodka for breakfast," she said, "with or without tomato juice." She was squatter than she seemed in the photographs and her eyes were hooded and dangerous. "That was for starters. Then wine all day. Cocktails before lunch, whiskey before dinner, more wine with the meals—first-growth clarets; nothing but the best for him—and brandy after, then malt whiskey as a little nightcap. A charming life, all in all. Not quite what I'd bargained for." She flicked her tongue across her lips, as though tasting the rancor. "But bargain is hardly the word. My drink bills were so large even the accountants were embarrassed. After all, there are limits to what one can write off as entertainment."

She paused for breath, then was off again before I could say a word. "I was optimistic enough to think he'd die of it. An older man would have, or even a man with more sense of decency. I thought of that every time I signed a check to my wine merchant. It's a good investment, I'd tell myself. How long can he keep it up? But he had youth on his side. Youth and youths." She looked at me balefully. "He had boyfriends, you know, as well as girls, and he brought them all home. A perpetual Roman feast, twelve months of the year." She gave me her Gorgon look again, then raised her voice and said slowly, "IN MY HOUSE."

There was a brief shock wave of silence around us. Then everyone started chattering again, loudly and nervously. "I won't forgive him that," she said. "MY HOUSE AND MY MONEY."

I tried to think of something to say, but her ferocity was overwhelming. Yet accountants or no accountants, no amount of revelry or great wines or twenty-year-old malts could have made a difference to a fortune like hers. "I financed my own humiliation," she meant. Money was a way of speaking.

Then suddenly the fierceness was gone and she gave me her famous smile, bright as a child's. "I wonder how he'll manage now. He's used to the grand life and that poor girl he married hasn't got a bean. Not as these things go." She laughed pleasantly, showing her beautiful teeth. "He's going to have to change his little ways, isn't he?"

I smiled with her.

"Diminished circumstances," she said. "Don't you just love that phrase? Him in diminished circumstances. That's one satisfaction, at least."

Although I knew the mileage the newspapers had got out of her troubles, I also knew she had had a year to get over it. The rich are supposed to be different from us, so it had never occurred to me that someone living her style of life could remain so hurt, so angry, so unrelenting, so money-conscious. Just like all the rest of us.

But perhaps the rich are different not because they are impervious to the anxieties of hand-to-mouth living, but because their money defines them:

> Only God, my dear,
> Could love you for yourself alone
> And not your yellow hair.

Great fortunes are like great beauty, blurring the image for the perceiver, coming between the possessor and what she imagines is her true self. For her husband, booze and promiscuity were probably ways of showing her she did not own him, while for her they proved how much he was exploiting her, how little he really valued *her*. I wondered if he was sober and faithful with his new wife and if what the gossip columnists were saying about her various lovers was true.

"He took his clothes when he left," she said, "and not another thing. My lawyers saw to that."

That also is a variant on the theme of mourning when it becomes displaced and rotted down into money: you pay your lawyers to do it for you. "The only good divorces," a Swedish judge told me, "are those when both the husband and the wife feel afterward that their respective lawyers have let them down." Meanwhile, the lawyers do their best to avoid disappointing their clients. They go about their lucrative business solemnly and with an appropriate show of sympathy, although the best of them are not fooled. "When people in conflict say what they want for themselves," said the distinguished Manhattan attorney, Morton L. Leavy, "there is some hope of sanity. But when they start saying what they want for one another, God help us all."

The only other hope of sanity when large sums of money are involved is for sense to prevail over sensibility. I once asked a wealthy friend why he did not divorce the wife he was always complaining about so bitterly. "My accountant wouldn't hear of it," he replied. "Everything's in her name: the business, the house, the cars, the weekend cottage, the villa in Tuscany. You name it, she owns it. On paper. So how could I leave her?" Then he added philosophically, "I suppose you could say the Inland Revenue does more to preserve the sanctity of marriage than any institution outside the Catholic Church." That was six years ago. This year they celebrated their silver wedding anniversary with their usual rancor.

(iii)

Children, money, lovers, possessions, work, bitterness, rage: there are endless ways of denying grief, of avoiding the pain and what the psychoanalysts call "the work" of mourning. The bereaved are often willing to exhaust themselves in order *not* to acknowledge what they feel. Yet sometimes when marriages break up, mourning may seem to be the whole story for one partner or the other, even after years of unhappiness and incompatibility. At first the friends say, "He's taking it very hard," or "She's inconsolable": meaning, it's excessive, overdone, in bad taste, boring. Later they become exasperated: "I told her he was dragging her down and divorce is the best thing that ever happened to her," they say, "but she just won't listen." In the end, they lose patience, make excuses, get the kids to say they are out when the grieving partner telephones.

On a rational level, they are right. When a friend says, "It's been wrong for years. You're better off without her," they cannot understand how you can agree and still go on being upset. They cannot, that is, understand how feelings can be so inviolable to reason, or how grief remains disproportionate because it is an expression of older griefs, of unfinished business from earlier days.

When, for example, Sylvia Plath's husband left her for another woman I think he reactivated all the anguish she had felt when her father died; as I wrote in *The Savage God*, "she felt abandoned, injured, enraged and bereaved as purely and defenselessly as she had as a child twenty years before." And perhaps for the first time, she was also free to express what she felt: her mother had not allowed her children to go to their father's funeral and had kept her own grief so resolutely to herself that Sylvia later accused her of being too busy to mourn. So when a second loved and powerful figure vanished abruptly from her life, Sylvia was grieving for two deaths in one. And this touched the deepest springs of her imagination, releasing the extraordinary torrent of poems that poured out of her more or less daily for the last six months of her life:

> The blood jet is poetry,
> There is no stopping it.

The image is more than usually accurate: the grief and anger she was transforming triumphantly into poetry was, literally, the lifeblood which had kept her going since her childhood.

But it was also that same grief and rage which destroyed her chance of getting her husband back. Had her reaction to his infidelity been less intense, less absolute, he would probably have returned to her when his affair had run its course. But in this area at least she lacked worldly wisdom; she was in the grip of emotions which had been lurking in her, waiting to erupt, since she was nine years old.

"In normal mourning," wrote Melanie Klein, "early psychotic anxieties are reactivated. The mourner is in fact ill, but because this state of mind is common and seems natural to us, we do not call mourning an illness." Sylvia Plath was able to redeem this sickness by turning it into poetry. For ordinary people the task is dourer, less spectacular and perhaps even more painful, since they lack anything as abiding as art to show for their suffering.

Consider, for instance, Carol and Paul, an odd couple who seemed to get along because they were so different. He was a squat, powerful little man with a bristling beard, tough as cowhide and very ambitious, while she was a nervous girl with long straight hair, self-effacing and so thin that she looked as if he could have crumpled her in his fingers like tissue paper. Wherever he went he was the center of attention, the man with more appetite and a greater buzz of energy than anyone else in the room. Later, after he had made a seamless transition from newspaper foreign correspondent to television personality, people gave him the stage as though by right, because his face was so well known. But even at the start, he commandeered it with a marvelous gift of the gab, unstoppable, impossible to resist. His specialty was surrealist outrage. He seemed to have a hot line permanently open to his uninhibited childhood. Everything the rest of us thought, then suppressed, he came out with—but disarmingly, as if it were the most natural thing in the world, so that the only possible response was laughter. Professionally, he learned to keep this outrageousness in check, but the people he interviewed knew it was there, waiting to be provoked, so they trod around him warily. He became very successful.

While he talked nonstop, she barely started. Over the years, I suppose I heard her agree or expostulate or occasionally laugh at his demented jokes. But I never really heard her talk—at length, as if she meant it. Not that I saw them regularly, but each time we met he seemed larger, more buoyant, more outrageous, while she seemed to have retreated further into the background, until finally she was as insubstantial as a shadow, and as silent.

An improbable combination, then, although what held them together was nobody's business but their own. Like most of their friends, I assumed their marriage survived because they had both been brought up as Catholics. Although he had left the Church even before he left school and her faith had wobbled severely, the teaching dies hard. So she was resigned to marriage as to a clubfoot. She had been brought up to believe it was a sacrament, as immutable as the Church itself; once you were in it, there was no getting out. Her parents had been unhappy and had stuck together; now it was her turn. She and Paul also had four children, all boys, as obstreperous as their father, with dirty fingernails and mops of electric hair.

The other thing that kept them going was his work: he was never at home. He traveled incessantly, shifting from one grand hotel to another, rarely bothering to unpack his suitcase. "Eighty different planes already this year and it's only July," he told me once. Then added, as though to convince himself, "I've kept a log." For a moment he seemed puzzled, adrift, then he launched into a baroque fantasia about an Air India stewardess, a curry and his bowels.

Nothing diminished his energy. He devoted his free time to the kind of sports which swallow up whole weekends: sailing in the summer, skiing in winter, golf in between. He would arrive home from the airport, dump his dirty clothes in the laundry basket, repack his grip and leave again—for Cowes or Wentworth or wherever the snow was good that weekend—sometimes with one of the older boys, more often on his own. I used to wonder if he was not pushing Carol to the point where she would say, "Stay with me. I need you." Perhaps, like most domineering people, he yearned secretly to be bullied. But she never obliged. "For God's sake, go," she would say in a dry, resentful voice, "otherwise you'll just hang around and be bored." So go he would, if only to get his own back. That, too, was part of their compact.

Had her friends asked—which they did not—she would have had her reasons. In the second decade of their marriage, when all the boys were safely at school, Carol took up the piano again. She had played well as a girl but gave it up when the children started arriving. Now she was working for a teacher's diploma, taking lessons, practicing three hours a day. It seemed to go with her silence, to fill it out and make it eloquent. It also went with their separateness, being something Paul took no part in, something he was ignorant of, although he seemed disproportionately pleased when she began ticking off the grades which would lead her to qualification. I suspect he thought she was trying to prove her independence as well as her talent, and that appealed to his competitive spirit. At a party once, between a hysterical disquisition on the emetic properties of jalapeño peppers and an even more hysterical story about driving into a snowbank at fifty miles per hour with a Nobel Prize winner in the passenger seat, he told me about Carol's renewed skill as a musician—proudly and with no jokes, as though Grade Eight from the Royal Schools of Music were not far short of the Nobel Prize itself. When I mentioned this to Carol later that evening, she looked at me icily and said, "He's so inured to success in his own career, you'd have thought he could have taken my paltry efforts in his stride. I'm sorry he's so surprised." Then she turned her back on me and began talking to someone else. For a woman who cast herself in the role of victim, she seemed startlingly unforgiving. Perhaps she wanted me to know that nothing had changed merely because she now had an interest in life. Their marriage endured on the same basis as it always had: because they were Catholics and saw almost nothing of each other.

So nobody was surprised when Paul left her for a twenty-five-year-old research assistant who skied, sailed and played a passable game of golf. I even wondered if Carol would notice he had gone and, if she did, if she would not feel relieved.

Then stories began to circulate. Paul and his girl had arrived home at one in the morning to find Carol lurking in the shrubbery by their front door. She had leaped out at them, nails flailing like a rabid cat's, shouting "Whore! Bastard!" A neighbor had called the police. After that, Carol had taken to haunting Television Centre whenever Paul's show went out, glaring at him when he passed her in the reception hall, intent and silent, as though trying to cast a spell. Finally the doormen, who all knew her from the old days, were ordered to keep her out. The Gothic stories continued: Carol had taken an overdose; Carol had had a breakdown; Carol had been discreetly hospitalized in a private nuthouse near Primrose Hill; Carol had won a prize at the Brent Music Festival. All the rumors had in common was, they were out of character. Then word came that Carol was taking Paul to the cleaners. And that, at least, was true. The alimony settlement was savage enough—and Paul famous enough—to rate a paragraph in *The Evening Standard*.

Then silence. Carol found herself an older man with a sweet temper and Paul settled down with his adored and adoring young lady. "Thank God," he announced, "I can't afford to marry her." His jokes, however, were fewer and kinder, and he seemed fonder of people, as though domestic happiness were contagious. Everybody, it seemed, was living happily unmarried ever after. If something was missing from the lives of their friends, that was because odd couples are hard to find. They had lasted nineteen years and we were all getting too old for readjustments.

So when I saw Carol a year or so after the divorce became final, three years after Paul walked out, I was feeling almost nostalgic for what I remembered were the good times we had all had together.

"Good times?" She looked at me as if I were a close encounter of the third kind. "All I remember is misery. Nineteen years of misery."

She was as ghostly thin as ever and her dark hair still hung straight as a waterfall, without a trace of gray. But there were tense lines around her mouth and eyes, and tension in the way she sat, held in on herself like a coiled spring. All that remained of her old passivity and self-effacement were the funereal clothes.

I started to interrupt but she cut me off abruptly. "Maybe the first few months were OK. After all, we were both so young. It seemed romantic and grown up to be off on my own with a handsome husband who made me laugh, and not much money. Us against the world. But within half a year that dream had gone bust. It was each for himself. There was no 'us.' "

"What woke you up so fast?"

"We went sailing, what else? He had a friend with a boat at Burnham. The idea was to sail to Ostend at Whitsun, eat a nice meal and sail back again. Three men and a boat and me, aged nineteen and pregnant. The first night out a storm came up like nothing I'd ever dreamed of. The boat was thrown around like a plastic toy. At first I was desperately sick, then just desperate. I thought the mast would break, that we'd capsize. Outside there was nothing but howling darkness. Inside everything was creaking and groaning and sliding around. After a while, I was too frightened even to vomit. At one point, when the owner was on deck and the rest of us below in the cabin, there was a terrible cracking, wrenching sound. This is it, I thought, we're going to die. So I turned to Paul and said, 'Hold my hand. I'm terrified.' And he wouldn't. He just looked at me like dirt and said, 'We don't need your hysteria.' 'We,' please note. As though I'd made a fool of him in front of his pals, made him look soft."

She glared at me, bright-eyed with anger. I had never suspected her of such vehemence.

Then the fire went out of her, her voice steadied. "I think now he was as terrified as I was and didn't dare let go in case he cracked. But I didn't see it that way at the time. After all, I was only a kid. What I saw was, he was giving me notice: when the crunch came I was on my own; there would be no support from him; ever. That was the first disillusionment. When we got to Ostend I said, 'I won't sail back. I'm going home by ferry.' All he said was, 'Go then,' and gave his pals a sheepish, furtive look. So off I went, on my own again. After that, I knew how it was going to be."

"But that was twenty something years ago. How can you still remember it? Why should it still make you so angry?"

"You don't understand." She shook her head sorrowfully. "I remember everything. Every slight, every insult, every hurt. Make no mistake, nothing is lost. Don't you think it's the same with him? In the end, none of us gets away with a single thing. A bad marriage is like the Last Judgment: it is all totted up, it all has to be paid for, every last lousy error."

I looked at her in wonder, thinking, The shadow has taken substance at last. She has been storing this up for years. Who would have guessed? Paul's bits and pieces were gone from the sitting room: the signed photographs of him with celebrities, the cartoons, the booty from his unending trips abroad. In their place was a grand piano piled with sheet music, Mark Rothko prints on the walls, and chaste Scandinavian rugs and curtains. The room was full of her presence.

"After that," she continued, "nothing went right. Before the Whitsun trip my pregnancy had been quite straightforward, but when I got back I went on being sick, violently, as if I were still shut up in that bloody boat. The baby was born six weeks premature. By then Paul was in Washington investigating some scandal or other and couldn't get back. So you see . . ."

She paused, raised her head and looked at me steadily with

wide, serious eyes. ". . . I was on my own when my first child was born and on my own when he died." A single large tear welled to each eye. She blinked them away. "Because he did die, poor little thing. He caught pneumonia in that sanitized box they were keeping him in and just died." Two more tears fell like stones. She blew her nose noisily. "I couldn't even hold him and comfort him. They wouldn't let me."

"And you blamed Paul?"

"How could I?" She made a brief cutting movement with her hand. "But it was my firstborn, you see. You don't ever really get over that." She blew her nose again. "And that was it. I was never really happy again."

I mumbled, "I didn't know."

"Why should you? It's not something Paul and I ever talked about, even to each other. Instead, I got pregnant again straightaway. Doctor's orders. Then pregnant again after that. And so on. Four more children in seven years. But none of them was Ben. All they did was wear me out. I suppose there are women who can cope, but I don't seem to be one of them. Physically, I felt wrecked; mentally, too, because of Ben. I think now I should have waited for more children. I wasn't in a fit state. But at the time I didn't feel that option was open to me. Once a Catholic . . ."

"And Paul was never there?"

"Never."

"If you felt so down, why didn't you make a fuss?"

She laughed. "Because I felt so down. Anyway, he was an ambitious man with a difficult job to do. I wouldn't have wanted to hold him back. And if I had, he'd have hated me for it."

"But what about the times he was in London? What about the weekends?"

"The weekends?" She brooded a little, as if she could not remember there ever being any weekends. "At first, when we had Peter and Bill in that flat in Bina Gardens, there was no room. It was bad enough being there on my own with two small kids and pregnant again. To have Paul there too was suffocating. Besides, he worked so hard during the week I felt he needed a break. I suppose"—she cocked her head, listening to herself—"I suppose I thought he ought to want to get away, even if he didn't."

"So you encouraged him? You pushed him out?"

"What else was I to do? Whenever he stayed it was worse. He used to get up around midday, wander into the kitchen in his pajamas and stare out of the window at the rain. Why do I remember it always raining on Saturdays?"

"That's England," I said.

She took no notice. "He'd stare at the rain and say, 'I'm bored. Christ, I'm bored.' I learned to dread that moment more than any other. That's why I encouraged him to go off sailing or skiing or whatever it was. Anything not to hear him say, 'I'm bored.' With me, he meant, and with the kids. And there wasn't a single thing in the whole world I could do about it."

She brooded again, then said in a puzzled voice, "You know, I think I felt sorry for him being married to me. I wasn't really on the ball in those days. I was so depressed and exhausted, it was all I could do to cope with the kids. So there wasn't much left over for him. And he was always so bloody full of life. Which made me feel even more inadequate." She was silent a moment, then roused herself for another effort. "You see, he isn't the sort of person who could ever be happy around children or the home, so there didn't seem any point in not giving him a long rein. The trouble was, I didn't think ahead, I didn't plan for the future. I just muddled along from day to day, imagining that our curious way of life suited us both: me depressed, him irrepressible. I thought that if I gave him a good length of rope he would feel free and grateful and then, maybe, hang himself. In fact, it wasn't hanging him, it was hanging me."

Another silence. She began to pick at the sleeve of her black sweater. For years, I thought, she has hidden behind nervousness and diffidence. Now I was seeing the face behind the face, unwaveringly depressed yet somehow whole. To break the gloom I said, "It can't have been all that bad. At least he made you laugh."

"In public. You try living with that famous sense of humor. I felt I was choking. Choking and beaten, like a battered child. Looking back on it now, even the jokes seem like an hallucination."

I started to interrupt but she cut me off impatiently. She did not want to argue; she wanted, after all those years of silence, to be heard.

"Don't you remember? He'd go into a room and insult everyone present. And they'd fall about with laughter. I used to think,
Am I the only one who hears what he's actually saying? Maybe
it's all my imagination. Maybe I'm going round the twist. Those
faces he's pulling: that's them. Why don't they see it? Why are
they all cackling away like hens?

"Then maybe once an evening, I'd catch somebody's eye and
see that shocked, dazed look. And I'd know there was one other
person who saw the emperor had no clothes on. Or perhaps I'd
see a couple of waiters exchange glances, shrug, roll their eyes
to heaven. Then I'd know I wasn't alone. I'd know I was sane.

"And there's another thing: half the time the jokes were
about me—me or my parents or the Catholic Church. I don't
think even the priest would have blamed me in his heart if he'd
known why I stopped going to Mass. Or why I went through
with the divorce, for that matter. I was Paul's straight man, his
whipping boy. He needed me. Perhaps that's why the marriage
lasted as long as it did."

"But everyone thought that was part of the pact," I said.
"He made jokes, you laughed at them. It's a kind of love."

"Love?" she echoed. "Love didn't come into it. We were
married, that's all. And because we'd been married as Catholics
in the church, I thought, Well, this is forever; this is something
you've got to put up with, for better or for worse. I see now that
that attitude must have been very difficult to live with. Paul is
an intelligent man and he must have realized that I was simply
enduring him. Maybe that's what gave him the courage to break
away. What did he have to lose?"

"After the children came, did you never want to make yourself attractive to him? Is that what you're saying? You made no
effort; you just let things slide."

For the first time, she blushed. "I wanted to rub his nose in
the dreariness of it all. Since I didn't seem able to tell him in
words, I wanted him to be able to look at me and *see* how I felt.
Sometimes I used to go out to the airport to meet him, especially
when I knew he'd been somewhere exotic: Bangkok, Bali, San
Francisco. And somehow I'd work it so that I never had time to
put on makeup and wash my hair. So there we'd be at the barrier, a shabby wife and four snotty-nosed, squabbling kids. I'd

see his face freeze as he came through customs and my heart would leap with pleasure. This is what you've got, I was telling him. This is marriage. All the rest is dreamland. It was my revenge, you see."

"For what?"

"For the hard time he gave me, for the exciting life he led when I wasn't around, for my depression."

When Paul had lived there the room had been as exuberant as he was, full of bright colors and children's debris. She had stripped it right down to match her image of herself, painted the walls a cerebral gray, sanded the floors and tidied away the knickknacks, the roller skates, the unfinished model airplanes. The rug in front of my chair was black and gray and black, like her dress. I studied its chaste abstract pattern, avoiding her eye. "You seem to be saying one of two things and I don't know which," I said. "Either feeling resentful was how you got your kicks or you wanted out of that marriage as much as he did. Which is it?"

She shrugged as if it did not matter. "Both probably." But her mouth was unsteady.

"Then why were you so devastated when he left?"

She laced her fingers together like a child making a church, but fiercely, so that the knuckles showed white. "I've thought about that for three years. Maybe that's all I've thought about. I'd like to say it was because, being brought up as a Catholic, I'll always feel married to him. But it's nothing as easy and straightforward as that. I think that what really happens is, you get wounded when you marry. It's like napalm. Gradually, the wound becomes a running sore all over your body. So you cover yourself with plaster. Well, you know what it's like tearing plaster off: painful, terribly painful. That's how it was with me. I was in a body plaster. Every inch of me was covered. There were none of those little gauze strips to protect the injured flesh. So when the plaster was all ripped off, it was agonizing. Even though I knew it was necessary, even though I knew the wounds would never heal until the plaster was removed, it was still excruciatingly painful." She went on twisting her hands in the childhood ritual: Here is the church, here is the steeple, open the doors and here are the people. Her voice was low and intense.

"You see, all of a sudden you're left. The plaster has gone and you're standing there with every wound exposed. And it's agony. But you know it has to be like that. No way are the wounds going to heal unless you pull those plasters off."

I looked at her with astonishment, trying to remember the old Carol, that nervous and apologetic Bride of Frankenstein. Her voice, as she spoke, had gradually steadied and her face was serious and thoughtful. She seemed unaware of my presence. She was like someone inspired, lifted up. This divorce—or the pain of it—had been the making of her.

"Do you reckon," I asked gently, "life will be better if and when the wounds heal?"

She nodded, her expression still thoughtful and inward. "It's been three years now and mostly they have healed. At least, the ones with 'Paul' written on them have. I can think of him now more or less without bitterness. But there are others which aren't right yet: the ones with 'marriage' written on them. I wouldn't want to try again."

"But I'd heard you have a very nice man now."

She looked at me bleakly. "Oh, Charlie," she said. "Yes, I suppose he is everything I could wish for: gentle, sweet, helpful." She shook her head desolately. "He makes me feel trapped. Maybe divorce has turned me into a cynic, but when he tells me he loves me I don't know what he's talking about. I don't know what love is anymore. I think it is something he wants to feel in order to gratify himself. I think it's a form of self-indulgence to talk about love. Is that an awful thing to say?"

"Not necessarily."

"When I was small my mother was always asking, 'Do you love me?' What a thing to say to a child! I'd answer, 'Yes,' and feel embarrassed. Then she would ask, 'How much do you love me?' It made me want to curl up and die. But I'd stretch my arms as wide as I could and say, 'This much.' All the time I'd be thinking, 'It's not enough. It's not what I mean. It's inadequate. It's wrong.' Now it's happening again. I keep thinking of that line in *The Hustler* when Paul Newman rounds on the lot of them and yells, 'Everybody wants a piece of me!' That's what I want to say to Charlie and the kids and my bitch of a mother. They can carve it on my tombstone when I'm gone." Her eyes were large and dark in her pale face, her hands trembled. "When Charlie says he loves me I feel threatened by it. I feel he's threatening my freedom. Although what that freedom is I don't know, since it depends on my alimony, and that's a dirty word these days. That's why I'm working so hard at the piano. I've got to make myself self-supporting."

We've had it all wrong, I thought, those concerned friends and I. Paul is only part of it. She is grieving for everything: for the premature baby she never had time to mourn, for her own childhood devoured by her steely mother, for a whole frozen world. When Paul left he awakened her to the permanent condition of her life. He may have done her a favor.

"It's none of my business," I said, "but being self-supporting won't necessarily make you any less depressed. And from what you've said, it sounds as if you've been depressed for as long as you can remember."

"It *is* none of your business." She smiled at me, without malice. "But you may be right. I've thought about that, too, during these last three years. The conclusion I have come to is that marriage . . ." She hesitated, choosing her words carefully, ". . . is a very . . . stultifying . . . condition. You don't realize how downhill you are going. I had a great deal of depression when I was married but I never really came to terms with how much. You go down and down, but slowly, every day another step, until you are walking through this valley where the sun never shines. And you don't even know you're in it. Then the marriage ends and everything changes. Maybe I first entered that ghastly valley when Ben died and only came out of it again when the marriage died. But I didn't understand that in any clear way. All I knew was that I had climbed back out. Suddenly, the sun was so blinding it hurt. I couldn't take it, I didn't even want it. It was only months later, when the sun had started to warm me through to the bones, that I began to think, Ah, fantastic! I've climbed out of that valley at last. It was only then that I realized how long I had walked in that deep cold shadow. All right, maybe there were flashes of sunlight down there. Yes. Not many. But it was only when I had finally climbed out and the sun started to shine and everything was bright and warm that I knew where I had been and how long I had been there. Of course, the deluges of depression still come from time to time. But in the end they make me see how life-giving the sunlight is."

All these years of silence, I thought, and now this gift of tongues. Grave face, clear eyes, eloquence. She has turned twenty years of victimization into a victory.

Perhaps she read my thoughts, for without warning her mood swung. The lines crinkled around her eyes and she grinned slyly, just as Paul used to grin when he put the knife in. "I can think of another way of putting it, less high-flown," she said. "Being married to Paul was like standing on a vibrating shelf. You know what I mean: the shelf vibrates and the things on it begin to move until gradually they get to the edge. Then they fall off. Nineteen years it took me to get from one end of that bloody shelf to the other, until finally I was teetering on the brink. I should have jumped. Why I waited to be knocked off, I can't think."

Then she was laughing as she used to laugh in the good old days when Paul made jokes about her, in her presence, to anyone who would listen. But now she was making his jokes about herself.

VIII

Collusion

(i)

The world is full of marriages incomprehensible to outsiders, but enduring: warder and prisoner, swinger and homebody, beauty and the beast. Love, in the conventional romantic sense, does not seem to come into the equation. They are held together by need, each silently colluding with the other's unacknowledged longings. Perhaps that is what Plato really meant by "the desire and pursuit of the whole." If so, it has less to do with Romeo and Juliet than with Lord and Lady Macbeth; less, that is, with what the psychoanalysts call "the ideal object"—dreamed of and unattainable—than with "projective identification," the mechanism by which parts of the personality that are hard to handle are split off into another person.

For example, a lively and sweet-natured lady novelist is married to a dour businessman who, since she became successful, has given up his small company to manage her affairs. She says "Yes, of course," to whatever her publishers ask; he draws up contracts of spun steel and insists on exorbitant advances. She makes friends, he alienates them. If the friends complain, she shrugs helplessly and promises to telephone next time she is in town. But she does not call, nor is she unfaithful to him, and the marriage has lasted thirty years. Before they married she had been a girl about town, living the bohemian life, writing fitfully, drinking too much. Now she lives like a nun or an athlete in training, working undisturbed week after week, since none of the friends is willing to brave the iron figure of her husband who guards the door and the telephone. The books she writes have become steadily richer and deeper over the years, although her friends find them curiously at odds with the person they know: malicious where she is witty, and altogether unforgiving. They blame it on the influence of her husband without pausing to consider that perhaps she is able to remain warm and outgoing because he is savage enough for them both, just as he can maintain his icy, rebarbative control because she is weak and affectionate. Her real marriage is to her work; she endures her husband as a penitent endures a hair shirt, a necessary severity.

Mutual assistance pacts of this kind can last a lifetime. They are not necessarily happy marriages in the accepted sense of the term—on the contrary, they are often founded on hatred or contempt or distaste—but they may be the only way the partners can get through life without crumpling under the pressure of urges they will not properly recognize as their own, like a stunt man with a wife who is frightened to cross the road: he takes the risks she secretly yearns for, while she personifies the fears he feels driven continually to conquer. The same coin, different faces.

Outsiders refuse to see it this way. Arrangements of this kind set their teeth on edge. They seem irrational, unjust, stupid, particularly to the new young women whose consciousness has been raised to their own rights and injuries. They are baffled by the doggedness with which their unliberated elders cling to preordained roles. They call it slavishness and blame it—indignantly and a shade condescendingly—on ignorance, apathy, social conditioning.

"If you want to know how much women of a certain age will sit still for in the name of marriage," said a social worker in New York, "go and see Naomi."

So I took a train and went out to see her in a Long Island suburb which had been glamorous when F. Scott Fitzgerald was incubating *The Great Gatsby*, but now was full of affluent doctors and psychiatrists. Saks, Lord & Taylor and Bergdorf Goodman have branches there, and the local delicatessens flog Jackson's teas, honeys from Fortnum & Mason and S. S. Pierce cans.

Her house was off down a tree-lined street, with a lawn in front and a swimming pool behind. There was a rusty basketball hoop on the wall of the three-car garage where her Buick was parked aslant, as though to make the oil-stained wastes look full. Naomi must have been lurking by the front door, for she opened it the instant I rang and led me into a large, hushed living room with woven tweed curtains and a great deal of expensive Danish furniture, rosewood and leather.

She was fifty-eight years old and, like the Buick, too small for the place: a dowdy and apologetic woman, her gray hair in a bun, and still, despite everything, devoted to her husband's glittering medical career. She pointed out the droop-nosed silver coffeepot given him by a grateful sheik, the Henry Moore maquette from a British industrialist, the framed scrolls and citations, the signed photographs of her husband with film stars and prizefighters, with military men in braided uniforms and medals, with a recent vice-president. She handled them like holy relics, as though devotion were her mode of life, her defining characteristic. It was in the lines of her face, the sag of her pudgy shoulders and the expression of her eyes, at once determined and unsteady, as bewildered as a lost dog's. In the photographs, her husband, who was two years older than she was, looked twenty years younger: a tall, vigorous man, whose silver hair seemed like some quirk of early middle age. Even his skin looked young. On a side table, hidden among the pictures of him with his famous clients, was their wedding photograph. Apart from the color of his hair, he had hardly changed, whereas all that remained of her was the bewildered expression in her eyes. She was like the picture of Dorian Gray, aging for him while he stayed young.

The man in the photographs had the vaguely military air eminent surgeons acquire from giving orders no one will ever question. Certainly not his dumpy and devoted wife, who seemed anxious at first to make excuses for him. She told me he worked impossible hours under impossible pressures, that he was constantly flying off around the world to perform operations or attend conferences—to which he never took her. She seemed proud of all this, or perhaps she was simply glad to have someone to talk to in that big, echoing house.

Then she said, "I know what you're thinking and the answer is yes. Of course there were other women, but I didn't mind. Not that there was much I could have done about it if I had minded, not with all the traveling he did and the fact that he was famous in his field as well as charming. He had everything going for him: fame, looks, money, power."

"All the aphrodisiacs."

"So they say. But that wasn't it for me." She wagged an admonitory finger, a stickler, suddenly, for detail. "We had a different arrangement." Since I was a stranger, none of this would be held against her, so she might as well get it right. She cleared her throat and took the plunge. "The truth is, I never knew what he saw in me. That he should have married me at all was a permanent astonishment." Her voice was low and unemphatic, without self-pity or resentment, simply stating the facts. "I always knew it was a one-sided affair, but only once in all that time did he ever say so."

"Once?"

"It was my fault. I suppose I'd known about the girls for years. But I pretended not to. Then finally it got too much. Friends started dropping hints—you know how it is—so I challenged him, like a fool, and we had our one real fight. 'I only married you because you pursued me,' he said, 'and because my mother thought it was time I settled down with a nice Jewish girl.' Of course, I was terribly hurt, but he was upset, you see. Later he apologized and said he had been having trouble at the hospital. Maybe he was; his colleagues have always been jealous of him. Or maybe one of his girls was playing up. Either way, he was miserable. In the end, I couldn't blame him. But I didn't want to hear him say those things again, so after that, I let it go."

"Why couldn't you blame him?"

"Because he'd never talked that way before. Because he was

always polite, even thoughtful, despite the pressures on him. And he was right about his mother. She was one of those kind, old-fashioned women who care only about the well-being of their beloved sons. That's why she wanted him to marry me, not one of his glamour pants. She knew I'd take care of him. I suppose I'm like her when it comes down to it: a homebody who adores him, someone who is willing to wait, a Rebecca. He was my hero in high school, my teenage crush. The other girls pinned up photographs of Tyrone Power and Gary Cooper. I pinned up clippings from the school paper about him."

She wore a dark, shapeless sweater and her skirt was heavy tweed, like the curtains but more somber. It was as if she dressed in order not to be seen. Then her jaw tightened and the expression in her eyes was no longer lost but stubborn. "It's not true I pursued him, but I did hang around in a speechless way. When he started to take me out I couldn't believe my luck. It seemed the sort of one-in-a-million shot that happens once in a lifetime. And when he finally asked me to marry him I thought, Well, now I have everything I've ever wanted."

Silence.

"So I did my best. I made a good home for him—and for his mother, too, in her last illness. I took care of everything—the kids, the bills, the house—so he could get on with his career without worrying. That was my pleasure. If he wanted to play around, it seemed a small enough price to pay. That's how he was, how we were, how the world is now. All that work and jetting about: there's too much strain, too much loneliness. It's not natural. Anyway, the girls came and went, but I stayed. And I'll tell you something: he always seemed glad to be back."

I waited for her to continue.

"Then you know what?" Her hand went up to her mouth, as if to stifle a laugh, but no laugh came. "He went and fell in love. Every winter he goes off skiing in New Hampshire with our daughter. Skiing's one of his things, one of his many things. And Natalie loves it, of course. Not the skiing, I guess, as much as the week alone with him. So I always leave them to it, so as not to spoil their fun. Well, last winter they go up to Conway as usual and she starts in on the skiing lessons again. But this time her teacher is a young woman: twenty-eight years old, blue eyes, long blond hair, always smiling. With a *tuchas*, as my uncle Manny used to say, you could crack nuts on. If you will forgive the expression. Twenty-eight years old to his sixty. To my fifty-eight. Who can argue?" She shrugged helplessly. "Not that I ever did."

"A bit late in the day, isn't it, for Don Juan to start playing Romeo?"

"But that's the point." For the first time, her voice rose irritably. "It's not just another affair. Those I'm used to. This time he's really fallen in love. Head over heels, like a teenager. He's moved out and settled in with her and . . ."

Her voice faded, the clock ticked, she stared intently at the tips of her Roots shoes. "And the trouble is, I can't really blame him. All my life I've loved him and now he's in love. So you see . . ." Her voice and face brightened. She seemed like someone who had just won an intricate argument. ". . . *I know how he feels*."

I waited while the brightness faded.

"Maybe now," she said carefully, "he'll understand how I've felt for the last thirty-five years." She shook her head briskly. "But that's just wishful thinking, isn't it? At the moment, he hardly even remembers I exist."

"Remind him, then."

"What's the use? He wants to marry her. He said the strangest thing to me the other day: he said, 'I want to settle down.' What does he think we've been doing all these years?"

That's what you have been doing, I thought. Now it is his turn. I wondered if the ski instructress with the long blond hair and cute ass would be as unfaithful to him as he was to Naomi. Maybe he wants to know how it feels. Elderly men sometimes marry young women because they are afraid of age and what Philip Larkin calls "the only end of age." But perhaps the surgeon was weary of being young. At the end of Oscar Wilde's story, Dorian Gray stabs his portrait and becomes old and withered and corrupt in death, while the painting reassumes its youthful beauty. To each his own different truth and different peace. But there was no chance of a Roman spring for Naomi.

To change the subject, I said, "At least you still have the house."

She surveyed the overfurnished room without pleasure. "Who needs it? I mean, what am I doing rattling around in a huge place like this? My son is married, my daughter's away at college. There is nothing to fill my days anymore." She broke off again, then added apologetically, "I'm not coming on like a martyr, you know. I knew the risk I was taking. It's just . . ." She gathered herself, then mumbled, "It's like being widowed."

"I'm sorry," I said, but she turned her head away. When I tried to talk again about practical matters—Did she have a settlement yet?—she seemed to think I was criticizing her. "I could find a job, I suppose, but who would employ me at my age, except out of pity? Which I don't want. The only thing I know how to do properly is run a home and look after my family. That's my function. He's a surgeon, I'm a housewife. Why should I have to stop?"

The stubborn, mulish look was back on her face and for a moment I thought I understood why her glamorous husband had broken away. It must have felt like being lashed to a monorail train, driving round and round the same obsessed circuit of devotion.

"What am I supposed to do?" she said. "Take up pottery? Go in for social work? Ask favors? I looked into all that, but those girls who run the office . . . The one who sent you, is she a friend of yours?"

"An acquaintance."

"At my age, who needs their understanding? Worse still, who needs their indignation? Anyway, he's being very generous. He says I can have the house, the car, whatever money I need."

"Then take him up on it. Find yourself a lawyer and get it all down on paper, signed and sealed, while he's still full of guilt. In a year's time, you'll be feeling less forgiving and he'll be feeling less guilty. But you'll still need the money. Get a settlement quick."

She nodded. Yes, she had not thought of it that way. Yes, I was quite right. But . . .

"But?"

The lines deepened around her mouth and her voice dropped even lower. I had to lean forward to hear what she was saying. "But it's not that simple." She began to speak fast, as though

parroting an argument she had been through countless times
before. "Next month's our thirty-fifth anniversary and I want
him to come home for it. I've been planning it all year, long
before this thing happened. Anthony, our eldest, is flying in from
the Coast with his family, Natalie's coming down from Benning-
ton. A little party for us and the children and a few of our oldest
friends." The low drone of the monorail on its remorseless circuit
stopped. She fumbled in her bag for a tissue, blew her nose, then
said more loudly, "It's been thirty-five years, for God's sake. All
I want is one afternoon out of his new life. Nothing more."

"Forgive me," I leaned back and peered at the Henry Moore
in order to avoid her dark, sad gaze, "but what has that got to
do with a lawyer?"

"Don't you see?" Her voice rose reproachfully. "You know
what they're like, stirring things up. If there's a lawyer on his
back bullying him about settlements and money and property,
he won't come, will he?"

She glared at me for a moment accusingly, as if I were
trying to undermine the last of her happiness. Then the fire went
out of her, though not the stubbornness. She ducked her head,
tightened her mouth and mumbled, "I do . . . so . . . want him
. . . to . . . come . . . to the party."

(ii)

DENYING

Later, thinking about Naomi in her big empty house, I remembered some lines by Sylvia Plath:

> Love is a shadow.
> How you lie and cry after it.
> Listen: these are its hooves: it has gone off,
>   like a horse.

At some point during their thirty-five years together Naomi's
script had been changed into something more equivocal: "Why
speak of love?" asks a character in T. S. Eliot's *The Cocktail
Party*. "We were used to each other." Her husband's unfaithful-

ness rested secure on Naomi's fidelity, and through him she led, by proxy, the exciting life she was otherwise not adapted to.

The generation which came of age in the sixties and after has no time for such ambiguities. It talks of depression as if it were a social evil with social causes, and sees no percentage in what were once considered the saving graces of marriage: trust, tolerance, affection, humor. To the feminists, a folktale heroine like the Patient Griselda is a traitor to her sex—"a lackey," they might say, "of male imperialism"—and modern marriage is staked out in terms of rights and property, like a precarious business partnership.

Professor Shorter blames this change on the second sexual revolution, in which eroticism displaced romantic feeling: "Because sexual attachment is notoriously unstable, couples resting atop such a base may easily be blown apart. To the extent that erotic gratification is becoming a major element in the couple's collective existence, the risk of marital dissolution increases." On one level perhaps nothing has changed: there has never been any loneliness like that of the marriage bed when the kissing has stopped. Twenty years ago, before the sixties had begun to swing, an elderly lawyer told me that, in his long experience and whatever the nominal excuses, the majority of marriages failed because the sex had failed. Yet he was implying, I think, something rather different from Professor Shorter. For the lawyer, sex was the seal which validated the relationship between husband and wife, a tender, pleasurable, healing connection which made up for discord and misunderstanding outside the bedroom, and without which no amount of goodwill would finally suffice. As Professor Shorter sees it, sex has now become an end in itself, a narcissistic pursuit to which the relationship is secondary. And when this happens, marriage is transformed from a stable institution into a battlefield where those ignorant armies clash, literally, by night.

But in societies still haunted by the ghost of the Puritan ethic, where hedonism and selfishness are embarrassments no one is anxious to admit to, erotic experiment has to be dignified as self-discovery. Whence, in the sixties, the clatter of closets resolutely opening and the solemn pursuit of the one true polymorphous perversion. Whence, too, the proliferation of how-to compendiums, *The Joy of Sex* next to *The Joy of Cooking* on the family bookshelf and the old bibles of self-improvement—Emily Post's, Dale Carnegie's—replaced by books with titles like *Creative Divorce: A New Opportunity for Personal Growth*. Contemporary marriage and contemporary copulation often seem to be undertaken in the same spirit as psychotherapy or est, TA or TM. They are forms of existential social climbing which have nothing to do with the drab routine of making a life with another person, with compromise, tribulation and boring detail, with fretful children and illness and bills. In Edith Wharton's *The Custom of the Country*, Undine Spragg changes husbands to match her expanding perception of Edwardian society. In *The Serial*, Cyra MacFadden's marvelous epic of Marin County, California, the dim-witted Undines of the 1970s do the same whenever reality falls short of their sexual-spiritual ambitions.

In these crumbling circumstances, old-fashioned infidelity now poses as freedom "to do your own thing," disaffection as a "life-style," collusion as self-fulfillment. What is missing is the sense of loss: *Listen: these are its hooves: it has gone off, like a horse.* To someone like myself, whose twenties coincided with the 1950s, that most private and inward of recent decades, talking to the uncommitted young who pretend not to know about loss and wasted time is like talking a language without grammar: the sense gets through, but not the mood.

As an example, I offer this fragment of party conversation with a young English writer, tall and languid, but handsome in an indeterminate way, with pale hair flopping forward over a pale forehead. His manner was diffident, enervated, but practiced: a kind of wan and cultivated helplessness, like a hothouse orchid, not quite of this world. Whenever I met him I had trouble linking him with what he wrote; it seemed harder, tauter than he did and not at all stupid, whereas socially he seemed to be pushing indolence to the point where it blurred with debility. A question of upbringing, I suppose. He had been to an exclusive school where languidness, carefully nurtured, is a means of survival. He was also currently unemployed. In other words, a representative of a new breed: Harrow and social welfare, strictly of the eighties.

We were talking about books when he said, "I haven't read that but my wife has."

"Your wife?" I had seen him with all sorts of girls, though never more than once with any one of them. "When did you get married?"

That seemed to amuse him. "Five years ago. But why should you know? We never go out together."

"Never?"

He nodded. "You might say, each of us has signed a separate peace."

"You mean divorced?"

"Heavens, no." Languid creases appeared around his mouth, indicating amusement again. "Not even separated. I mean, you can't have a divorce where there isn't a marriage, can you? There has to be some kind of knot before you can cut it."

"Yet you *are* married, technically speaking?"

"Technically speaking, we have a marriage license issued by the Kensington Registry Office. Technically speaking, Lisa uses my last name when it suits her. To sign checks and things. But technically speaking doesn't make a marriage, does it?"

"In the circumstances, why did you ever bother?"

He considered this in silence for a moment, his pale brow wrinkling with the effort. After all, it was a long time ago. "Well . . ." He made an elegant, dismissive movement with his hand. "She just moved in. Nothing particularly romantic, although we quite fancied each other at first. But the reason she moved in was, she had nowhere else to go. She's German, you see, and was over here to learn the language. Her parents had paid for her to do one of those courses at Saint Someone-or-Other's in Hampstead, along with all the poor little rich girls from Rio and Hong Kong. When it was all over they said, 'That's it. No more money. Come on home.' And she didn't want to. So how does a German girl get by in London without a work permit?"

"Au pair?"

He smiled tolerantly. "She isn't exactly the type of girl you could imagine wiping the kids' noses, doing the chores and fending off hubby when the little wife is off at evening classes learning about macramé. Pity you haven't met her. You'd know what I mean; see the irony of it and all."

"So what did she do?"

"Moved in with me. You know the scene: at the end of our

first evening together I said, nervously, 'Come back to my place.'
And she came. And she stayed. I was terribly innocent in those
days. Not a virgin precisely, but all I'd had was whores. So when
this beautiful and intelligent girl moved in, scattering trails of
Kleenex behind her like the Primavera, I was flattered. Flattered and touched. I even liked the Kleenex. The fact is, I'd
never met anyone who used it before, except the whores. All
those nice young English girls I used to dance with at parties
used handkerchiefs. Irish linen handkerchiefs. So even that little
detail added to the fascination, the strangeness of her. Like her
being foreign and clever. She reads a lot, you see, far more than
I do: philosophy, psychology, linguistics. She's full of ideas. No,
I do her wrong. She has a real feeling for ideas, a real understanding. One of God's intellectuals, in a way."

"You make her sound like a paragon."

"Paragons are for poetry. Off the page and in the kitchen is
different. I find"—he peered intently at the bubbles in his glass
—"I find it hard, actually, to let myself go emotionally. If you
know what I mean. But then, so does she. We have that in
common." He peered, sipped, peered again. "Anyway, there she
was: installed. Once the first flush was over, we didn't take much
more notice of each other. Just went on leading our lives as
before. I had my girls—though not whores anymore; she cured
me of that—but she never asked. She had her men, but I never
asked either."

"Weren't either of you ever jealous?"

He looked at me slyly, to see if I was trying to catch him
out. "Absolutely not. That's not an emotion either of us has ever
experienced."

When I did not respond he seemed disappointed. "Anyway,"
he went on, "she was used to that sort of thing. It ran in the
family. Her parents had been the same: leading separate lives
together under the same roof. Mine too, I suppose, though I
never really saw that much of them, what with boarding school
and all. It's one way of rubbing along through life. I think she
rather expected it."

"Why bother to marry then?"

"It meant she could stay in England legally, without any
hassle from the Home Office. Oh, and I forgot: she got pregnant

almost at once. No question of who was the father, I'm afraid.
Not that I would have doubted her word. I mean, why would she
have wanted to lie about something like that?"

"Why wouldn't she?"

He shook his head. "You're missing the point. That's not her
style. She simply doesn't care enough about things to lie about
them."

"I see."

"Do you? I wonder."

"Sharing the same bed and having your sex elsewhere: *that*
I don't see."

"Who said we share the same bed?"

"Don't you?"

He grinned appreciatively. "Good guess." He pushed his
glass at a passing waiter to be refilled, then drank off half of it
immediately. "I suppose it adds to the poignancy of the situation.
And whatever else we lack, no one could deny that what we have
is poignant in its peculiar way."

"If that's what turns you on."

"To each his own. No need to be sniffy."

"Not sniffy, just puzzled. I mean, haven't you ever fallen in
love?"

He ducked his head apologetically. "I wish I could."

"What about her?"

"Not that I know of. Not that she's ever mentioned. Maybe
she wishes the same."

"That's not a separate peace you've signed. It's a nonaggres-
sion pact." Each protecting his own passivity in order to continue
with the half-lives they prefer. Like two cripples with one leg
apiece: together they get on fine.

He seemed obscurely pleased by this. "That's one way of
putting it. Certainly, I'd never want to move out. You see, we
have this beautiful little child. I couldn't let him go. Nor my wife,
come to that. I like her company. As I said, she's much cleverer
than I am. And she cooks for me when she's around. I wouldn't
want to lose all that comfort, would I? As it is, I have the comforts of marriage and the convenience of divorce. Who could ask
for more?"

He smiled his self-deprecating smile, so I smiled back and

changed the subject. What was he doing these days? Meaning, what was he writing? He, however, misunderstood me.

"I had this job in the parcels office at Paddington. But we went on strike, then there was a cutback, so now I'm unemployed. But what with the job and the union and the wife and the child, I qualify for a supplementary benefit. And that does it. It means we can just scrape by. So you see," he added triumphantly, "there *are* advantages in being married. If we'd been divorced, we'd be in all sorts of financial trouble. As it is . . ." He drained his glass and looked around for a waiter.

"What about the writing?"

"Oh, *that*." Again the downward ironic gesture. "I had an idea for a novel about Brazil, where I spent time as a child. But somehow I don't seem able to get down to it. You see, what with the supplementary benefit, there's no need. Maybe if I didn't have it . . ." His voice trailed away. He peered irritably into his empty glass, then looked around again for a waiter. "You don't have a cigarette, do you?"

I shook my head.

"Ah, well . . ." He wandered off across the room to where a very pretty young girl was talking to an elderly man. Both were smoking. "I say"—I saw him flash them his diffident, charming smile—"I wonder if I might possibly scrounge a cigarette off you?"

The girl smiled back at him brilliantly. "Have one of mine," she said before her companion had a chance.

(iii)

KNOWING

Perhaps the separate peace he claimed to have signed was just another fiction, like the ones he could no longer muster energy enough to write down. For all I know, his wife was also an invention, since I have still never seen her or met anyone who has. But whatever the truth, he had judged his act to perfection. I was as shocked as he intended me to be, though not by his passivity. What shocked me was the languid ease with which he dealt himself out of the culture, patronizing emotions which had driven his fellow authors at least since Chaucer's time. Jealousy? Our servants can feel that for us. Or our elders. It was as if I were talking to him about a once deadly and fashionable sickness, like consumption, which modern medicine has done away with. There is no answer to such comprehensive denial.

Yet I do not believe any marriage, however liberated, is immune to jealousy. Even in the most "open" arrangement there is always a payoff: the sadistic pleasure of confessing, the masochistic thrill of forgiving, the devious excitement of being turned on by the thought that one's partner has already been turned on by someone else. No matter how dogged the experiments and rococo the combinations—switching partners, "tripling," four-in-a-bed, or rugger-scrum Sandstone-style orgies—jealousy and guilt are never absent when two married people are unfaithful to each other. They can only be sublimated into a perverse aphrodisiac.

A chic young American would probably dismiss this attitude as a "Freudian hang-up," middle-class and middle-aged, while a genuine Freudian would add that delusional jealousy is a form of paranoia and the primitive intensity of conjugal jealousy is Oedipal in its origins: one marriage echoes another, jealousy of one's partner reawakens the jealousy a child feels for its parents, archaic, based on ignorance and fed by the imagination.

Perhaps this is why the fundamental torment of adult jealousy is not the sense of betrayal but the uncertainty. The jealous are driven by the need, above all, to know: to put a face on the fantasied lover, to fix a time and place for the meetings, to have evidence, witnesses, accomplices in their sickness. Othello cries out to Iago:

> Thou has set me on the rack.
> I swear 'tis better to be much abused
> Than but to know't a little . . .
> I had been happy if the general camp,
> Pioneers and all, had tasted her sweet body,
> So I had nothing known.

Iago counters his demand for "ocular proof" by tossing Desdemona's lost handkerchief in his way, remarking contemptuously,

> Trifles light as air
> Are to the jealous confirmations strong
> As proofs of holy writ.

Proof, in fact, is not the point. All that is needed is a focus on which Othello can concentrate his madness.

For Shakespeare, jealousy was like the Black Death, a deadly sickness which descended without warning out of the clear air. The merest suggestion by Iago is enough to infect Othello mortally. In *The Winter's Tale*, Leontes lacks even an Iago; his frenzy is self-generated:

> Alack, for lesser knowledge! How accursed
> In being so blest! There may be in the cup
> A spider steeped, and one may drink, depart,
> And yet partake no venom; for his knowledge
> Is not infected: but if one present
> Th' abhorred ingredient to his eye, make known
> How he hath drunk, he cracks his gorge, his sides,
> With violent hefts. I have drunk, and seen the spider.

He has seen nothing, imagined everything, and the knowledge he boasts of is delusion. All he knows for certain is his own prurient apprehension which convulses him like the spider in the image, an abomination to be vomited up. He and Othello are vulnerable to jealousy in the same way as hemophiliacs are vulnerable to wounding: the slightest suspicion may be terminal. They are paranoias waiting to be fulfilled.

The jealous batten on imagined proof to protect themselves from the alternatives, craziness and conspiracy. "Jealousy," said Elizabeth Bowen, "is no more than feeling alone among smiling enemies." In a poem called "A Birthday Present," Sylvia Plath wrote a brilliant fugue on this variation on the theme of knowing: the conviction that the whole world is in on a secret from which only she was excluded. "There is this one thing I want today, and only you can give it to me." This birthday present, this one thing she wants, is truth: "Only let down the veil, the veil, the veil." Any knowledge, even death, is better than the fever of uncertainty:

> If it were death
>
> I would admire the deep gravity of it, its timeless eyes.
> I would know you were serious.
>
> There would be a nobility then, there would be a birthday.
> And the knife not carve, but enter
>
> Pure and clean as the cry of a baby,
> And the universe slide from my side.

For the jealous, the only peace is in knowing, even in knowing the worst.

Sylvia Plath had an uncanny gift for writing out of the eye of the storm, using her poetry to create a point of calm in the turmoil of the last months of her life. Had she lived longer, perhaps she might have attained the more worldly detachment of Colette, who looked back on the jealousy she had once called "a sojourn in hell" and found her claims grossly exaggerated. The jealous, she suggested, profit from their sickness by transforming their debilitating curiosity into a physical discipline:

> It is a kind of gymnast's purgatory, where the senses are trained, one by one . . . The sense of hearing becomes refined, one acquires visual virtuosity, a rapid and hushed step, a sense of smell that can capture the particles deposited in the atmosphere by a head of hair, a scented powder, the passage of a brazenly happy person—all this strongly recalls the field exercises of the soldier or the hypersensitive skill of poachers. A body absolutely on the alert becomes weightless, moves with somnambulistic ease, rarely collapses and falls.

For Colette in middle age, jealousy was no longer a sickness; it was just another aspect of the manifold sensuality of which, in *The Pure and the Impure*, she was a connoisseur. Whence her leisurely attitude toward it, her ability to savor it for the special pleasures it can yield: "All the rest is, according to one's character, as boring as any solitary sport, as immoral as a game of chance." The triumph of the sensualist is to derive pleasure even from one's own afflictions. That young English writer might have

appreciated Colette's irony, but he would not properly have
understood the concentration of thought and feeling required to
transform his style of denial into her style of wisdom.

Without those saving strategies, one is stuck with the thing
itself, that unique combination of revulsion and fascination, of
the need to know with the fear of knowing.

> O curse of marriage,
> That we can call these delicate creatures ours,
> And not their appetites!

But at least Othello had tragedy and poetry to dignify his agony.
A modern instance like Max, thirty-two years old and assistant
sales manager in the London branch of a multinational engineering company, has to take his consolations where he can find
them:

"What do I remember best?" he said. "The afternoons, I
suppose. Those bloody awful afternoons immediately after the
separation when I used to collect my small daughter from school.
The lawyers had agreed I could do it twice a week because the
child and I were very close. Thank you very much."

He ran his fingers through his short, thick hair and eyed me
truculently. He was at the critical stage of drunkenness, between not caring and caring too much. Drunk enough to talk
easily, almost eloquently, but also drunk to the point where the
next sip might make him maudlin.

"Anyway," I said.

"Anyway." He took the next sip. "She used to come running
down the walled passage from the school door to the street, then
launch herself full-tilt, arms outstretched like wings, from the
top of the three stone steps straight into my arms. Out of breath
and excited."

Another pause, another sip of whiskey.

"It was one of those fine, dry Octobers which are the English
substitute for summer: the air gold as the leaves, the grass losing
its color, the shadows lengthening sooner. I used to take her off
to Regent's Park so she could let off steam after being cooped up

all day in a dusty classroom. She'd dash around like a puppy let off the lead, play hide-and-seek, chase the ducks, roll me on the grass and bounce on my chest until I cried, 'Pax.' The same old schoolkid language, just like when I was a boy. For both of us it was a proof that we were still together, despite appearances. It was also, for both of us, enough to break our hearts, since we knew it was all a lie. You see, I . . ."

All I saw was, he was about to drift off. So I interrupted in a brisk, matter-of-fact voice: "It could have been worse. The lawyers could have made it once a month, not twice a week."

He looked at me with distaste, then took another drink. "You're missing the point. What made it a lie wasn't the separation but the silences. Like the silences in the last year of my marriage. You see, this bouncy, slightly desperate child could answer all the questions that had been eating me up: Who was he? What did he look like? But of course I couldn't ask her. She already had too much to contend with. That's the point."

"I see."

"Do you?" He shrugged, then drifted off again, talking to himself, as if he had forgotten all about me. "Odd that one should know so much about somebody and yet know nothing at all. I'd learned to recognize the scent of his lemony after-shave in my wife's hair. Likewise the smell of excitement he aroused in her: the damp female smell, like mushrooms. Sometimes, when she undressed at night, I imagined I could trace the marks his hands had left on her breasts and on the smooth curve between her waist and hips. I'd lie there and imagine him slowly laying claim to her. Just make-believe, of course, make-believe and sickness. What I really saw was my own desire for her rotting down to a kind of fetid, rank-smelling compost in which any dottiness could grow. Once, however, when we took the child swimming, I did notice a small bite mark on the inside of her left thigh. It was half-hidden and discreet, as though made by a fastidious mouth. Yet I had no idea what he looked like.

"For months, in fact, I had no proof he even existed except for the vague new scents I smelled on her, which I concentrated on like a gundog. Then the firm sent me to Frankfurt for a sales conference that dragged on for a whole week and when I got back her eyes were shining, her skin was clear, her whole body was somehow richer—you know, as if it were slightly swollen with lovemaking.

"It was a sticky September afternoon and the plane was packed with businessmen like myself, getting back into the fight after the summer break. Then I had to sit sweating in the rush hour all the way in from Heathrow. When I got home I stripped off and went into the bathroom, taking my dirty clothes with me. While the shower ran, I opened the laundry basket to deposit my things. On top was one of my daughter's tee shirts with a dribble of caked egg down its front, and under that were sheets. But this was Friday and, according to the usual routine, the beds were changed on Mondays. I stared into the wicker basket and the thumping of my heart seemed louder than the shower. Then I pulled out the sheets. There were wide pale stains all over one of them; at the center of each stain a stiff, yellowish core. I had a sudden, sharp image of unimaginable pleasures and my wife laboring towards them with her knees raised."

He was a large blunt man with a beery complexion, but for a moment he sat so still that he seemed to shrink slightly, as though the vision of what he had lost, or never had, had diminished him irredeemably.

Finally, he went on, "That was it, of course. I left the next day."

"Did you say why?"

"How could I? You don't tell a woman who already despises you that you've been examining the sheets she slept in, like a child looking for evidence of its parents copulating. I mean, it's not done, is it?" He sat still again while he considered the depths of his past humiliations. "Anyway, it wasn't necessary. She was so glad to see the back of me she even forgot to ask why I was going."

He giggled suddenly, like a naughty schoolboy, then was silent.

"Well?"

"Well, I still don't know which hurt most: the proof of all that ecstasy or the simple fact I couldn't put a face on the lucky man."

"But your daughter knew."

He nodded. "And I couldn't ask her. Oddly enough, I was

with her when I got my answer. It was the end of one of those
exhausting afternoons. We'd played hide-and-seek, we'd played
grandmother's footsteps, I'd pushed her on the swings and
rowed her on the lake. Then just short of home we stopped at a
tea shop for a bite to eat. It was one of those olde worlde places
with steps up to the entrance. The first thing I saw when I
opened the door was my wife sitting with him at a table directly
in front of me, staring at me petrified, as if I were a ghost. That
was the first glimpse I had of him: a long thin back and her
widened eyes. He was yattering away with great animation.
When he moved his head I saw a fragment of an attenuated
Mervyn Peake profile, straight out of *Gormenghast*, all nose and
chin and no lips, with a wiry mop of hair, the color of dirty sand.
He was rattling away nineteen to the dozen, not looking at her.
Which was just as well since she was pale as death. The two of
us stared at each other a moment, both frozen, like a movie still.
Then she gave a tiny, almost imperceptible shake of her head. I
turned and went out, closing the door behind me before my
daughter could see.

" 'It's full,' I told her. 'Let's go somewhere else.'

"It was all over so fast that later I wasn't even sure it had
happened. But gradually I realized I had all I needed: a profile,
a slope of the shoulders, a rather anxious voice. Poor bastard, I
thought, how's he going to cope with her?

"After that it was all right. More or less. I was at peace at
last. When they married I even went to John Lewis and bought
them a present: one of those Cafetière machines she'd always
hankered after but never got around to buying. And it wasn't
hypocrisy. I really wished them well. It was the not knowing
that almost killed me."

IX

Appearances

"Technology," wrote Elizabeth Hardwick, "annihilates conse-quence." She was speaking of contraception, but in less special-ized ways technology has also played havoc with the traditional roles of husband and wife:

> Industrialization . . . has transformed the functions of marriage and family life. Basically, the wife used to be the producer of goods (bread, cheese, clothing), the performer of essential services (edu-cating the young, ironing shirts, nursing the old and ill); the hus-band was the provider of food or money, the defender—and ruler —of his wife and children.
>
> But factories, transportation, schools, hospitals, and modern merchandising changed all that. Man and woman no longer need marriage in order to survive, and marriage has ceased to be basi-cally practical and productive but has become instead a special kind of friendship. When it fails to provide us with companionship, sex, and the satisfaction of our individual emotional needs, we are deeply dissatisfied—no matter how many goods and services the spouse provides.

Thus Morton and Bernice Hunt in *The Divorce Experience*. They approve of the change, perhaps because they subscribe to the vaguely psychotherapeutic belief in self-fulfillment as an ultimate good and divorce as an opportunity for what another seize-the-day writer on the topic calls "personal growth." But there is a difference, often overlooked in the polemics of divorce, between the reasonable expectation of happiness and old-fashioned selfishness. When the Hunts talk of marriage as "a special kind of friendship" they are implying what is both best and worst in contemporary attitudes to the institution: best is the rejection of marriage as a prison walled in by religion and society, with death as the only way out; worst is the idea that it is *merely* a friendship, based on casual choice, subject to casual change. This misses the point of friendship as well as marriage, since both, if they are serious, depend on loyalty and endurance. "The mutual conquest of difficulties," wrote the polar explorer Apsley Cherry-Garrard, "is the cement of friendship as it is the only lasting cement of marriage."

But in the high emotional run-up to marriage—particularly young marriage—when you are gasping like a landed fish with love, the notion of friendship seems absurd, faintly insulting. Friendship is for the elderly, a poor second best for those who have given up, while love is the uncompromising thing itself, pure and purifying. The besotted young have no trouble understanding what Crashaw, in another context, meant by "Love, thou art absolute, sole Lord / Of life and death," but they are confused by tenderness, by the moment, for example, in Jan Troell's *The Emigrants* when the inarticulate Swedish farmer tries to tell his wife he loves her and can only come up with "We are the best of friends." Yet "We are the best of friends" is no less a declaration of love than "Oh, my oblivion is a very Antony, / And I am all forgotten," and it takes into account a truth which Cleopatra, like all the other famous doomed lovers, did not need to concern herself with: no marriage will survive unless you believe your partner, in the end, is on your side and wishes you well.

In the end. But marriage brings out the worst in people as relentlessly as it brings out the best, and small dissatisfactions accumulate grain by grain until even friendship is smothered

under the drift. Anna Karenina hated her husband for his coldness and she also hated him for the way he cracked his finger
joints; Tolstoy reserves judgment as to which idiosyncrasy drove
her into the arms of Vronsky. When people are in love, any
outrage is acceptable because the whole is worth more than the
parts. But when love wears out, the smallest quirks of character
and physical tics are transformed by the terrible intimacy of
married life into intolerable deformations.

How else to explain those otherwise incomprehensible divorces between couples who have stuck it out together for
twenty or thirty years, then suddenly split up when they seem
too old and exhausted to start again? John Berryman put it this
way in one of his short stories:

> I gathered she "left" him—that is, kicked him out, as he more or
> less forced her to. In short, a usual case. Why people divorce each
> other is their own business, inscrutable. They seldom, in my ex-
> perience, know why themselves—know what was most important,
> I mean, along the camps of the Everest of dissatisfactions nearly
> every human being feels with any other human being he knows
> inside out. Maybe nothing is more important. It's the mountain,
> and you must get too weary to climb on.

Harriet and Jake were like that. Both had the grace not to
offer the obvious excuse—"We only stayed together for the children's sake"—because they knew no one would have believed
them. They were the glamorous couple in the lives of all their
friends and they seemed to have everything the rest of us fumbled after: beauty, brains, charm, humor, endurance. With all
that on their side, it goes without saying they were complicated
people, so we admired them because they had decided to make a
go of it, and then were appalled when they went the way of
everyone else. If they could divorce, no one was safe.

The experts say that the couples most vulnerable to disaster
are always those who appear to be most ideally matched, as
though all that perfection in other people's eyes were too heavy
a load to carry. Harriet and Jake, however, carried theirs for
twenty-four years, a whole generation. They seemed to find one
another interesting, were easy enough to make jokes about each

other without malice and in public, and even went on dancing together long after their contemporaries had given up. To throw all that away at fifty seemed pointless and perverse.

They offered no explanations at the time, although later, after they were both remarried, I got the outline of the story bit by bit: he felt he was drowning, she felt eliminated. "In short, a usual case," as Berryman says, although no less puzzling for that. I think now that what happened was they set up a pattern right at the start and the pattern took over. They established roles and were unable to get out of them.

It seems he had black moods which descended irregularly and without warning, like epileptic fits: not ill-temper or sulkiness or depression such as everyone is prone to, but day after day of pure blackness, blotting out everything—her and the children, his work and hers, their social life, their sex life. "It was like a black hole in deep space," she said. "Everything got sucked in." If she tried asking him what was wrong, he walked out of the house. She should have stopped him the first time that happened, but she didn't and it set a precedent.

She didn't for two reasons. First, she was used to it. Her father had been perpetually gloomy and silent, a severe Bradford businessman who divorced her mother when Harriet was sixteen but continued to pay out dourly for his errors, even after Harriet and her sister had left home. He gave her money in a loveless way and always seemed disapproving and disappointed, whatever efforts she made. Second, Jake at that time was an artist, so she gave him the benefit of the doubt. Perhaps that blackness was where the paintings came from.

The paintings themselves were tiny, Klee-like things, obsessional but exquisitely controlled, every detail locked into place as though by unanswerable logic. But he didn't paint much, worked slowly when he did and spent long hours at hobbies into which he could channel his rage for perfection. For example, he spent weeks stripping down the engine and suspension of their old Mini, not because he drove fast—she was more dashing at the wheel and, on the rare occasions when they went out together, she drove—but because he loved the idea of having, hidden away under the hood of their shabby little wagon, a perfect piece of machinery, polished, tuned, spotless. Since he found it hard to prosper as a painter, he used this hobby to tide him over the lean periods and finished up working four days a week modifying sports cars in a specialist garage.

By then both their children were in nursery school and Harriet was working again as a publisher's editor. So she told him the garage job wasn't necessary, they could get by on her salary and the blood money her father was still paying. "I prefer it this way," he answered. "At least I don't have to talk to other painters."

She, too, preferred it since his black moods seemed rarer when he wasn't painting, and without them they lived more or less as their friends imagined: affectionately and with humor, enjoying each other's company. If he was often out, coming and going without explanation, that was not only because his moods had established in her the habit of never questioning him but because she also kept herself to herself. She believed in privacy and was careful to allow her children, as well as Jake, free air in which to move about without intrusion. That, too, was part of her attractiveness.

One evening he came back from the garage with a face as black as thunder, ate his meal in silence, then announced casually, "I've sold the Mini. Bought an old Rover in its place. Boring as hell, but they never go wrong." Then he got up without another word and went upstairs. The Rover was parked outside, slab-sided and gray, solid as an old battleship. He was right: boring as hell. She felt let down. When she went back inside he was staggering down the stairs with a load of old copies of *Autosport* and *Motor Sport* which he dumped in the garbage. Then he settled down in his armchair with *Hi-Fi News*, *Wireless World* and *Popular Hi-Fi* and did not speak to her for the rest of the evening.

He taught himself the intricacies of hi-fi as he had taught himself about motor engines: meticulously, obsessionally and with remarkable speed. He bought some secondhand equipment, was dissatisfied and began to experiment with his own modifications. He spent so much time at the local hi-fi shop discussing technicalities with the engineers that in the end he was offered a job. He accepted without consulting her and once again she felt let down.

But the job went well. His charm and know-how brought in

the enthusiasts and the shop began to market his modifications. Finally, he designed and built an amplifier which would take him nearer to that ideal of perfection he had always been after—in his paintings, in his car and now in the technology of sound. A pundit from one of the trade magazines listened and was impressed, the owner of the shop found a backer and Jake became a manufacturer. On a very small scale: just him and two young men as obsessional as he was, in a couple of rented garages in Kenton. But they sold as much as they could build and at least he had a reputation among the cognoscenti—more, he remarked, than had happened to him when he was painting.

By then he had given up painting altogether, although the moods did not go away. When Harriet nerved herself to ask the family doctor about them he listened to her at length, tapping the side of his square head judiciously with a pencil, like a sculptor testing a block of marble. He appeared not to like what he heard. But "No," he answered, "if he sleeps, eats and works, these aren't psychotic episodes." Psychotic episodes. After that, she watched Jake with renewed interest and wondered what was filling the silence in his skull: slew factors, mains ripple and diodes, or just blackness? Neither alternative seemed to fit his long, intelligent face and witty mouth. Then the moods passed, he was as amusing and attractive as before, and they went back out into the world again to see their friends. Marriage, she concluded, was no remedy for isolation, and she left it at that.

One afternoon she came home from the office and found a bonfire blazing in the middle of their ragged garden, Jake standing in front of it, legs astride, arms crossed, oblivious to the children who danced and whooped around the fire, pretending to be Red Indians.

"What's all this?" she asked.

"Folly and conceit." He did not look at her. "Youth. I'm burning my pictures."

"Oh." She stared at the flames and tears began to ooze down her stiff face.

"I'm too old for such foolishness," he said.

"It's *our* youth, not yours alone."

He turned and looked at her with distaste. "Why are you crying? They're my pictures."

"It's the smoke," she said and went back inside.

After that, their marriage began to slide. She was used to his being hardly ever at home, but now the quality of his absences changed. When he returned late at night there was a charge and tension about him which did not include her. He no longer reacted to her moods and he talked to the children as though by long-distance telephone. She was certain he was sleeping around, but he was too sharp and controlled to let anything slip and their noninterference pact prevented her asking him. Whenever she tried, he did not even bother to answer.

The one clue which made her certain he was having affairs was his sudden, overbearing jealousy of her. She was a woman whom age does not spoil: tall, strong-boned, alert, with a mane of black hair, a clear English complexion and a certain Yorkshire forthrightness which drew men to her without any effort on her part. Now she could scarcely smile at another man without Jake accusing her afterward of infidelity. It was the only time he noticed her. In the end, to spare the pointless scenes, she made herself cold and aloof with everybody. Anything for a quiet life. Her admirers dropped away and Jake became the life and soul of the party.

They continued to make love, but the quality of that changed, like the quality of his absences. Since they were now middle-aged and experienced, they were able to obtain the expected satisfactions, but mechanically and without tenderness, because this was something they knew how to do together. No amount of expertise could disguise from her that his mind was elsewhere and her body a distraction from whatever it was he was focused on. It reminded her of his technician's way of listening to his continually changing audio equipment: as if the music somehow got in the way of the purity of the hi-fi. Even while he was making love to her, she felt eaten up with jealousy of the women who engaged his full attention. Afterward, she felt more isolated than before and often dreamed she found him with another girl, always a friend of hers. Then she would wake desolated because he had left her. But that, too, she kept to herself, knowing that if she tried to talk to him about it, he would make her feel stupid. A gift he shared with her father.

One evening they went to one of those parties where the hosts say, "Bring the children," and when you get there you realize the children aren't children any longer. The room was filled with young men and women with fresh skin and clear eyes who danced together as if they could go on all night, inventively and with a litheness which put their elders so much to shame that none of them dared join in. Harriet and Jake sat on the sidelines along with the other parents, drinking, gossiping, old friends together. Occasionally, she glanced over at the young people moving raptly to their awful music, and when she looked away again the familiar faces around her seemed more ugly: cheeks lined and baggy, thin hair gone gray, bad breath, blood-shot eyes. "Mirror, mirror, on the wall . . ." She knew how Snow White's stepmother had felt.

Late in the evening a friend took Harriet aside and told her, whispering, she had seen Jake in Chez Victor, holding hands across the table with a young unmarried woman they all knew. "Never took his eyes off her," said the friend. "That's how I saw him before he saw me."

She and Harriet were sitting on the staircase. Rock music boomed in the room below. On the next flight up a young couple were locked together like sky divers with a single parachute. The friend's face was solemn, her eyes large with concern, although she seemed to be enjoying herself.

"I know all about that," said Harriet dismissively. "Boys will be boys, even in their forties."

She was surprised by her own fluency and calm. Perhaps it was because she finally had a face to match her fantasies. She was also surprised that the friend let it go there and seemed satisfied.

But when they got home at two in the morning she was neither fluent nor calm. Unlike Jake who merely shrugged: "Take it or leave it."

As usual, she felt at a disadvantage, so she tried again, this time humbly: "Why bother?"

He rounded on her indignantly: "You're drowning me. You and your bloody forbearance."

She had no answer to that. One man's reality is another man's dream world, but where did that leave her?

So she, too, began to take lovers, but discreetly and not from among their friends; younger men mostly, in the hope that some of their youth might rub off on her. After a lifetime of fidelity, the secretiveness excited her. She arranged elaborate alibis for her absences and made sure of having bits of proof to leave around when she returned: the stub of a movie ticket, an art-gallery catalog, something inexpensive in a Fenwick's shopping bag. If she went off for a weekend, she typed elaborate conference memos to herself on office paper. Since Jake no longer asked her, she displayed these tokens of innocence to her uninterested teenage children, hoping they would mention them to their father. But the secretiveness excited her more than the sex. After twenty years with one man, she found everyone else inept, even the gentlest. At first, it was enough that they were different, but that stimulant did not last. Her heart wasn't in it and she seemed to view her lovers from a long way off. When they fell in love with her she was vaguely pleased, mildly flattered, but all she could feel in return was a distant maternal fondness. She also worried about what her father would think, although it was years since they had seen each other.

As for Jake: his public charm and cleverness were his means of keeping the world at bay, so she assumed his liaisons were as loveless as hers and he remained, in his way, as loyal to her as he was to anyone—loyal but shut off, loyal to his own inadequacies—and dependent on her being there to run the household, keep an eye on the children and bring in a salary. After the night of the party, both silently accepted that they would live their own lives while remaining together for convenience' sake, out of habit and apathy. What really held them together was jealousy, but it was hard for two intelligent, middle-aged people to admit that the lovers they pretended to make so much of were all they now had in common. Mutual infidelity was shaming enough. To acknowledge that they needed it in order to stay married would have been more humiliation than they could reasonably bear.

And not strictly true. For two middle-aged working parents, falling in love is a windfall, like a spare tenner bet on an outsider who goes on to win the big race. Nice when it happens, but don't rely on it. Meanwhile, Harriet and Jake remained attracted to each other and made love regularly enough, often with relish now there were fewer pretenses. And when Jake wasn't off in one of his black holes they also—after a lifetime's practice

—enjoyed each other's company. Most important, they kept up appearances and so remained, to outsiders, a rather glamorous couple, she with her youthful figure, energy and vivid clothes, he subtle and quick as a knife. While their friends' marriages disintegrated around them, theirs went on for better or for worse. But after two decades, nobody questioned too closely just what was entailed by "worse." Survival was more than enough. And habit: neither could imagine a life which did not include the other.

The years passed, the children left home, Jake designed a preamp to go with his amplifier, then a head amp to match them both. He moved out of the garages in Kenton into a small unit on an industrial estate in Tottenham. He went to Japan to discuss the possibility of building a moving-coil cartridge to his own impossible specifications. Two or three times a year he flew to the States to attend audio exhibitions and confer with the dealers who handled his equipment, although he never asked Harriet to go with him. Not that she could have spared time from her own work. She was now a senior editor at a sedate publishing house that specialized in philosophy and psychology; her name was on the company notepaper, and she could have told the family doctor a technical thing or two about psychotic episodes.

Their compact—about privacy and keeping up appearances —would probably have lasted them out if it had not been for the day on the Thames. Denis and Dolly, their closest friends and their only contemporaries whose marriage had not foundered, had invited them for a Sunday on their rented motor cruiser. But when Sunday came Jake had already vanished down one of his black holes. "I'll go alone," said Harriet. "The hell you will," he answered, and that was all he said until they got to the river and he started drinking.

From Henley to Sonning the Thames was like Regent's Street at rush hour. Motor cruisers paraded up and down, their roofs and decks strewn with sunbathers. At every lock little day boats jostled each other, children tugging importantly at the painters while their fathers barked orders and their grandparents sat uncomfortably in the stern, blinking at the sunshine. Young men in rowing boats displayed their muscles to their girlfriends, who giggled and pulled the wrong rudder-lines. The banks were lined with fishermen and picnicking families. At Sonning both the pubs were packed.

But above the lock the crowds thinned out and a cool wind blew down the long ugly reach to Reading. They chugged past the sheds of the Reading Working Men's Boat Club and the Reading Tradesmen's Boat Club to the gasworks at the mouth of the River Kennet, then turned around, chugged back and moored at a little island below Sonning Hill. As they passed the Working Men's Boat Club a second time, Jake said, "Forget the fucking thatch and the flowers. There's the real England: class distinctions and industrial blight." He was into his fourth whiskey by then and nobody bothered to answer.

He was finishing his fifth by the time the rest of them had swum and dried and spread out the picnic lunch in the cockpit. When Harriet handed him a plate of food he stared at it, head cocked, and asked in a puzzled voice, "What's this for?" Nobody laughed.

"I've got coffee in the thermos," said Dolly.

Jake shook his head. "I'm sticking to mother's milk." He tipped more whiskey into his glass.

While the others ate and chatted, he leaned back against the plastic cushions and conducted their conversation with the leg of a chicken. They took no notice of him.

"I was in Tesco the other day . . ." Harriet was saying.

"Do me a favor." Jake leaned forward and tapped her on the shoulder with his drumstick. "Not another diatribe on the price of margarine." Then he turned to Denis and said, "Did I ever tell you about Nancy, the girl with nipples like honey?"

Denis went on eating.

"How about Sue and Sandra and Lucy?"

Denis sighed and wiped his mouth carefully on a paper napkin. "Time to go," he said.

"We haven't finished eating," said Dolly.

"We can finish as we go."

"What about Linda?" Jake continued. "Surely I've told you about Linda, the love of my life in New York?"

"Can I help?" Harriet asked Denis.

"Let her," said Jake. "You'd be astonished how helpful she can be. Or maybe you already know."

"You're drunk," said Denis wearily.

"No more than is strictly necessary."

Denis started the engine and held the boat into the bank while Harriet clambered ashore to untie. Then he reversed slowly away from the island, swung the bows around and headed back toward Sonning Lock, letting the current take them, the engine almost idling.

Jake wagged the chicken leg at him. "My son, the navigator. What have you done to him, Dolly?"

"Eat something," Dolly answered. "It'll make you feel better."

"I feel fine."

A cruiser went past, a gray-bearded man at the wheel. Three people were asleep on the cabin roof, two more on the forward deck. Jake jabbed the drumstick in its direction. "The Ancient Mariner and his ghost crew." He picked up the whiskey bottle in his free hand and sang out, " 'Water, water, everywhere, / Nor any drop to drink.' " He took a swig at the bottle. " 'Nor any,' " he repeated. "I like that old-fashioned circumlocution. It goes with my old-fashioned wife."

"Dolly's right," said Denis. "Have some coffee, for God's sake."

Jake pushed his plate of food away. "You sure I never told you about Linda? Lovely legs—straight up to her tits."

Harriet picked up her plate, climbed out of the cockpit and went to the bows. She sat staring at the muddy little waves and the impassive fishermen on the bank. A moment later Dolly sat down beside her. "Take no notice. He's drunk." She put her arm around Harriet's shoulders. "Don't let him get to you. Not after all this time."

Harriet straightened her back. "May he rot in hell," she said.

Then they sat in silence while Jake continued his litany of girls. "Remember Tamsin?" he was saying. "You met her once at the Terrazza. Tamsin at the Terrazza. Tamsin of the tiny tits."

"Insulting," said Dolly.

Harriet looked at her friend's worried face and thought, She's putting on weight; she should do something about it. Aloud she said, "His whole life with me has been one long calculated insult."

When they reached Sonning Lock, Harriet went back to the

cockpit. "I'm going," she announced and dressed hurriedly while they waited for the gates to open. Then the boat slid forward into the lock and she stepped ashore. "I'll get a taxi to Henley and pick up the car." She tilted her head at Jake who was glaring at her sullenly. "You can drive him back, Denis. Or put him on a train."

The downriver gates inched apart and the boat sank sedately out of sight.

When Jake wandered in after midnight Harriet was already asleep. She sat up in bed and eyed him with distaste as he swayed in the doorway. "You know what the man said?" He grinned foolishly. "Being married means never having to say you're sorry. Or is it the other way around? Being sorry . . ."

"Sleep in the spare room," she said, "and turn that bloody light out."

Abruptly the room was in darkness again. He slammed the door.

As she drifted back to sleep, it occurred to her that this was the first time in their life together he had ever even started to apologize.

He was still asleep when she left for work the next morning and when he arrived home that night his face was shut as a gravestone. He went straight out into the kitchen, made himself a sandwich, then carried it into the sitting room and turned on the hi-fi. She put down her book and looked at him, waiting for a word. But he did not speak.

"Well?" she said finally.

He bit into his sandwich, then listened a moment, head to one side, mouth tight. "The treble's a bit bright." He went over to the bank of shimmering equipment and began to fiddle with the knobs.

Harriet went upstairs. I've swallowed my last insult, she thought; this time he must make the first move.

He slept in the spare room again that night, then the next and the next, all through the week. Neither of them said a word.

When she came in from shopping on Saturday morning he was sitting in the kitchen, drinking coffee and reading *The Times*. She dumped her shopping bags on the other end of the table and started to unpack them. He watched her while she moved busily about the room, then said, "I might as well move out."

She picked up a carton of eggs and began to transfer them to the rack on the refrigerator door. "Good idea," she answered, without looking at him. She walked over to the sink and dropped the carton in the rubbish bin. Then she turned to him. He was watching her carefully, his expression alert and tense, as though he were auditioning a new piece of equipment. She wondered when she had last merited such concentration.

"I'm going to need a few days to find a room."

"Take your time."

And that was all she said.

It was two weeks before he found a place to live and during that time they scarcely spoke. He seemed dismayed that she did not give in and say, "Don't go. Not after all these years." But it was also impossible for him to break the habit of a lifetime. To apologize now would tilt the balance of power irredeemably in her favor; he would drown without trace. So he watched and waited, certain she would relent even at the last moment when the trunk of his car was stuffed with electronic gear and his suitcases were packed and waiting in the hall.

"Good-bye," he said and kissed her on the cheek.

She did not respond. She felt like a weight lifter concentrating herself for an Olympic effort.

He picked up the suitcases and shuffled down the path. She watched him go, thinking, Soon he'll be an old man.

"Good luck," she called and closed the front door. Then she went up to the bedroom, opened her address book and telephoned all her boyfriends, current and past.

My real life is the one I don't lead. She remembered the line from a story in *The New Yorker*. Well, now was her chance. There was no one to put her down and she couldn't get over the sense of relief. She could tune her old Japanese transistor radio to a pop station and there would be no Jake to say, "How can you listen *to* that *through* that? You're like the ads in the trade papers: 'Garbage in, garbage out.' " And she would switch off obediently, ashamed of her bad taste and her bad ear. Her unapproachable father had brought her up to believe that her instinctive preferences were not worth much and those who disapproved of them knew better, were better. But her father was out of touch, her husband gone. It's been a lifetime, she thought, forty-six years. I must use what's left. *My real life is the one I don't lead.*

But the men she saw did not seem to notice either her age or her inadequacies. They flattered her, bought her dinners at expensive restaurants and treated her tenderly in bed. In her surprise she seemed to shed years: her eyes cleared, her face filled out, her body regained some of its suppleness. When she went to parties she danced with the exclusive young and did not feel self-conscious.

"You're behaving like a teenager," said Dolly disapprovingly.

"High time, too," she answered. "Our kids were encouraged to have their adolescence while they were adolescent. We missed it. When I stand for Parliament there's only going to be one plank in my platform: a law forbidding marriage before the age of thirty."

"You'd have chances," said Dolly. "Have you worked out the details?"

"Everything. You'd buy the marriage license at the post office, like all the other licenses. Renewable every two years by mutual consent. That would keep everyone on their best behavior. And each year the marriage lasted beyond the first two, you'd get a bonus: a tax rebate payable to the wife, so she could splurge on a new coat or a holiday alone. It would give us something to look forward to. After all, we're the ones who keep it all going."

"All the same, it's hard on your children," said Dolly enviously.

One evening Harriet stopped at Denis and Dolly's house on her way back from work and found Jake there, gloomily drinking. She kissed him on the cheek, just as she kissed Denis and Dolly, and asked him how he was, what he was doing. He shrugged: "You win a few, you lose a few." But he looked at her oddly and for the half hour she stayed his eyes never left her, although their expression slowly changed from astonishment to irritation to wistfulness. She realized he was still waiting for her to make a gesture. He feels sorry for himself, he wants me back, she thought, and was filled with unreasoning hilarity. When she left she kissed him again cheerfully, out of the goodness of her heart, as though she were giving money to Oxfam.

Jake was outraged. But when he got back to his bachelor room later that evening the young lady who was sharing his life that week was no consolation. He lay awake for a long time, watching the shadows run on the ceiling, and the next morning startled the girl by announcing that, since it wasn't working out, maybe she had better leave. "I didn't know it wasn't working out," she answered, "but don't worry, I'm leaving."

He began dropping in on Harriet, sometimes announced, sometimes not. It was like the long courtship they had not had time for in their youth. He lounged in his usual armchair and kept up his usual wry commentary on friends and business and politics. But all the time he was watching her and she knew he was waiting for a sign, for a weakness. She also knew he was as bored as she was by the new company each of them was keeping: her well-meaning boyfriends, his tinny young girls. They had only to reach out. But she refused to make the first move and, although he now wanted to, he didn't know how. He could only come back on the same terms, yielding nothing.

Her mother died in June and within a month her father had followed her. Harriet assumed grief had nothing to do with it, since they had scarcely spoken for thirty years. He must have wanted to outlast her to prove a point, and then there was no further reason to drag on. He left his daughters a cunningly selected portfolio of sound investments and a big house in Bradford, which they sold. Even after death duties, there was enough for her to get by on without working. She had had no idea he was so wealthy. She would have liked to thank him and explain how sorry she was to have let him down. Yet at the funeral all she felt was relief.

The next time Jake telephoned to invite himself around, she cut him off in midsentence. "There's no point," she said. "I want a divorce."

There was a long silence. Then he did an accent: "Now you tell me."

"I'm not joking. I'm going to see my lawyer tomorrow." It had not occurred to her before, but now it seemed logical.

Another silence. "OK." He kept up the accent. "Whatever you say, boss. I'll see mine."

"Fine," she said and rang off.

The divorce went through quickly and without fuss. Harriet was now better off than Jake and there was no child maintenance to quarrel over. She bought out Jake's share of their house with money from the sale of the mausoleum in Bradford. One house for another; the symmetry pleased her. So did the fact that Jake bought himself an apartment at the other end of London with the proceeds. She felt vaguely responsible for him and even fonder than before. But it was the same fondness she felt for her grown-up children now they had gone off into the world: full of history and regrets, but distant.

After that, they saw more of each other, not less. Friends noticed them talking amicably together at parties and began to invite them to dinner as a couple, although the invitations were separate. Over the years Jake's irony had rubbed off on her and now she seemed witty as well as freer and more assured, while he, no longer able to use her as a victim, was alert and affectionate. The friends made jokes to them about the way they had exchanged roles, then took each of them aside: "This is nonsense. Why don't you two get together again?"

Harriet used to reply, "Perhaps we will. In our old age."

She even believed it. Having already spent most of a lifetime together, it seemed unnatural not to finish what they had begun. But on equal terms. Meanwhile, there was this interim while each of them belatedly made up for what they had missed by marrying young. That also seemed natural in this liberated age.

Then Jake went off on an extended trip to America and Japan, and Harriet settled down four nights a week with a sad, comfortable man, a little older than herself, who spent the other three nights with an invalid wife in the country. Harriet knew the wife had been too ill for too long for him ever to leave her and liked him for that.

One Saturday morning Jake telephoned.

"You're back." Despite herself, she heard her voice quickening. "How was the trip?"

"The trip was fine. You'd be surprised how keen the dealers are on our stuff."

"Why should I be?" It irritated her to feel so pleased to hear his voice again.

"How's it with you?"

"Also fine. I've shed my winter coat, taken off ten pounds." I'm flirting with him, she thought.

There was a long pause. Then Jake said, "I've got something to tell you." Another pause. But she knew what was coming. We're still married, she thought.

"I'm married," said Jake.

"Hang on," she said. "The milk's about to boil over."

In the kitchen she peeled off a piece of paper towel and blew her nose loudly. Then she went back to the telephone. "Who's the lucky girl?"

"Linda. A girl I know from New York."

The one with legs up to her tits. "Your old flame," she said.

He managed a laugh. "Not so old."

"I hope you'll be very happy."

Jake cleared his throat. "Look, Harriet, there's no need for us . . ."

"I know."

"Will you come and have dinner with us when we've got this place sorted out? We'll ask Denis and Dolly." When she did not reply he added anxiously, "You will come, won't you?"

"Of course. When you're sorted out." She wanted to ask, Does she look after you? Instead, she said, "I've got to go now. The milkman's at the door. You know what Saturdays are like."

After he hung up she took the telephone off the hook, put on her oldest jeans and began sweeping and polishing vehemently, as if her well-ordered house had not been cleaned for months. She rearranged the furniture in the sitting room, rolled up a rug she had never liked and dumped it upstairs in her son's old bedroom. At the back of her son's wardrobe she found a picture of her Jake had painted when they were first married. The only portrait he had ever tried. He had missed it when he lit his bonfire. She took it downstairs and hung it over the mantelpiece. Her expectant girl's face stared down at her and she stared back at it without pleasure. Then she went upstairs again and took a long bath. I'm free, she told herself. But she was not convinced.

She would have liked to telephone her lover in the country, but they had an agreement about that. So she called her sister whom she had not spoken to since they met at the solicitor's office to hear their father's will. The sister was younger than Harriet and had been married twice for a grand total of two years and seven months. She was the only person Harriet knew who had not been surprised when she and Jake divorced.

"Well," she said when Harriet told her the news, "that's one mistake you don't have to make a second time. God knows, you've had me worried."

"All the same . . ."

"All the same, you're forty-something years old, Harriet. Old enough to know better."

"I do know better. But we were married for twenty-four years. You can't just dismiss that out of hand."

There was a brief, embarrassed silence at the other end. In the background Harriet heard the chatter of a disk jockey. "Twenty-four years?" Her sister's voice was slow and careful. "Are you sure?"

"Of course I'm sure. Twenty-four years and three months. What's so significant about that?"

"You don't remember?"

"Don't be so mysterious," said Harriet irritably. "I've got enough on my plate as it is."

"Twenty-four years is precisely the time our dear departed parents were together before they divorced. Surely I don't have to tell you that."

"I'd forgotten." But as she spoke, an old circuit tripped in her head and she saw Jake and herself standing awkwardly by the Pither stove in his chilly studio. She was wearing a linen suit and both of them had confetti in their hair. The wedding guests had not yet arrived. They kissed and moved apart and, "Well," she said, "at least we have twenty-four years in front of us." "With remission for good behavior?" asked Jake.

She had known all along. *My real life is the one I don't lead.*

"I always assumed," her sister was saying, "our parents had proved definitively that marriage was no good, however hard you tried. Twenty-four years of misery and at the end all they had to show for it was lawyers' bills. So I arranged my life accordingly. Whereas you drew the opposite conclusion: it can be made to work, despite the odds. I always admired you for that, for that grim determination of yours to make a go of it. Now you've proved what you set out to prove. You've lasted the course."

There was a raucous burst of pop music behind her.

Garbage in, garbage out, thought Harriet automatically, and was suddenly furious. "Why me?" she shouted into the telephone.

"Pardon?"

"Why should my life be predetermined and not yours? You make me feel like someone out of a Greek tragedy. Don't argue. I know about that stuff. I've read the textbooks. I publish the bloody things. I've got grown-up children and I'm pushing fifty, yet I'm still a dutiful little daughter. That's what you're saying."

"I'm saying nothing of the kind," her sister answered huffily.

Harriet's anger vanished as abruptly as it had arrived. "I'm like wax," she said. "Everyone puts his thumbprint on me."

"You and the rest of the world."

"All those appearances we kept up," said Harriet wearily.

"Blood under the bridge," said her sister.

X

The Paperless Marriage

(i)

"Marriage," wrote the ecclesiastical historian W. E. H. Lecky, "gives either party an extraordinary power of injuring each other." In one form or another, that power to hurt has been the main argument against the ban on divorce down through the centuries. The great humanists of the Renaissance, Sir Thomas More and Erasmus and Vives, seventeenth-century reformers like Milton and the lawyer John Selden, the leaders of the eighteenth-century Enlightenment, Voltaire and Montesquieu, nineteenth-century social philosophers such as Jeremy Bentham and John Stuart Mill—in their different ways, all agreed that the Romans had been right and "the reasons for divorce are unnecessary; because whatever causes the law may admit as sufficient to break a marriage, a mutual antipathy must be stronger than them all."

Montesquieu wrote that in *The Spirit of the Laws*. In precisely the same spirit, the Law Commission which prepared the ground for the British Divorce Reform Act of 1969 claimed that it would "buttress" the institution of marriage by providing a way for "dead marriages" to be "dissolved with dignity." "Mutual antipathy," "dead marriages," "empty shells": behind the rhetoric lies the perennial conviction that the most effective means of safeguarding matrimony is divorce itself. In 1909 a witness before another Royal Commission on divorce had put it this way:

> In my humble opinion marriage should be encouraged in every way, and divorce should be encouraged, not for its own sake, but for the sake of marriage. Regarded as a human institution, marriage cannot hope to be a working success unless divorce is in the background as a reserve. With divorce as a protection against unforeseen calamities arising out of marriage, marriage becomes a wise investment having regard to the circumstances generally. Without divorce I look upon marriage as a dangerous, mad gamble.
>
> I look upon divorce as a policy of insurance. I take it it is a fact there is no marriage, however judiciously and carefully it may be arranged, whatever may be the absolute good faith of the parties to it, which is not an experiment. You cannot prevent it being anything else, and I therefore look upon divorce as a policy of insurance, providing an opportunity of relief and release to married couples who, through no fault of their own, without any moral blame, have come into contact with unforeseen difficulties and calamities which make married life intolerable.

It sounds like a long-winded version of George Bernard Shaw's aphorism, "Divorce, in fact, is not the destruction of marriage, but the first condition of its maintenance." Yet Mr. Plowden, the witness, was a Metropolitan Police Magistrate, not a Shavian iconoclast, and he appears to have been embarrassed by his own daring; whence his insistence on "insurance," as though to emphasize that what he was saying was mere prudence and sound business sense.

It is a logical step from divorce as an insurance policy against some domestic act of God to the modern concept of marriage as "a special kind of friendship." But to change that friendship back into enduring marriage it is necessary to make moral strengths out of what seem to be twentieth-century defects. Professor Shorter, for example, has argued that modern contraception and the sexual revolution that followed it have destabilized the institution of marriage. And perhaps this is true for those whose sexual freedom arrived late. But for the young the ability

to make stupid mistakes without the shotgun of unwanted pregnancy permanently at their heads has been a great blessing: if
they decide to marry, the chances are they will know more or
less what they are doing and what they are seeking. They may
have gained this precarious knowledge through promiscuity or
years of serial monogamy—solemnly living together as though
married, but without the ultimate legal sanction—so in the end
they will have paid as much for it as their elders in terms of
trouble and confusion. But at least they have some experience
on which to base their decision, and experience in the ambiguities of the shared life is the best hope for a decent marriage.

Hence the statistical truism that the younger a couple mar-
ries, the more likely they are to divorce. In the United States
and Britain, the risk of divorce among those who marry around
twenty is about one in two, roughly double the national average,
while those who delay their final choice until thirty will probably
last the course. In other words, the old-fashioned concept of
youthful virtue and clean living is a recipe for marital disaster.
It is as though there were a second law of thermodynamics for
the sexual life, with weariness taking the place of entropy: the
greater the opportunity for promiscuity, the more attractive fidelity appears. The youngsters who take for granted that there
is no good reason not to go to bed together if they want to seem
to behave with noticeably more restraint and discrimination than
their middle-aged parents who swung so remorselessly when
they got their belated chance a couple of decades ago. The dreadful young of the sixties—with their fancy dress, their dope, their
Maoist-Leninist parroting—have been replaced by a generation
that is bedwise in the same way as slum children are streetwise:
knowing the dangers, the possibilities and the odds, watchful
and, they hope, not easily fooled. Listen to two of them talking
in *The Petting Zoo* by a novelist, Brett Singer, who is still in her
twenties:

> "I don't even know if I want to marry him anymore."
> "Don't get married," Bonnie says. "Whatever you do, don't get
> married and don't get pregnant either."
> "Then what should I get?'
> "Get rich," she says. "Get smart. Get laid. Take care, old friend,"
> she says softly.

The oldest generation has no illusions about the advantages their grandchildren enjoy. "What did I know when I married?" a seventy-year-old woman asked me bitterly. Her husband was sitting across the room, but his hearing aid was switched off and he seemed to be sleeping. From the perspective of the late twentieth century, the elderly see the innocence they were once proud of as the great debilitator, the enemy of happiness. After fifty years of making do and getting by, they remain secretly outraged by the memory not of their romantic rashness or their parents' coercion, but of their stone ignorance of the ways of the world in their youth. They are haunted by the idea that there might have been someone else—now long dead—waiting just around the next corner, someone more interesting, more tender, more appropriate, with whom they might have lived a better life. "Not that I'm complaining," added the grandmother, as her husband stirred in his sleep.

Early in this century, a witty bishop of New Jersey formulated what he called "the Metuchen theory," according to which ninety percent of small-town Americans married their high-school sweethearts or, at their most adventurous, someone who lived within five blocks of home. Free choice barely came into it; all that mattered was that the future partner be presentable and at hand. Cheap travel, the long-distance telephone and the contraceptive pill have opened the world up for the young in ways their grandparents never dreamed of, leaving the old with an abiding resentment of the closed society and enforced innocence which deprived them of opportunities their grandchildren now take as if by natural right. The ability to sow wild oats with impunity and behave badly for a spell without doing harm seems like an excuse for celebration to those brought up to believe that the psychopathology of everyday life was expressed mainly through slips of the tongue.

In *The Sea and the Mirror*, Auden's autumnal postscript to *The Tempest*, Prospero, sailing philosophically home to Milan and death, looks at the happy lovers and meditates:

> Their eyes are big and blue with love; its lighting
> Makes even us look new: yes, today it all looks so easy.
> Will Ferdinand be fond of a Miranda
> Familiar as a stocking? Will a Miranda who is

No longer a silly lovesick little goose,
When Ferdinand and his brave world are her profession,
Go into raptures over existing at all?
Probably I over-estimate their difficulties;
Just the same, I am very glad I shall never
Be twenty and have to go through the business again,
The hours of fuss and fury, the conceit, the expense.

A modern Prospero, waiting equally philosophically in the Registry Office while Ferdinand and Miranda legalize their arrangements four years after they began living together, would probably draw the same conclusion. But he would envy the young couple the blessed realism which enabled them to delay their decision until both were indeed as familiar to each other as stockings and both relatively confident that the stockings fit.

"Marriage gives either party an extraordinary power of injuring each other." Before the change in the divorce laws, the worst advertisement for marriage was the callousness with which husbands and wives treated each other. Couples who lived together without an official document to validate their union invariably seemed more alert to each other's needs and more tender toward each other's sensibilities than those whom only death could part. When the unmarried fought they seemed more circumspect, more fearful, as if they knew that victory was not necessarily to the strong and that if they attacked too savagely the injured party might simply pack and leave. In comparison, badly married couples were like old club professionals in the ring, both certain that no matter how hard they hit each other they would always bounce back off the ropes.

In modern marriages the ropes no longer hold. Divorce, a friend told me ruefully before his third, is the fire in which marriage is now tested. Nothing, he meant, can be taken for granted and bad behavior must be moderated, like any other transaction, to what the market will bear. When divorce is a constantly open option, marriage lasts as long as the partners choose to make it last. The outraged wife no longer runs home to mother; she goes to a lawyer. This, too, is a new development. A generation ago divorce was still a prerogative of the relatively affluent who could afford the legal fees, the alimony, the contumely. The best a working-class wife could do was apply to a local court for a separation order and maintenance—which her absconding partner usually did not pay. Now she has a democratic right to the genuine article. "When legal aid services were expanded around the country as part of the anti-poverty program of the mid-1960s," wrote Joseph Epstein in his excellent book, *Divorced in America*, "legal aid lawyers more often found themselves called upon to assist the poor in attaining divorces than to protect them from the harsher abrasions of capitalism—landlords, credit contracts, garnishments of wages—that anti-poverty legal-aid programs were initially devised to combat. In one such program, Judicare in Northern Wisconsin, in 1966 *The New York Times* reported that 84 percent of the cases handled involved divorce actions." Eighty-four percent! The political moral is clear and not at all uplifting: no matter how deprived and exploited one's social circumstances, unhappiness begins at home.

(ii)

In Scandinavia the radical young drew the obvious conclusions and tried for a time to do without formal marriage. If legal papers are worth so little and do such harm, they said, let us have marriages without papers, marriages based solely on free choice and goodwill. It was a dream of a brave new world, but like all dreams it produced its own special confusions.

I learned about them in Copenhagen, the coziest, most bustling of the Scandinavian capitals, busier than Stockholm, Oslo and Helsinki, and warmer in every sense. But it is also more at the mercy of European fashions, as if all the theories which have washed across the Western democracies in the last twenty years have ended up there, among the bookshops and the bicycles. The radical politics of Paris and Berlin, the hedonism of swinging London, American feminism: all the pipe dreams of 1968 have taken on a kind of mild substance in Copenhagen.

There is even an officially sanctioned hippie commune in what were once the army barracks of Christiana: candlelight, squalor, macrobiotic food, a little dope and a lot of bad art—clumsy pottery, batik, indignant free verse—swarms of bedraggled children whose bemused parents wander around in sandals among the oriental-hallucinogen murals daubed on the grimy buildings. In its heyday there were guided tours of the place,

featuring impromptu lectures on communal living. It was a land-
mark to be proud of and, unlike Haight-Ashbury, it still hangs
on in a marginal way, a souvenir of the sixties preserved for
posterity.

A token, too, of the way they live now. The political dreams
may not have survived inflation and recession, but in personal
relations Copenhagen remains determinedly post–'68. That,
they tell you, is when it all started: when the contraceptive pill
ceased to be on doctors' prescription and became generally available on demand; when the laws against abortion were relaxed;
when there was a boom in the building of day nurseries, and also
an economic boom which created jobs for women as well as men.
Everything combined to produce what a sociologist primly described to me as "an explosion of cohabitation." He meant "the
young in one another's arms," everywhere, publicly and without
benefit of clergy. It was for a while a waking dream of the liberated society, but Danish style—that is, with decency and a sense
of proportion.

And the young continue to dream it in a slightly liverish
way. Birgitta, for instance, is a tall, strong-looking young
woman of twenty-two, with a cloche of dark hair around her
broad, pleasant face—Danish faces are flattish and wide, like the
Japanese. Her blue eyes have the puzzled, peering look of someone who is nearsighted and does not wear glasses. But then,
everything about her is puzzled and faintly dejected, as though
she were inextricably involved in a game and no one will tell her
the rules.

The name of the game is "the paperless marriage" and it is
played with considerable energy. Elsewhere, it is called "living
together," but in Denmark they have given it an appropriately
radical, post–'68 title, a gesture of freedom in a form-filling age.
In theory, a paperless marriage is a model for the future, a
marriage without bureaucracy, without ceremony, without legal
equivocation. It is a free union of equals who agree to make a life
together, but independently, keeping their own names, their
own property, their own proper distance. It is a form of marriage
for those on the run from one marital disaster who are terrified
of being trapped in another, yet hanker for something more stable and satisfying than an affair. It is also marriage reinter-

preted according to the politics of feminism, the dice for once loaded in favor of the women and no allowances made for traditional patriarchal authority. If the union breaks up, for example, the father has no rights over the children; however strongly he feels for them, the mother can keep them away from him legally, without appeal, particularly since it is now the custom for children born out of wedlock to take their mother's surname.

A paperless marriage, then, is relentlessly modern, unyieldingly feminist. Nevertheless, Birgitta, who had separated from her paperless husband one month before, was clearly in a state. Which was why she had been invited to dinner. My friend David and his paperless wife Suzanne thought I should meet someone who was going through this new style of divorce: a divorce without marriage, a blueprint for the future.

Over dinner the conversation was mostly about Per, the departed paperless husband, whom Suzanne detested. Had always detested, she now confessed, although she had not been able to say so before. Suzanne was small and intense, with dark liquid eyes, like molasses, and a mass of auburn curls. "The worst type of male chauvinist bully," she said, "possessive and unfaithful." She glared at me indignantly, bristling with loyalty.

Birgitta took her cue: "When I complained about his girls he made fun of me." Her voice was low and miserable. "But the one time I went out with another man he blacked my eye."

"Jesus," said David, and smiled nervously at Suzanne.

But when I asked, "Why did you put up with it?" Birgitta rounded on me angrily: "We were married, for God's sake."

I glanced over at my friends on the other side of the table, but they were gazing at her, their faces full of sympathy.

"Not exactly," I said.

Birgitta's annoyance increased: "What difference does a piece of paper make? I *felt* married."

"You're well out of it now," I said placatingly.

She shook her head. "You don't understand. It's not that easy."

"You mean the apartment and things?" I had already heard about that from the sociologist. A paperless marriage was ideal, he had told me, until it breaks up. At that point, every possession—from children to teacups—can be argued over endlessly, bitterly. The legal wrangling and expense were so inordinate that young couples were beginning to marry again in order to protect themselves against disaster. "You need so many papers in a paperless marriage," he had said, "whereas if you're married, all you need is the license." The paperless marriage had been made prematurely obsolete by easy divorce.

But not in Birgitta's case. She shook her head. "Yes and no. I moved in with him but"—she blushed vividly from the base of her neck to the edge of her fringe—"but I kept my own apartment. I needed somewhere I could escape to." She swallowed some wine and her puzzled expression cleared for a moment. "I suppose I didn't trust him."

"That seems sensible," I said, "in the circumstances."

"In the circumstances," said Suzanne, "it was the wisest thing she did." She gave me another hard look, as if I were the offending husband.

"So what was the problem?" I asked. "Children?"

Once again Birgitta shook her head. *That* was the problem, she explained. What was? She went on shaking her head. Like one of Muriel Spark's "girls of slender means," she seemed racked by "strong but obscure emotion." "*That* was," she repeated. "I got pregnant and . . ."

I refilled her glass. David and Suzanne paused over their food, their faces expectant and solicitous. They had heard the story before.

There was a long silence.

"And?" I said finally.

"And he wouldn't let me go through with it." She peered nearsightedly at her plate, her face reddening again, this time with shame and indignation. "When I asked him why not, he said, 'Because we aren't married.' Did you ever hear such male chauvinist arrogance?"

"Bastard," said Suzanne.

"I told him being pregnant made it a marriage."

"What did he say to that?" asked David. The paranoia of liberation was getting to him too, and he shifted uncomfortably in his chair. The two of us had been type-cast as sexual imperialists, colonialists of the hearth, and he seemed crushed by the role.

"He called it part of the sentimental feminist mystique."

"Bastard," Suzanne repeated, glaring at me.

Birgitta went on: "He said it was a question of keeping the baby or keeping him. So . . ." We waited. "So I had an abortion and . . ." She swallowed more wine. Her eyes were brimming. Suzanne reached across the table and took her hand. David and I studied the abstract pattern on the tablecloth.

"And . . ." Suzanne coaxed.

"And I hated him for it, of course. What else was I to do?" She burst into tears.

Suzanne came round the table and took the weeping girl in her arms, murmuring to her like a mother to her child. David poured more wine and avoided my eyes. "The bastards," crooned Suzanne, over and over again. "The bastards." In the plural. She made me feel like an aging Nazi confronted by his victims.

A little later, while Suzanne was out in the kitchen getting coffee, I asked, "How long were you together?" Simply to break the silence.

Birgitta peered at me indignantly. "A year," she answered, eyes brimming again. "A whole year."

Soon after midnight David and I drove her home through the wet Copenhagen suburbs. When I opened the car door for her she pecked David on the cheek and shook my hand formally. Then she hesitated, suddenly embarrassed. "I'd ask you both in," she said, "but Per wouldn't like it."

"Per?"

"He's terribly jealous."

"But I thought . . ."

"Oh, well," she said, "he still drops in from time to time. Usually when I'm not expecting it." She giggled like a schoolgirl. "You know how it is," she said.

A sudden flurry of rain made her run for the door of the apartment building. I waved to her as we drove away. She was standing in the doorway, a stolid and forlorn figure under the rain and wavering streetlights. She waved back briefly, then went inside.

"Poor kid," I said. "I wonder if the boyfriend will turn up tonight."

"Of course not," said David. "I've met him. He's not the type to get his feet wet just for the sake of a girl."

We drove for a while in silence back through the dark streets and the rain.

"I can't help but admire him," I said at last. "But don't tell Suzanne."

"The Victorians had a name for him." David peered grimly through the streaming windshield. "A cad."

"They had a name for that paperless marriage, too."

A truck thundered past, sending up sheets of spray. David muttered at it.

"A long engagement," I went on. "To a cad, as you say, who finished by leaving her in the lurch. Seduced and abandoned, they called it. Like Tess of the D'Urbervilles."

"Poor Tess," said David. "Poor Birgitta." He turned off into the side streets where the new leaves heaved and shuddered under the rain. "I can't exactly say I admire Per." He glanced at me quickly. "But back in the fifties when I was his age, I sure as hell used to envy guys like that. The ones who could treat girls badly and get away with it." He grinned ruefully, wiping the steamed-up windshield with the back of his hand. "Not an art I ever mastered," he said. "But don't tell Suzanne."

We drew up in front of the neat brick building where David and Suzanne lived their well-ordered paperless marriage.

"The one thing I don't understand," I said, "is why she thinks of it as a marriage. OK, so nobody has long engagements anymore. But they still have affairs that don't work out."

David opened the car door and turned up the collar of his jacket. "How else is she to think of it?" he asked. "That's what it's called these days. It's a question of semantics. She doesn't want to get left behind, does she?"

Inside the apartment the lights were out. The dining-room table had been cleared and wiped, the dirty plates were piled in the kitchen sink. On the drying rack was a note in Suzanne's rounded, art-school hand: "Your turn to do the dishes."

David stared at it gloomily. "I wonder what my old mother would have thought of it all, God rest her soul." He sighed. "I'll wash," he said, "you dry."

XI

The Future?

(i)

In her dim and muddled way, Birgitta was grappling with the responsibilities of enlightenment, a peculiarly Scandinavian preoccupation. For more than a century the Nordic countries have seemed saner about marriage and divorce than the rest of Europe, perhaps because they came to Christianity later and their free and easy folk customs lingered on longer than elsewhere. Peasants and early industrial workers lived together unmarried and without opprobrium until their first child was born and only began to marry before pregnancy when they became wealthier and middle class in their habits, while for the upper classes, divorce was relatively simple even a hundred years ago. In their arts, too, there is a continual tension between the stuffiness of the past and the freedom of the future: in *A Doll's House* Ibsen created the first feminist heroine, a woman willing to abandon husband and children in order to make a life for herself on her own terms, and when Strindberg, who hated the play, attacked him for it in the preface to *Getting Married*, his counterproposals for women's rights were very like those now claimed by the feminists.

For the private citizen, then, enlightenment begins in Scandinavia, and the rest of us, in our more optimistic moments, often imagine the future will look like Sweden with a more forgiving climate: democratic, wealthy, technologically advanced and with unobtrusive birth-to-grave social welfare. It is a kind of talisman for the Western democracies, a proof that the future might be worth having and that the problems it will pose will not be those of deprivation, class envy and sexual inequality, but the more reasonable, though equally complicated difficulties of controlling the bureaucracy and making sense of free time, of freedom itself.

The Scandinavians share this image of themselves as social pioneers. "We are working on that," say the officials, whatever problem you mention. "A commission is studying it." Yet the solutions remain elusive, perhaps because the relationship of the individual to the state is always unequal. The expert who gives advice, the authority which gives money, invariably have the advantage, and state compassion is not in the end a substitute for mutual dependence or personal initiative. Even if it were, there are no official solutions to unhappiness. The young, who have inherited the most enlightened attitudes in the world to marriage and divorce, remain as hard pressed as the rest of us —or more so, since they have nothing to blame but themselves.

(ii)

It was late April when I went to Sweden and the trees were still reluctant to put out their leaves. All over Stockholm people were sitting on steps and benches in sheltered corners, lifting their faces gratefully to the pale sun. But once out in the wind and shade, they turned up the collars of their overcoats and hurried for shelter.

Not even that much of the spring had penetrated Karen's office, a large and severe room with a dead wall outside the window. To compensate for the gloom she had pinned up opposite her desk a single splash of color: an orange sun on a background of jarring green, simple to the point of caricature, like a small child's image of summer. Apart from that, the room contained no intrusions from the world outside: no family photographs, no posters, no personal bits and pieces. On her desk were neat piles of books and papers, a clean blotter, a stapler, a jar of sharpened pencils. The books lining her shelves were in alphabetical order and the wall she faced was blank, except for the orange sun. It was all very professional.

As she was, too, at first glance: a young woman in her twenties with the trim, taut figure of someone who looks after herself, eats carefully, exercises daily, does not drink too much. Her face had that curious Scandinavian purity: clear complexion and clear blue eyes, beautiful teeth, neat mouth, fine blond hair, becomingly cut. An impression, above all, of physical clarity, translucent, like a Christmas rose. Yet she lacked the freedom, the sense of something unpremeditated and bounteous, that would have made her really beautiful. In its place was endless competence and an intellectual lucidity which might quickly turn to impatience. She belonged to the admirable tribe who do well whatever they want to do because they continually exert their intelligence—cool, controlled, but distant, not quite approachable. She reminded me of Hemingway's marvelous phrase, used by Kathleen Knott as the title for a book on Sweden: "a clean, well-lighted place."

Karen was also one of the new generation of women: educated, successful, liberated as though by natural right, taking for granted the battles of the sixties, neither belligerent nor guilty about her equality, an inheritor of that brave new world which seems so peculiarly Scandinavian, since nowhere else has the combination of natural resources, efficient economies and small homogeneous populations produced such universal prosperity and enlightened welfare. Talking to her was like entering a time warp and talking to some space traveler from the future.

But like a space traveler in an alien environment, there was something uneasy about her. She seemed wistful, as though diminished by all that liberation and puzzled that it should have provoked more difficulties than it solved. Her mouth and her voice were tense, as if she sensed some area of interior darkness which resisted the light of her intelligence, cutting her off from herself as well as from other people, so that she felt as she seemed—remote. She spoke English fluently, as she did six other languages, but with a faint weariness that implied her gift of tongues was more a source of depression to her than of pleasure and her intelligence a burden she would like to shed along with all the other burdens. Even her good looks irritated her when men ogled her in the street or across restaurants. She resented the disorderly world that made it hard for her to live the life she wanted, in peace and isolation.

Intelligence and resentment, wistfulness and competence: that effect she produced was shifting and double, like a trompe l'oeil drawing: looked at one way there were two faces, looked at another, two urns; and each image obliterated the other. I felt at once overawed and also, irrationally, a little sorry for her.

For sorry was not how one was supposed to feel for someone with her poise and success. Her translations had won national prizes and the plate on her office door in the theater announced that she was CHIEF LITERARY ADVISER. In Stockholm her name was known, at least among people who read books and go to the theater. She was a figure to be envied and reckoned with, not pitied. Nor was she one of those embattled feminists who consider such a response an insidious form of male condescension, although she was feminist enough to know her rights and to have used them to obtain an apparently trouble-free divorce of the kind the unhappily married have been dreaming of for a thousand years.

Unlike her mother, whose marriage had broken up a dozen years before for reasons which now seem merely comic: after a lifetime at home she had decided she wanted to take a job and her husband had not thought it proper. She was fifty at the time and he was five years older, with rigid views as to what a woman's place is and is not. When she insisted, he marched out, full of outraged rectitude.

Karen was thirteen when her parents divorced, but even then she was the one they came to for advice. Not to confide in, not to enlist on one side or the other, but for advice, as if she were the parent and they the children. Since then the sense of always being a little older than everyone else, a little more in control, a little more detached, had never left her, although she had forgiven them at last and even grown close to her mother.

"We're very much alike," she said, "at least in our divorces. But she's a frail creature, not anyone I could ever bring my problems to. She has enough of her own, poor soul, and she brings them to me. I suppose there's a certain irony in that, although she doesn't see it. Or is that how it always is with parents as they grow older and more querulous? The children begin to treat them in the same way as they once treated the children." The question was not for me but for the orange sun pinned on her wall behind me. She made a tentative gesture toward it, as if for reassurance. "Except that it was no different when I was a child. Perhaps responsibility is a quirk you are born with, like being double-jointed."

Karen's husband, like her father, was handsome, athletic, profoundly conventional and not as bright as she was. They were both students at Uppsala. She was eighteen, he was four years older, which seemed significant at the time. More significant even than their love affair, which both of them came to sensibly, without hang-ups and with varying degrees of prior experience. This also was one of the ambiguous freedoms their generation had inherited. They approached sex as they approached everything else, knowledgeably and with common sense, not as something to make a fuss about. Like most of the young women she knew, she discovered it was possible to have an orgasm every time without its ever seeming to mean very much. But nobody had told her that. They talked about the devaluation of the kroner, but not about the devaluation of pleasure. Instead, they went on making the same old exaggerated claims—in books, in films, in advertisements. She felt shut out, irritated, woeful.

But young love affairs have an impetus of their own, and to their friends Karen and Karl seemed an ideal couple, good-looking, confident, ambitious—people who would go places. And Karl was besotted with her, which was both flattering and reassuring to a girl of eighteen whose father had walked out. So after a year they moved in together to a single student's room in a corridor of single rooms, with a narrow bed and scarcely enough space for her books and clothes, let alone his. They spent a year like this, working side by side at the small wall desk, to a background of other people's music and chatter, of feet continually coming and going outside the door.

Later she was able to salvage only one joke from the whole

unsavory mess: "We got married in order to get a student's apartment. That's what Uppsala was like in those days. Now they are less fussy." But now, when she repeated this, her voice was matter-of-fact, the joke no longer funny, even as a conversational gambit.

When I muttered something about practical reasons being as good as any, she interrupted me: "We had a kind of love for each other. At least, we called it love."

"What would you call it now?"

"Security. Someone to be with and to be with me. Someone to talk to. If I wanted to say something, I could turn round and there he was, listening."

I wanted to ask, When did he stop listening? When did you stop talking? But she gave me no chance.

"We had interests in common: we both loved travel, we both loved food. No young-married risottos for us. I used to cook elaborate dinners out of Julia Child and Elizabeth David and we would eat them by candlelight, just the two of us." She tapped the blotter as she talked, with a pencil as sharp as a stiletto. In less than five years, the romantic young wife had become a true literary professional: unable to read or think or even talk without a pencil in her hand. "I came to loathe those cozy evenings. Just the two of us in the candlelight. My husband had the idea that family life excluded other people. No one was allowed to intrude on our privacy. No one and nothing." She studied the dead wall outside her window, as though to remind herself of her earlier imprisonment. But when she went on she seemed to be apologizing: "I'm one of God's readers, you see; an important part of my life has always been led through books. In those days particularly, when I was stumbling about trying to find out who I was, I read all the time. Read and wrote about what I read, trying to learn to think for myself. But Karl looked down on that and in the evenings he wouldn't allow me to read, because that was something I couldn't share with him. According to him, family life meant sharing everything. Not withdrawing into a book, secluding oneself, leading an imaginative life of one's own, but sitting hand in hand in front of the television. So far as he was concerned, family life was candlelight, television and gossip. He called it togetherness, I called it intrusion. But in those days I lacked self-confidence, so I went along with it."

Her voice was calm, stating the facts without bitterness, without indignation. Yet she seemed spectacularly not lacking in self-confidence.

"But you were a bookish girl when you met him, and you had two years together before you married. Both of you must have known what you were getting into."

She smiled at me tolerantly, refusing to be ruffled. "That was part of the romance. He was a plodder, very slow with his studies, while I did almost enough courses to get two degrees at once. So I used to help him with his work. Think how alluring that was for both of us. For him, I was the little wife who was also like some marvelous bright child, a flattering adjunct to his personality. Intelligence is an aphrodisiac; so is stupidity. His intellectual slowness made me feel powerful and motherly; it canceled out the age difference. For a time, at least."

"And then?"

"And then I grew up. We develop, you know, and at enormous speed in the early twenties. Gradually I realized we were developing in different directions. He had no interest at all in the things that interested me—books, plays, films. He just went to the trotting races or watched TV. If fate was especially kind, he watched the trotting races on TV. For me the world was just beginning to open up, whereas for him that marriage was all there was to it and all there would ever be. He was a kind of primitive determinist; he looked on life as something utterly preset. You do what your parents and society expect you to do: finish your studies, find a wife, find a job, buy a little house, buy a little car, buy all sorts of expensive objects to act as a barrier between you and the world outside. Then you plant a garden, have children and that's it. Nothing more happens."

"Until you die?"

"Until you die."

In the corridor outside two people were talking in subdued voices. A telephone rang in another office. A door closed. From the theater downstairs came the faint sound of a piano. It was all very discreet.

"For a man with a system," I said, "he got his timetable rather muddled."

Her perfect little nose wrinkled with distaste, briefly, almost involuntarily. "How was I to blame? My only crime was to get my degree two years before he did. Maybe that was the first fly in the ointment. But directly I graduated I became pregnant, and that was according to plan."

"Your plan or his?"

"Our plan. We had a modern marriage in that way at least." Then her pure face relaxed, her voice quickened, and the chill vanished in a sudden burst of feeling, like the weather outside. "I can even tell you where and when I conceived. It was July, so we were traveling as usual. Driving to Turkey, to be precise. When we got to Zagreb we went to the theater . . ."

"How . . .?"

"I studied Serbo-Croatian. It's one of my languages."

"Silly of me. I should have guessed." I smiled, but she took no notice.

"Anyway. There was this marvelous play by a local author I'd never heard of. It knocked me out. I'm sure that's the night Kristi was conceived. I could feel it happening. The next morning I went back to the theater and got a copy of the text. I translated it during the last couple of months of my pregnancy when there was nothing much else I could do. In a way, it changed my life as much as my daughter did, although I didn't . . ."

Her voice trailed away. She began doodling arabesques on the blotter.

"Go on."

She looked up at me and her face snapped shut again like an electric door.

"We were terribly short of money. Karl was so slow with his studies the state cut off his grant. So I had to find a job. That meant Stockholm. The baby was five months old by then and Karl was home all day working for his degree. So we changed roles. He stayed with the child while I worked, translating documents for an import-export company. I left the house every morning at six, took the train to Stockholm, did a day in the office, then traveled back to Uppsala—it's an hour each way—and was home by six."

"It must have been a strain."

"I *lovved* it." She pronounced the word with a short "o," Scandinavian style and alluring. "I felt, finally I am starting. My life is beginning."

"What about your daughter's life?"

"We found a Czech girl who came from nine to four. Then Karl took over until I got back. He and Kristi grew very close at that time."

"Meaning they aren't now?"

"Meaning things work out one way or another."

"How long did this go on?"

"Seven months. Then my father helped us buy a little house outside Stockholm, which shortened my day considerably, and Karl finished his degree. He mooned around for a while, feeling sorry for himself, then managed to land a job in the legal division of the Patent Office."

"At which point you could stay home again?"

"Not at all. My job paid far more than his, so I had to go on with it. We couldn't have managed on his salary."

"And the child?"

"The local authorities helped us pay a daily mother to look after her. They thought it odd, despite all our women's liberation, that I should be the chief wage-earner. But facts are facts."

"With his old-fashioned view of marriage, your husband must have thought it even odder."

A brief shake of the head, a slight tightening of the mouth. I wondered what it took to ruffle her implacable calm.

"You underestimate him," she said evenly. "He had an infinite capacity for ignoring whatever failed to fit his view of himself or of the world. He was impregnable, like a missile silo; nothing penetrated. He just shrugged and said, 'It's hard luck the state pays so badly. But it's only temporary. When I qualify as a lawyer I'll be earning plenty for both of us.' And he believed it. He didn't allow himself to feel a flicker of inferiority toward me because, according to his lights, that wasn't how things were. In his style of marriage the man ran things, and he always contrived to make reality look like that. The harder I worked, the more successful I became, the more his contempt increased. And in some crazy way, I believed him."

Her voice was quiet and reasonable, but the puzzled look was back on her face and once again I felt sorry for her. "You must have wanted to. You said you married him for security. It's like *The Wild Duck:* the old hunter shoots rabbits in the attic,

the failure daydreams on the sofa about his nonexistent invention. People collude with each other's delusions for their own
private needs."

She sat still to attend to this, pencil poised above the blotter, head tilted as though listening to something a long way off.
"I don't learn languages, they just stick to me." She made it
sound like a weakness. "It's a knack, like playing the piano by
ear. So I shared his low opinion of my abilities. This is the way
things should be, I thought. I worked, I came home, I cooked, I
washed the dishes, I played with my child and cleaned the house,
and the days just passed. Then one morning I woke up and it
was all different."

"Why? Did you meet someone?"

She looked at me for a moment without answering and her
deep blue eyes were cold and unamused. I understood briefly
how her husband must have felt: reduced.

"The only people I met were friends of Karl: dull little couples who talked about nothing except television and horse racing
and children and the price of steak. In that order. The people I
worked with, like the people I studied with at university, had
their own lives elsewhere. There was no question of my meeting
them outside. I wasn't allowed to go anywhere by myself. My
husband was too possessive. Togetherness, remember?"

"So what happened?"

"That play. I showed it to a friend at work whose boyfriend
was an actor. Who showed it to the director of this theater. Who
decided to put it on. And it was a big success. Everybody came,
everybody talked about it. Suddenly people wanted to meet me.
I won a prize for the translation and eventually I got this job. In
short, I discovered that out there in the big world I was being
taken seriously. So very slowly I began to think that maybe I,
too, should take myself seriously, maybe I should find out who I
really am and what I really want, rather than just take Karl's
word for it."

"And your husband, did he begin to take you seriously, too?"

Again her nose wrinkled with disdain. "My husband," she
said carefully, "came to the first night under sufferance, but he
never even read the thing."

"Did you honestly expect him to?"

But she ignored the question, off on her own track: "What

he felt, I think, was indignation. A certain indignation. For him, the world was not like that. He stood shoulder to shoulder with the Victorian patriarchs: a woman's duty was not to be success- ful, except as a wife and mother. *Kirche, Küche, Kinder.* Bare- foot, pregnant and in the kitchen. She could earn, too, since this was 1975. He paid that much lip service to the women's move- ment. But ·public success was something else. Suddenly he be- came edgy and insecure. He complained, he picked fights, he made fun of me and tried to get our daughter to join in. Then he decided he wanted another child."

"And you? Was it still a modern marriage?"

"More and more modern. I said no. Because I'd be tied down. Because there'd be no way out."

"By then you were looking for a way out?"

"I had no alternative," she answered in her reasonable voice.

She had no alternative. She was Nora of *A Doll's House* one hundred years on, with her marriage behind her and a profes- sional life established. The atmosphere in her office was subdued and orderly. Elsewhere in the spacious building actors were re- hearsing, secretaries and scene painters and carpenters were going about their business without fuss. Outside, on this unnat- urally cold spring day, lay the foreign city, handsome, prosper- ous and chilly, like its inhabitants.

She had no alternative. I wondered how many denials and disappointments had gone into that simple statement, how many sleepless nights during which what had once been a marriage disintegrated into a reminder of everything she now wished to put behind her: the excesses, stupidities and ignorance of her youth.

Likewise her youthful desires. When I asked about them tentatively she answered without hesitation: "It became a fail- ure. The more he wanted to hold me back, the more I wanted to run. Naturally, that made it impossible to feel anything for him sexually."

"Naturally," I echoed.

"The last months were terrible. There was violence and . . ." She moved her hands vaguely from her breasts to her face. ". . . and all sorts of horrors. He went up and down like a seesaw. Up and down. One moment he was throwing things at me, the next he wanted to make love, to . . ." She hesitated, then said slowly and distinctly, ". . . to force himself on me. It was very upsetting."

I watched her calm, pure face and wondered which had upset her more, his violence or his shambling attempts at tenderness.

"He was always nervous," she went on, "always on edge. And the child noticed everything. I knew it was up to me to be strong and calm and sensible. So I never lost my temper in front of her, never shouted, never threw things, like he did. I just sort of . . ."

She drew a long deep breath, then exhaled sharply and shut her mouth tight. "Like that."

She remained silent for a while, unmoving, lips together as if still holding her breath. When she went on, her voice was lower and less reasonable. "Everyone makes claims on me—my husband, my child, my parents. I'm the one who always has to be sane and strong and reliable, the one who never breaks down."

"You do it," I said, "then you feel contempt for them for making you go through this farce. Is that it?"

She shrugged. "Contempt. Compassion. What's the difference? I felt like a lonely mother with two children, one a baby daughter, the other a teenager with all the hang-ups of adolescence."

"How long did this last?"

"Until he started working on the child, waking her up in the middle of the night, saying, 'Your mother doesn't love you anymore,' sitting tipsily on the end of her bed and weeping, 'She's going to leave us because she doesn't love you anymore.' Imagine what that does to a little girl. That was when I knew I had to do something radical."

"Like divorce?"

She nodded. "But I couldn't say so at first. I told him we should try living apart for a while. Anything to soften the blow. He countered by saying he hadn't done anything wrong, so he wasn't going to move. I suppose he hoped I would be held to him by inertia, it would be too difficult to set up house again on my own." She smiled grimly. "Well, in that, as in other matters, he underestimated me. But I wanted to find somewhere near, so

my daughter could have the same friends and the same neighbor-
hood and the same woman to look after her while I was at work.
It took me six months, but I managed it."

"How did he take that?"

"He was outraged. When I arrived with the mover's van he
stood at the top of the stairs and threw my things down at me.
Yet oddly enough, when it came to the formalities of divorce he
was quite helpful. Not that the formalities amount to much. We
have a no-fault system here, so there was no question of one
party proving the other guilty in court. No question of alimony
either, since we were both working. All you have to do is put in
an application. Then, if there's a child under sixteen involved,
you must wait six months for the divorce to become final. It's no
more complicated than buying a dog license. Nevertheless, he
did his best. Maybe he wanted to show me what a good lawyer
he was."

"Were things easier after you left?"

"Not at all. I was stupid to find a house so close. He kept
dropping in, telephoning, always wanting to know if I had someone there."

"Did you?"

"Never. But he and his family wanted me to. Then they
would have been able to explain everything. For me to have
moved out for no obvious reason was beyond their understanding. His mother came bustling around after I'd gone. He was her
spoiled darling, you see, and she had always detested me. So
around she came, poking her nose into things. And she found the
cupboards were untidy. That was all she needed. She told him I
had left because I was a socialist and didn't clean properly. In
the world they inhabit those two things go together. After that,
they felt easier in their minds. They had their explanation."

I looked at her but could see no relationship between what
she was saying and her clear young face. The attitudes, confusions and humiliations she described belonged to my generation
or her mother's, whereas she was slim, confident and no more
wrinkled than a fresh apricot, an inheritor of the sexual revolution, the women's movement, the pill and all those elaborate
legal reforms designed to alleviate domestic misery by making
divorce easy. It seemed absurd that so many years of rhetoric,
goodwill and good works should have had so little effect. In the

end, only the social stigma had changed. When she was a child she tried desperately to keep her parents' divorce a secret. She told her school friends her father had been posted abroad by his company and was terrified of their finding out the truth, as if divorce were something shameful and obscurely contagious, like madness in the family or a suicide. Her own daughter has no such problems: they discuss the matter together openly and calmly; the child watches TV programs on the subject; the parents of most of her friends are separated. Everybody's doing it, everybody's talking about it, and nothing has altered. The legal mechanics are simpler and cheaper, the arguments in favor more convincing, but the bitterness is unchanged.

"So it ended there," I asked, "after the statutory six months?"

"With people like that, these things never end. Every other day he's on the telephone, saying he's changed, begging me to come around and see for myself how different he is, how different everything is. 'Come for dinner,' he says. 'Come for coffee.' And sometimes, like a fool, I give in. But when I get there the same old candles are burning and all he wants to do is make a pass at me, or knock me about when I turn him down. Then he weeps and tells me how much he loves me, how unhappy he is and how lonely, how empty and awful the house is without me. It's all make-believe, except"—she ran the tip of her tongue slowly around her lips as if to make the words taste better—"except that he's right in one thing: the house *is* awful. He leaves the dirty dishes in the sink when he goes to work in the morning, and when he comes back at night they're still there. They weren't when I was around. So now . . ."

She broke off abruptly. It was hard to tell if she was enjoying herself or angry.

"Does he tell the world, too, that he's still in love with you?"

She shook her head. "He's a public official, a lawyer. He has his dignity to maintain. He tells people we have agreed to separate and now we are good friends, doing the sensible thing. Which is precisely what I want—for the child's sake as well as ours. To everyone else he's the responsible father, the noble husband with a wayward wife. Only I am privy to the secret of his broken heart." Her gentian blue eyes looked at me, through

me, became bored with what they saw and moved for relief to
the picture of the orange sun. "Maybe it's even true. Maybe he
still believes he loves me, inasmuch as he knows what love is and
is capable of feeling it. Certainly, he's suffering in his fashion,
and love is the name he gives that unfamiliar process."

"What name would you give it?"

"Disappointment? Disbelief? Self-pity? Humiliation? Who
knows? He told me once he felt as if he'd put all his money on the
wrong horse and couldn't bring himself to admit it. I can believe
that. I've seen him do it when the trotting races were on television. He just shuts his eyes and turns his head away." Her eyes
closed, her head ducked cruelly in pantomime. "That's what he's
doing now: shaking his head and telling himself over and over
again, 'It's not true. She'll come back. She'll realize how much
we have in common. All this is just an idea she's got into her
head. A dream. She'll wake up and be lonely.' "

"Are you?"

"Never. It's not an emotion I have ever had. I've always
liked being alone, even when I was a child. Now when I come
home in the evening I can't believe my luck. I chat with my
daughter, read to her, play games. Once she's in bed I can listen
to music or read a book and there's no one to say, 'Why must you
shut yourself off? Why don't you watch television with me?' If I
want to go to the theater or the movies, I don't ask permission,
I hire a baby-sitter. I'm not answerable to a living soul except
Kristi, and she's a pleasure." She shook her elegant head. "No,
it's not loneliness I feel now. It's wonder. How did I endure all
those years in someone else's pocket? If I ever marry again, it
will be as an equal, a free person, complete in myself, not as a
dependent."

Her voice, as she spoke, had imperceptibly lightened and
intensified. She was Nora again, vindicated and whole. Finally,
some passionate nerve had been struck, a nerve her bumbling,
self-righteous husband had never been near, a passion from
which his pomposity had always shut him off. "Beyond all this,
the wish to be alone." She was a perfectionist in life as well as in
her feeling for languages, her translations, her work in the theater. She was fastidious, rational, uninvolved, yet obsessed with
the ideal of an intellectual and emotional clarity to match the

physical clarity of her presence. The disorder of the fallen, imperfect world would always be distasteful to her. Perhaps in a different age with different values she would have ended in a nunnery. The impossible ideal is the same: a life in perfect order, purified, uncluttered.

To achieve this she was willing to put up with any amount of chaos. Soon after she moved, for example, the pipes burst in the new house and flooded the cellar. For three hours she sloshed around in gum boots, under a single naked bulb, lugging empty packing cases, bottles of wine, old trunks and garden furniture up the cellar stairs, across the kitchen and out the back door to dry in the mild sunlight. "Terrible." Her eyes were large with the recollection of it. "Trial by water. But I never doubted for a moment that I'd done the right thing. Not for one moment. That, in fact, is all I have salvaged from the whole mess."

She sat straight-backed and very still, like a pale statue in a whitewashed northern church, a statue carved for its own sake as a beautiful object, not the kind anyone ever prayed to expecting an answer.

"What is?"

"Conviction," she said slowly. "The conviction that if you feel strongly about something, then you must do it, whatever the cost. Because when you get old it's better to regret the things you *have* done than the things you haven't done. The more you attempt, the more chance you have of getting some of them right. And at least you can say you've tried."

A telephone began to ring in the office next door. She paused, listening, tapping the blotter impatiently with her pencil. When the ringing stopped she picked up a file, opened it and nodded to me dismissively. "As for the inconveniences," she said in a businesslike voice, "the financial strain and the rest: none of them cancel out the pleasure of being on my own again."

(iii)

I have a Turkish friend, a photographer, who is married to a Swede and lives in Stockholm, which he detests. Whenever the Scandinavian gloom becomes particularly insufferable, he rounds on his Swedish friends, jabs his fingers at them in the sign of the evil eye and barks, "Europe ends at Copenhagen. This is the North." Talking to this self-contained, sad, powerful young woman, I understood for the first time what he meant.

Loneliness, alienation, *ensamhet:* the names may change but the emptiness remains the same. Whenever two or three are gathered together to discuss Nordic problems, this is the one they all agree on. It is there at the center of Ingmar Bergman's films, "a strange, aching void," he calls it, fueling the despair with which his characters try, and fail, to get through to each other. "Loneliness is absolute," says the husband in *Scenes from a Marriage.* "It's an illusion to imagine anything else." And for once in that movie the wisdom and evidence is overwhelmingly on his side. "In Scandinavia," a psychiatrist told me, "people marry because they are lonely. Then two years later they get divorced, and when you ask them why they say, 'Because we felt lonely.' "

The chill at the heart is like the chill of the climate, a fact of nature, immovable. They even blame it on the unforgiving weather, on the long dark winters—as little as four or five hours of murky daylight in the capitals, and in the north none at all—which make people huddle into their clothes and scurry from home to work and back like creatures scuttling from cage to cage. To make matters worse, this otherwise meticulously organized society is curiously lacking in informal places to meet. The first time I arrived in Stockholm, on a cold Saturday night in late autumn, the streets were full of drunks yet there seemed nowhere to sit and drink. For a couple of hours I wandered around the city center searching for a bar, until I realized that all the singing, shouting youths weaving about on Karlavägen were carrying their own bottles. So I gave up and went back to my hotel, where I had a bottle of my own and a book. That was in the 1960s, yet even now, when isolation is beginning to be recognized as an official problem, all the authorities can come up with for their cities of the future are "community centers." However lavishly equipped they may be, they will be no substitute for the British pub or French café, each with its own special character and code.

In Scandinavia social life exists almost exclusively in the

home. For this reason, casual relationships are rare and difficult to handle. If you wish to take them further, you have to invite your new acquaintance back to your house. Which means committing yourself before you know whom or what you are committing yourself to. Most people don't even try. Like Karl, they believe married life excludes other people. Perhaps that famous northern passion for the Mediterranean is not just for the sun, but for what the sun allows: a social life led casually out in the streets between people who are not eternally bundled up in heavy clothes.

"Europe ends at Copenhagen. This is the North." The Turk was right and the sociologists and psychiatrists may be wrong. Loneliness is not necessarily a problem to be eliminated, but a saving grace in an inhospitable world. Whence the tensile strength of those addicted to the solitary life and the unfailing, shuffling vulnerability of those who are not. Whence Karen and Karl.

> It is not enough [wrote Montaigne] for a man to have sequestered himselfe from the concourse of people: it is not sufficient to shift place, a man must also sever himselfe from the popular conditions that are in us. A man must sequester and recover himselfe from himselfe . . . We carry our fetters with us: it is not an absolute libertie; we still cast back our lookes towards that we have left behind; our mind doth still runne on it; our fancie is full of it . . . Our evill is rooted in our minde: and it cannot scape from it selfe . . . Therefore it must be reduced and brought into it selfe: It is the true solitariness, and which may be enjoyed even in the frequencie of peopled Cities and Kings courts.

But there is a difference between solitariness and loneliness, between sober self-sufficiency and that sense of incompleteness for which God, as a remedy, created Eve: "And the Lord God said, It is not good that man should be alone; I will make him a help meet for him."

For long centuries marriage was a celebration of the end of loneliness, the wedding ceremony a culmination of the Platonic desire and pursuit of the whole, since those who are in love, even secretly, find it impossible not to announce their happiness to the world. "It's a lovely thing to have a ceremony together," said Liv Ullmann, "to promise something together in a ceremony. You don't love each other more or do more for each other because you are married. But I think we all need some kind of manifestation, because we are all a little insecure." Until recently, marriage, in theory, was the end of insecurity. The couple stood up before witnesses and were asked, "Do you X take Y to be your lawful wedded . . ." "I do," each replied. And that— for the last thousand years—was that.

But the rules of the game have changed with the divorce laws. When insecurity and loneliness now return in new disguises the couple stand up again before different witnesses and say, "I do no longer." In a world of multiple options, where relationships are assumed to be shifting and unstable, marriage ceases to be an immutable institution and becomes instead a form of work, as absorbing and demanding as all the others. Perhaps more so in a society like Britain, where the labor laws and the divorce laws pull in opposite directions: it is almost impossible for a company to fire an inefficient or troublesome employee without the whole staff coming out in sympathy, but a troublesome husband or wife can now be divorced with startlingly little fuss.

Yet by some perverse sociological magic, the instability of contemporary marriage and the sheer difficulty of keeping it going—the patience, tenacity, alertness and compromises it requires—have made it suddenly seem valuable in a new way. It answers a problem of the future: when the electronic Utopia arrives, what will we do with our time-out? Today's solutions are those of exhaustion: television and bingo, football and the racetrack, booze and drugs, are all convenient antidotes to labor and stress, but in a more relaxed world they will merely transform the two-day week into so many two-week days.

The Scandinavians, in their perennial role of harbingers of the future, are pinning their hopes on marriage. The Norwegians, for example, have experimented in work sharing: the husband and wife alternate in the home and work shifts at the same job. Disrupt the pattern, they are saying, and you change the values: the boredom and exhaustion of both domesticity and salaried work are reduced, the family is strengthened. And when the children see as much of their father as of their mother, the conventional sex roles shift, the stereotypes are broken. No more moonlighting at family life, no more isolation within the nuclear family. In time, the system might even bring life back into the neighborhoods.

For the moment, the experiment is not a program but a controlled piece of social engineering with specially selected families. Its solutions don't apply even in oil-rich, sparsely populated, serious-minded Norway. But it is a start, and less self-defeating than most: when the technological future arrives, better to think in terms of regeneration than of new forms of loneliness; better people talking to each other than more soap operas for more channels; better to reinvent the family as a way of life than to dream up still more mindless and insulting ways of filling the long hours between sleep.

But the problem of leisure is also the problem of personal freedom, and easy divorce is its precondition. In 1670 a lawyer called Pufendorf quoted approvingly an ancient Hebrew authority who said, "Nothing is more useful to marriage than the right to divorce, which is likely to keep both parties agreeable to each other and to maintain peace in the family." Peace in the family depends now, more than ever, on goodwill and also on free will. Neither will make adult sexual life any less troublesome or ambiguous, but at least they make it hard to believe that the troubles and the ambiguities are not of one's own doing and one's own choice. They deprive both victims and bullies of the comforting delusion that they are forced into their roles by unjust laws or empty religious dogmas or irresistible social conventions. No one is going to live happily ever after second time around, or third, or however many it takes, if happiness does not happen to be what he or she is after. But there is a modest chance that they may finish as consenting adults making a life together in the knowledge that it can easily be unmade, each responsible for his own choice and behavior and character. This may not be the beginning of wisdom, but it is certainly an end, even when it turns out wrong.

XII

—————◈—————

Postscript: Going Home

Unlike Copenhagen, Stockholm does not turn its back to the water. The ships sail right into the center, the smaller ones tying up between the Old Palace and the Opera House. The evening after I talked to Karen, I walked in the gathering dark the length of Strandvägen while two yachts raced lazily in the cold air from the amusement park at Djürgarden to the quay in front of the Diplomat Hotel. Two ghostly, solitary presences going about their graceful business almost in the heart of the city.

The next morning I was woken by a strange noise, far off but insistent, growing rapidly to a full-throated scream. I got to the window in time to see a big racing bike at peak revs flashing past the hotel, its rider stretched flat along the tank as though molded to it. The pure high note of the engine faded down Strandvägen, as eerie and beautiful as a visitation in the otherwise silent city.

I looked at my watch: four fifteen. But the sun was already high in the china blue sky. I stood for a while, watching, but nobody came, nobody went. I felt I had been let in on a secret: there was, after all, an hour of release in this formal, law-abiding city; the future was not altogether reasonable. If I listened carefully enough, maybe I could also hear the stirrings of resentment and rage and frustration, like the scream of that polished, exquisitely tuned engine, when the rest of the world was asleep. But it was unlikely. Somehow the yachts and the racing bike and the resolute, wistful young woman who had talked to me about her failed marriage seemed to blur together in the unnaturally bright dawn. They were all part of the same tense melancholy which broods over this beautiful northern city where even unhappiness seems to be at a remove, far off, vanishing, someone else's. It is a place for the uncluttered life, for not quite getting through. As Stendhal said of London, "It is not so much a city as a numerous multitude of hermits."

But London has changed, mellowed by age and wealth and then the decay of wealth, and, a Londoner myself, I had listened to too many voices talking about lives as cluttered and confused as the Old Curiosity Shop—as every marriage must be and every divorce, even up there beyond Copenhagen, where Europe ends. Order, silence, detachment and unwavering reason are for saints and purists, religious or secular: for monks and nuns, bachelors and spinsters. Those who commit themselves to the desire and pursuit of the whole, whether they find it or not, disqualify themselves from perfection and clean, well-lighted places and must settle for the rackety but comforting human muddle of marriage and children and disillusion and love. "What is the answer?" Gertrude Stein was asked as she lay dying. Her last words were, "What is the question?"

It was time I went home.

Two thousand cigarettes.
A hundred miles
from wall to wall.
An eternity and a half of vigils
blanker than snow.

Tons of words
old as the tracks
of a platypus in the sand.

A hundred books we didn't write.
A hundred pyramids we didn't build.

Sweepings.
Dust.

Bitter
as the beginning of the world.

Believe me when I say
it was beautiful.

Miroslav Holub, "Love"